FAITH'S NEW AGE

FAITH'S NEW AGE

A PERSPECTIVE ON CONTEMPORARY RELIGIOUS CHANGE

❖

LLOYD GEERING

COLLINS
ST JAMES'S PLACE, LONDON
1980

William Collins Sons & Co Ltd
London · Glasgow · Sydney · Auckland
Toronto · Johannesburg

First published 1980

ISBN 0 00 215282 7
Made and printed in Great Britain by
William Collins Sons & Co Ltd, Glasgow

To
Bruce, Jane and Jessica

CONTENTS

Preface *page* 9

1 Understanding Religion in Today's Changing World 13
2 The First Major Threshold of Religious Change 29
3 Some Significant Steps Leading to the Modern World 49
4 The Second Major Threshold of Religious Change 66
5 From Religion to Philosophy 92
6 From Religious Tradition to Either History or Myth 112
7 From Theology to Anthropology 132
8 To a Religion Without God? 149
9 The Impact of Science on Religion 168
10 A New Queen of the Sciences? 188
11 The Copernican Revolution in the Science of the Soul 208
12 From Absolutism to Relativism in a Pluralistic World 231
13 Secularization – a Process of Religious Change In Two Stages 251
14 Why did Secularization Come out of the West? 276
15 A Prophet of the New Age 300

Notes 320
Bibliography 334
General Index 345

PREFACE

This book has developed out of a course of lectures which I have been giving for several years to second year students of Religious Studies at the Victoria University of Wellington. The course has been entitled, for want of a better name, 'Religion in Change'. The ambiguity was deliberate. The aim of the course was not only to gain a clearer understanding of how religion is faring in the modern context of rapid social change; it was also asking to what extent religion (or at least the manifestation of man's spiritual search) is itself in the process of radical change.

As is made clear in the first chapter of this book, it is necessary for this purpose to define religion in fairly broad terms. Such a procedure is fully accepted in modern University Departments of Religious Studies, where one often finds courses offered in the modern development of atheism and humanism as well as in the history of the more traditional religions. Indeed, even to do justice to the great diversity of man's religious experience in the past, it is necessary to look at religion as something which is applicable to almost everybody. No matter who a person is, what his particular beliefs are, or what cultural tradition he stems from, his religion is that in which he expresses his ultimate, or most basic, concern with life. Since religion, therefore, is by its very nature of the widest possible interest, it seemed to be a desirable project to put the substance of these lectures into a form suitable for publication and with the general reader in mind, rather than the specialist. Consequently as little as possible background information is assumed, and explanatory notes about key persons are offered where it seemed necessary.

The above-mentioned course set out to provide a balanced overview of the changes which have taken place in man's religious experience and to establish some kind of perspective from which to view, and to understand more clearly, the particular changes which are so obviously taking place in the religious sphere today. A simple pattern or paradigm of religious change began to emerge. It consists of analysing man's religious experience into three phases, which may be referred to as the primal religions, the historical religions and the secular (or this-worldly) religions. In the course of historical succession these phases have been separated from each other by two transition periods or major thresholds of religious change. Although there is a degree of irreversibility in the sequence, these phases are not to be regarded as mutually exclusive. In much of modern society in the Western world elements of all three phases are still to be found, operating at different cultural levels, and sometimes even in the same person.

Because the second of the transition periods is much closer to us in time, and because it is only in the latter part of the twentieth century that it is becoming widely recognized that something of this order *has* taken place, the majority of the book (Chapters 3–12) is taken up with the description of it – the steps which led up to it, the nature of it and the evidence from the nineteenth century that an irreversible religious threshold has in fact been crossed over. The final summary and actual climax of the book is found in Chapters 13–14. The study of Nietzsche has been placed, not in the body of the book along with the other nineteenth century creators of modern thought, but at the end of the book, as a kind of epilogue, on the grounds that he best epitomizes the open-ended and enigmatic character of the new religious era.

If a paradigm, such as the one here expounded, can be established with any degree of credibility, it then becomes a very useful instrument with which to study and analyse what is happening in the rather confusing religious scene which confronts us in the world today. The above-mentioned course, therefore, went on to examine the way in which the long established religious traditions (religions of the historical phase) are reacting to and managing to cope with, the religious transition which has recently taken place. It examined in turn the variety of responses being made in the Christian, Jewish, Islamic, Hindu, Buddhist and Chinese cultures.

Not long after I began the preparation of this book it became clear to me that it would be impossible to deal adequately in one volume with all that I had attempted (admittedly too ambitiously) to cover in the course of lectures. Therefore I have confined this book to that section of the course which dealt with the exposition of the paradigm of religious change. It is at present intended to follow this with subsequent volumes, which are tentatively entitled *Christianity in Transition* and *Oriental Religions in Transition*. These would sketch the variety of ways in which the traditional religions are finding it necessary to explore new forms of expression in order to remain viable within the context of the new era.

Responsibility for teaching within a modern University Department of Religious Studies provides an excellent setting for the evolution of a book such as this. Perhaps in few places other than in such a department can one so readily bring together for discussion such a diverse collection of viewpoints on religious issues. I am grateful for the stimulation provided by continual dialogue with staff and students.

Since the study of religion leads one into so many areas of life and knowledge, which are covered in a modern university by many specialist disciplines, Religious Studies is itself becoming an increasingly interdisciplinary pursuit. In the writing of this book, I have been grateful for the help which I received from others within the University. In particular I wish to thank the following: Professor Peter Munz, of the History Department, has read the whole manuscript; Professor Michael Hill, a sociologist of religion, has read the majority of it; Mr C. J. F. Parkin of the Philosophy Department has read all the chapters which deal specifically with philosophers; Professor A. J. W. Taylor, a clinical psychologist, has read Chapter 11; Dr G. C. Hewitt, of the Zoology Department, has read Chapter 9; Dr Jim Veitch, a colleague in Religious Studies, has read Chapters 12–14. All have made valuable comments and suggestions, many of which have been incorporated in the final text. They in no way share any responsibility, of course, for the opinions here expressed or for the blemishes or errors which remain. I acknowledge their encouragement with gratitude.

Lloyd Geering
Victoria University of Wellington,
March 1979

ACKNOWLEDGEMENTS

The author and publishers acknowledge with gratitude the following permissions:

Routledge and Kegan Paul Ltd., London, for quoting from *The Origin and Goal of History* by Karl Jaspers, *Lectures on the Philosophy of Religion* by G. W. F. Hegel, and *The Essence of Christianity* by Ludwig Feuerbach. George Allen & Unwin Ltd., London, for quoting from *Elementary Forms of the Religious Life* by E. Durkheim. Penguin Books Ltd., London, for quoting from *Early Writings* by Karl Marx, and *Thus Spoke Zarathustra*, *Twilight of the Idols* and *Antichrist* by Nietzsche. Schocken Books Inc., New York, for quoting from the Reinhold Niebuhr introduction and the text of *Marx and Engels on Religion*. SCM Press Ltd., London, for quoting from *Thinking About God* by John Macquarrie and *The Life of Jesus Critically Examined* by D. F. Strauss. Harper & Row Inc., New York, for quoting from *Lectures on the Essence of Religion* by Ludwig Feuerbach. Bobbs-Merrill Company Inc., New York, for quoting from *Principles of the Philosophy of the Future* by Ludwig Feuerbach.

CHAPTER 1

UNDERSTANDING RELIGION IN TODAY'S CHANGING WORLD

❖

Everybody agrees that we live in a period of widespread change, even though there may be differences of opinion on how to interpret it. Of course there is nothing new in the phenomenon of change itself. As motion is basic to the physical universe, so change is a necessary component of life. Organic life manifests itself in cycles of change, leading from birth through maturity to decay and death. Moreover there could be no such thing as human history if we were not continuously experiencing change.

There are different kinds of change however. Change which occurs according to regular patterns thereby displays, at another level, an element of permanence or changelessness. Wherever such regularity is recognized, this type of change no longer unsettles and threatens man in the way in which sudden, unexpected and irregular change does. Even patternless change may move along at a more or less constant speed. Some periods of history, relative to others, have been like this. Such constancy provides, for the time being, an element of permanence and it similarly gives men confidence as they face the future.

On the other hand, when there is a sudden or significant variation in the speed of change men become much more sensitive to it. In our day, for example, we seem to be much more aware of change than our forebears were. At least three reasons can be suggested for this. First, owing to a variety of causes, the speed of change has been distinctly accelerating in this century. It is now much more noticeable within the lifetime of the average person. Secondly, although we can point to periods of accelerated change in the past, these were always confined to particular geographical areas. Never before has the whole human race been caught up simultaneously in change on a global scale, such as we witness today. Thirdly, more areas of human experience are being subjected to change all at one time than has apparently been the case before.

Even before Alvin Toffler's *Future Shock* and similar books were bringing the nature of modern change to widespread popular attention, prophetic voices had already been speaking of its epochal character. Nicholas Berdyaev wrote in 1936, 'We are living at a time of immense crisis, on the threshold of a new era. The very structure of historical development has suffered a profound change . . . This change can only be regarded as catastrophic. Volcanic sources have opened in the historical substrata'.[1] And about the same time Paul Tillich wrote, 'We are in the midst of a world-revolution affecting every section of human existence, forcing upon us a new interpretation of life and of the world'.[2]

Because, as human beings, we are at the very centre of modern change, and have the most to gain or lose by the direction it takes, we are in no position simply to ignore it once we have come to recognize its existence. Some, like King Canute, are passionately trying to hold back the tide of change. Some are afraid of it but do not know what to do about it. Some are content to be passively carried along by it. Some rejoice in it and are trying to steer it in a particular direction. Some appear to be shutting their eyes to it in the hope that it will go away. The choice of the most appropriate response depends on our having a clear and adequate understanding of what it is we are encountering.

Perhaps in no area of human experience now undergoing change is there more confusion than there is in religion. 'Something seems to have happened to the world, including its religions, which makes us grapple for words in an effort to clarify and interpret to ourselves, and for ourselves, what it is that has happened', said R. J. Z. Werblowsky in his lectures on changing religion in a changing world.[3] The confusion is understandable for, when change is minimal, it is usually religion which provides the stabilizing force in the community. When many other things are in a state of flux or uncertainty religion still speaks of that which is the same yesterday, today and for ever. It offers men a firm rock on which to stand amidst the sea of change. But when religion itself is caught up in the confusion of change (and never has religion been expressed in such diverse and contradictory ways as it is today) then, as in an earthquake, it seems as if the very ground beneath can no longer be relied on.

In this book we intend to examine the ways in which modern change is impinging on religion, to search for the causes and to discern the present trends. It will be suggested, not only that traditional religion is being threatened by changes from without but also that a more radical kind of internal change is taking place in the basic forms which religion may assume. It is hoped to throw some light on the present confused situation by suggesting that the most profitable way of looking at the present period of change is to see it as one of religious transition on the grand scale.

This is only possible, however, if we are prepared to define religion in reasonably broad terms. Before proceeding further, therefore, we must look at the problems created by the fact that this word can mean quite different things to different people. In a quite seminal book entitled *The Meaning and End of Religion*, W. Cantwell Smith even made a plea for the dropping of the term altogether owing to the confusion to which it leads. While this course of action does not seem at all practicable, we can learn much from his observations. He points out, for example, that the reification of the term 'religion' to denote a definable set of beliefs and practices is a comparatively modern phenomenon. (Indeed this may itself be a sign of the impending religious change.) When one is reared within a homogeneous culture one need never be aware that one has a religion in this modern sense of the term. Thus for a long time in Western Christendom the word religion referred to the life of piety or devotion, which, in the circumstances, meant Christian devotion.

It was as the horizon of Western man was extended to include some acquaintance with the great civilizations of the Middle East, India and China that the usage of the word religion began to change to allow for the observable fact that there was more than one way of being devout or religious. From that time onwards the word religion was often used to refer to the particular set of beliefs and rituals to which a person or society gave allegiance. Only as the word became thus reified could it, for the first time, be used in the plural. The human race was now seen to be divided among a number of religions such as Islam, Hinduism, Buddhism, Confucianism, etc., all parallel to Christianity, the religion of Europe. At the same time as the variety of religious experience became clearly evident, it was necessary to give names to the particular religious traditions. Terms like Hinduism, Buddhism, Confucianism were not in use before the nineteenth century.

But what exactly do all these religions have in common? What is the essence of religion? Here we come up against the notoriously difficult task of defining religion, once the term has become reified. For there is no one belief, one practice, one goal, let alone a common core of such, which they all share and acknowledge to be at the centre of their tradition. To the Western mind religion involves belief in one or more gods. By this criterion, however, Jainism,

Theravada Buddhism and Confucianism could no longer be categorized as religions.

The problem of definition is further compounded by the very nature of modern change itself. A significant number of people today have consciously abandoned allegiance to any of the traditional forms of religion and say they have no religion. Since it is acknowledged that, in past history, every human society manifested a way of life which can be called religious, does this mean that for the first time in history a section of mankind is really becoming religionless? It largely depends on how we define religion.

It is true that there is widespread questioning of traditional forms of religion today. But this is not the first time in human history that this has taken place. In the next chapter we shall be referring to a period of such questioning in the ancient world. There emerged at that time new interpretations of the meaning of life which could well have been judged non-religious by the traditionalists of the day if they had possessed such a concept as our word 'religion' in its modern use. But as we look back from our present vantage point we have no hesitation in admitting the Jains and Buddhists to be religious in spite of their atheistic interpretation of life. We now see that the Buddha's rejection of the Vedas and of Brahmanism was not a religionless philosophy but a new form of religion. We need a definition of religion therefore that will do justice both to the variety of past religious forms and to the possibility that in the modern world there may be quite new forms of religion coming to birth.

We have just referred to Buddhism as a new interpretation of the meaning of life. That is a useful clue in our search for a satisfactory definition of religion. It was actually used by Carlo Della Casa when he said, 'Religion is a total mode of the interpreting and living of life'.[4] But why is it so necessary to say 'total'? Paul Tillich made this clear when he wrote, 'Religion is that which concerns us ultimately'. 'Religion is the state of being grasped by an ultimate concern, a concern which qualifies all other concerns as preliminary and which itself contains the answer to the question of the meaning of life.'[5]

In moving in this direction we are, in one sense, simply returning to the original sense of the word religion before it became identified with particular forms such as belief in God, in a supernatural world, etc. Derived from the Latin *religio* it originally meant 'devotion', 'piety' or what we may call a conscientious concern for the things which ultimately matter. Strangely enough we still sometimes use 'religion' metaphorically in this way when, for example, we say that a man is religiously punctual or has made a religion of some sport or interest to which he devotes most of his time and attention.

This approach to the definition of religion has the effect of shifting our attention from the particular and diverse forms in which men have in the past expressed their devotion, back to the nature of man himself. Man shows himself to be religious whenever and wherever he takes the questions of human existence seriously, acknowledges that life has depth and meaning, and makes his response to whatever he finds ultimate. It is the person who treats human existence as trivial or meaningless who is non-religious. This means, for example, that the sincere and concerned atheist is more religious than the half-hearted theist or nominal Christian.

The phenomenon of religion originates from within man himself and because of the fundamental nature of human existence. Only with rare exceptions, men everywhere and at all times have made some kind of response to the demands of human existence. They have tried to make something of life. They have looked for meaning and purpose. They have hoped for some kind of fulfilment. For such reasons mankind has been universally religious in the past. There is no good reason to suspect men will cease to be religious in the future, even though an increasing number appear to have grown dissatisfied with the religious forms of the past and are looking for new forms.

To understand religion it is thus necessary to distinguish between the mode of origin and the forms of expression. The latter consists of particular sets of beliefs, rituals and social structures. One such set may serve a particular society as its 'living religion' over a very long period of time.

But every such set is dependent upon an initial response (either individual or corporate) to the demands of human existence. Such a response is always made in faith. That is why faith has always been a necessary component of religion and is sometimes even identified with religion. Faith is the attitude of trust and hope in which a man responds to what he believes to be the ultimate significance of life. In each response of faith there is a content which is of supreme importance to the believer and this content determines the forms in which he expresses his response. The way in which the content is conceived, as well as the forms of expression, are open to endless variety. What is common to them all is the component of faith or trust in the initiating response.

No definition of religion is likely to prove entirely adequate. It is hoped, however, that this brief discussion will make clearer how the term is being used in this book. To summarize what has been said we now define religion as the response of faith to the ultimate issues of human existence, a response by which a society (or an individual) expresses its sense of identity, its purpose in life and its hope of fulfilment, a response which manifests itself in a complex of beliefs, rituals, life-styles and social structures.

We are now ready to discuss in a preliminary way how change is to be related to religion. The first observation arises from the way in which we have distinguished the initiating response of faith from the forms in which it comes to expression. Within the context of a living and healthy religious tradition the faith of successive generations of believers continues to add to and mould the set of forms in which the faith is expressed. There may come a time however when there arises some kind of hiatus between the initiating faith and the traditional set of forms. Although the society in question may still give nominal allegiance to the latter, it may no longer genuinely express the faith by which that society lives. In such cases a new set of forms may be embryonically taking shape. Some refer to it as a crypto-religion. If it finally comes to birth it will supersede the former religion, which then joins the company of the dead religions of man's past.

Let us now exemplify this hypothetical situation. It is an indisputable fact that at the present time the great major religions which have existed for two thousand years (some more, some less) are all suffering erosion from what has been called the acids of modernity. This is not to deny that they are also displaying some remarkable resilience. Such erosion is too often interpreted as a movement from belief to unbelief, from faith to doubt, from religion to non-religion. This judgment is dependent upon a perspective from some point within one or other of these religions. Just as it reflects too narrow a definition of religion, so also it betrays too limited a perspective. John MacMurray wrote in an essay on 'Religion in Transformation', 'The decay of religion is the first stage in a transformation of religion . . . The withdrawal of support from traditional religion is a necessary preliminary to a transformation of the religious form'.[6]

Simply to deplore the passing of the so-called 'ages of faith' is to fail to do justice to some important aspects of the contemporary religious situation. In the ancient world, for example, the person who asserted 'There is no God' could be dismissed as a fool. But the contemporary person who calls himself an atheist is very often no fool but a very intelligent man and, into the bargain, he may lead quite a virtuous life. Moreover, he very likely claims to have been led to make his atheistic assertions in the interests of what he regards as ultimate truth. It will not do simply to say he is misguided and to try to persuade him of the error of his beliefs.

Many of those who have come to sit lightly on the traditional forms of religion, or to abandon them altogether, have often done so because, not only do these no longer adequately express their personal response of faith, but they are actually in conflict with it. Their protest, in other words, is a genuinely religious one even though, from the perspective of past tradition, it appears to take an irreligious form. To use traditional religious symbols, we could say that it is the God they find speaking within them who is calling them to recognize the ancestral gods as idols and hence to abandon them. It must be freely conceded that not every example of modern apostasy can be interpreted in this way. As in the past, protest may also be an excuse to cover hidden motives of sloth, pleasure and self-indulgence. But wherever men have chosen, on the grounds of sincerity and truth, to walk no longer on the traditional paths of faith, their sincerity must be respected and the reasons for it sought.

Those who have remained loyal to the traditional paths have for the most part observed the modern erosion with sorrow and even dismay. They have often strongly resisted any change in the internal structure of their beliefs and practices, which may have been contemplated in the attempt to meet the challenges of modernity. Such resistance is understandable. Because religion expresses not just one aspect of life but the dimension of depth or ultimacy which embraces and permeates the whole of life, it is often the last thing in which one is prepared to tolerate change. Religious traditions which have been transmitted over any length of time consequently possess a strong inbuilt conservatism. It is one of the hazards of religious forms. In the Judaeo-Christian tradition this element of conservatism has been associated in particular with the priestly office, so often regarded as the vehicle for conserving the values of the past. In those periods when the priest has been the dominant religious figure the external forms of the religious tradition have been most strongly resistant to change.

But there is another side to religion, particularly in those traditions which originated around some historical figure. Here we find that religion may also be strongly associated with change and actually provide the initiators of change. These are frequently referred to as prophets. The respective roles of priest and prophet should be seen as complementary to one another rather than as mutually exclusive, even though, almost of necessity, they must often come into conflict in actual practice. Both play a desirable role in an ongoing religious tradition and on some occasions both roles have been combined in the one individual. Because the priest is conserving what is already known and accepted, there is usually little difficulty in recognizing his to be a genuinely religious role. However, since the prophet may feel called to proclaim something fresh and strange, he can be too readily mistaken for, and dismissed as, the enemy of religion. Of course, there are true prophets and false prophets and only time may clearly differentiate between the two. The true prophet, however, is the pioneer of genuine religious change and development.

In the light of this one would expect those religious traditions where the role of the prophet has rarely or never appeared, to have been relatively static, and those traditions which have known a succession of prophets, to have manifested the greatest degree of change in the course of their history. Generally speaking the history of religions seems to bear this out. In the latter category we may place early Israel, Christianity, Islam, Buddhism and their later derivatives. These also are the religions which have been most missionary. They have not only tolerated a certain amount of internal development but they have been strongly motivated to bring religious change to others by the process of conversion. In the modern period Christianity used to such effect the opportunities opened up by European imperial expansion that it has become the most widely distributed religion on a global basis. If there is, as we have suggested, a correlation between change and the prophetic character of a religious tradition, then it would be no accident at all that it is out of Western Christendom that modern global change has emerged.

In view of what has been said of priest and prophet, we can appreciate the more clearly why man, in his religious experience, has an ambivalent relationship with change. In so far as he relies on known and tried religious forms for spiritual support and guidance he does not wish them ever to change. But in so far as religious experience arises from man's own personal and inner response to the ultimate demands of existence he is bound to discard the inherited forms as soon as they cease to correspond to the voice and needs of the spirit within. This means that at a time of cultural change man finds himself pulled in two directions at once. Some will surrender to the one, some to the other; others may try to hold the two in a balanced tension. Inevitably this will lead to confusion, misunderstanding and bewilderment, such as we find in the contemporary religious situation.

How is one to understand it? How is one to get a clear picture of what is happening in the modern world with regard to religion? This brings us up against a very serious problem. Ideally one would look for an external observation post from which one could view the situation as a whole and at which one could abandon all presuppositions and let the facts speak for themselves. The success which has attended the physical sciences has been because such a stance has been largely possible. When it comes to the study of man himself this objectivity is much more difficult to achieve. In the study of religion, or what men regard as their ultimate concern, there can be no neutral observation point. This difficulty must be frankly acknowledged. This is why this book is subtitled 'A Perspective . . .' There is no absolute centre from which to view reality.

The recognition that there is no absolute centre, no neutral observation post, from which to view the changing character of religion is itself some evidence of the fact that we have moved into a new religious era. Up until relatively recently the Christian, Muslim, Oriental, etc., believed his own tradition did in fact supply the absolute and only valid point from which one could adequately view and understand man's nature and destiny. The change which is at present going on has been forcing us to concede that, however much we may continue to value one or more of these viewpoints, no one of them can be regarded as anything more than relatively true or useful. Moreover, the very conclusions we come to in a study of this kind will necessarily reflect the starting point from which we attempt to view the contemporary religious situation.

But though the problem is a very real one, to which there is no wholly satisfactory solution, the more we are alert to it the more we shall guard ourselves from the worst errors of subjective judgment into which it could lead us. It is necessary to acknowledge quite openly, and briefly to expound, the viewpoint from which this study is made. It is written from within the cultural tradition of Western Christianity by one who acknowledges that the basic values and the content of his ultimate concern have been moulded principally by the Christian faith. It is a viewpoint, however, which acknowledges that so much of what has emerged in the modern world (and which we have every reason to value) is inconsistent with Christianity in its orthodox or classical forms. The eternal verities which appeared to our forefathers to be so clear and certain apparently exist today, if they exist at all, in a very fluid form.

In a world which can too easily become chaotic, purposeless and meaningless are there any discernible signs which can help us understand just where we are in relation to the world of the past? When the early global explorers ventured out into the unknown oceans they made themselves simple maps to keep track of where they were in relation to the homeland they had come from. These maps were crude in comparison with those which later superseded them. But, at the time, they were better than nothing at all. It is always easier to improve on something which already exists than to start with nothing. What we seem to need today is some kind of map of religious history to see just where we are in the process of religious change.

This book is an attempt, in part at least, to provide such a skeleton map, in the full knowledge that it cannot expect to be complete or final. The most that can be hoped for is that it may be of some value to others who, sharing substantially the same starting point, are looking for some kind of guide. Many people today know the experience of being suddenly deposited by an airline bus in the middle of an immense unknown city. What a boon it is to find one of those large maps of the main city streets in which there is a large arrow saying, 'You are here'. This book is an attempt to say where we are in relation to man's religious past.

There is a further difficulty to be acknowledged. We have long since passed the time (if ever there was one) in which any one person can master all the available material which would have some bearing on a quest such as this. In the course of reading and research one is struck by the haphazard nature by which one sometimes stumbles across new data which proves to be strikingly relevant to the task in hand. It is little wonder that academic study has become more and more highly specialized. In order to master his subject the specialist must confine his attention to an ever smaller area of study. Today there is a tremendous body of knowledge available about the individual trees of the wood, but our pressing need is to get a clearer picture of the wood as a whole. In the area of religion, perhaps more than in most other subjects, how we come to understand and evaluate a particular tree depends very much on how we see the wood as a whole.

For the task undertaken in this book there is a wealth of material available from historians, sociologists, anthropologists, scientists, philosophers, theologians, scholars of religion and prophetic thinkers of various kinds. Only a limited amount of this ever comes to the notice of any one person and from this he must make a selection of what he regards as the most pertinent. With such a prospect it is clear that others could not only be led to interpret the material differently but also be influenced by different segments of material. In view of the diversity of opinion that this procedure could lead to, it is all the more striking to find that some broad consensus of opinion does exist among those scholars who have already given their attention to the task here being undertaken, and whose judgments will be reflected in what follows.

There is general agreement, for example, that the process of modern change in which the whole world has become enveloped originated in Western Europe and has been emerging there over the last four or five hundred years. Many non-Western countries have actually referred to the change to which their culture has been subjected as

'Westernization'. This is the reason why most of the book is devoted to a study of what was happening to the religion of Western Europe over that period. The key to the modern religious situation is believed to be there. The roots of contemporary religious change are to be found there.

This modern process of change is set, however, in the much larger context provided by the history of religions. Now it must be clearly acknowledged that the events of human history are always much more complex than any one simple theory will explain. Yet some broad patterns do emerge from an overview of history and these can be quite useful, provided they are not taken too literally, applied too rigidly or pressed too far.

The simple pattern which it is the intention of this book to expound is this. Within the known history of man there appear to have been two main thresholds of change over which man has passed in that response of faith to ultimate issues which we call religion. The first was during the first millennium BC, the centre of it being about the sixth century BC. This threshold is to be found in some three or four centres of civilization which were largely independent of each other. The second threshold is in our immediate past and present, originating in Western Christianity and now encircling the globe. There is a relationship between these two thresholds in that they may be seen as two successive steps in the one process, for which the term 'secularization', adequately defined, may prove a suitable description.

In the next chapter we shall look at the first threshold and draw attention to the specific changes there discernible, which enable one to give it such a label. Thereafter we shall concentrate on the second threshold, starting in Chapter 3 with the significant steps which led up to it. The centre of it, the watershed between the modern world and all that preceded it, is to be located in the eighteenth century. The aftermath of that watershed will then be examined in greater detail, first to make clear that a radical religious shift had taken place and secondly to show how the foundations of the modern religious era are to be found there. The seminal thinkers – Hegel, Strauss, Feuerbach and Marx – form an interconnected succession. The modern world owes more to them that it usually realizes. Though they may be hailed, in part, as the pioneers of the contemporary world they should be seen not so much as the creators of the modern world as the interpreters of the new era which had emerged with man's crossing of a major threshold.

Then we shall look at the way in which the physical sciences, the social sciences and intercultural encounter not only make the modern world different from the pre-modern, but constitute the common heritage of an emerging global culture. It then remains to draw the threads together, to show how the two thresholds may be linked together and to explore how and why the second threshold is to be related to the Christian tradition.

CHAPTER 2

THE FIRST MAJOR THRESHOLD OF RELIGIOUS CHANGE

❖

When one looks back over the history of religion, in all its complexity and diversity, one finds that at the beginning of the modern era (say the sixteenth century) the many human societies then existing, with only minimal contact with each other, were roughly of two kinds. For a long time Western man was inclined to label these the civilized and the uncivilized. In so far as the word 'civilization' etymologically refers to, and implies the presence of, the more complex social structure of urban life this division is justified. In the civilized world there was evident a sophistication of life which was lacking in the so-called uncivilized societies.

The civilized world consisted mainly of the great land mass of Europe and Asia, though it spilled over into some northern sections of Africa and into islands like Japan. The uncivilized world was to be found in the rest of Africa (the 'dark continent'), the Americas, Australia, Melanesia and Polynesia and in some small isolated pockets of Asia. There were some very marked differences between these two worlds in the quality of their life, the sophistication of their culture and, especially for our purposes, the type of their religion.

The societies of the uncivilized world were mainly tribal in character, their culture was still often Stone Age though some had developed the use of metals, and their religion fell into the category now often described as primal. The numerous primal religions were all unique in their particulars but manifested a number of broad characteristics in common. These we shall be describing shortly.

When we turn to the civilized world we find that it was composed of comparatively few independent types of civilization and each of these was based upon, and could be identified by, a nameable religious tradition. They were the Christian West, the Islamic Middle East, Hindu India, the Buddhist Orient. China had long been more pluralistic in that the indigenous Confucianism and Taoism had lived in peaceful, if at times uneasy, co-existence with the incoming Buddhism. Within these broad divisions there were also many lesser modifications, which there is no need here to elaborate, as well as other significant religious minorities, such as the Jews, the Jains, the Parsis, the Sikhs.

Culturally and religiously there was a very wide gap between the uncivilized and the civilized worlds. When Western man first became acquainted with the rest of the globe, from the sixteenth century onwards, he was able to appreciate the *cultural* gap from the beginning. He did not at first always appreciate the *religious* gap. To the Christian mind all non-Christians were pagans, irrespective of whether they were animists or Hindus, headhunters or Buddhists. Only in the course of time have Christians been forced to concede that there is a very significant difference between the levels reached by the religious traditions of the civilized world and those of the uncivilized world. It has been reflected in the fact that, whereas the missionary spread of Christianity has been relatively successful in the latter, it has rarely gained more than a somewhat unstable foothold in the various areas of the non-Christian civilized world.

Now if, as we have very good reason to believe, the whole human race at present on this earth is descended from a common biological and cultural stock in the distant, Stone Age past, how did this gap come about? Apparently the societies of the civilized world are the heirs of one or more stages of cultural development which had not occurred in the tribal societies. So far as we can judge, the kind of life lived in the latter (and this includes the kind of religion practised) has continued with comparatively little change for a very long time. It appears that the distant ancestors of all in the civilized world lived a life, many millennia ago, not dissimilar from that still extant in the tribal societies at the beginning of the modern era.

But whereas the structures and beliefs of tribal societies stretch back into pre-history the characteristics of the civilized world had beginnings which can be traced within the known history of man. Indeed each of the major religious traditions, by which we have above identified the various societies of the civilized world, looks back to an origin in a particular historical period. In some cases an historical figure is named as the founder or authoritative teacher. (By contrast, the tribal societies have to draw upon unhistorical myth with which to describe their origins and, in so far as these people look to founders at all, these are usually superhuman divine figures who belong to myth and not to history.)

These historical origins stretch from the second millennium BC (in the case of Abraham, Moses, and the anonymous authors of the Vedas and of the early Upanishads) down to the seventh century AD (in the case of Islam, the youngest of the great traditional religions). An expanse of some two thousand years constitutes quite a short period, however, when viewed against the background of the 100,000 years or more during which *Homo sapiens* has inhabited the earth, and, during quite a long section of which, man lived a Stone Age existence.

Within the period 1750 BC to AD 650 it is possible to point

to a relatively short period which was particularly fruitful with regard to the number of religious traditions which find their historical origin within it. In 1856 Lasaulx drew attention to this phenomenon for the first time: 'It cannot possibly be an accident that, six hundred years before Christ, Zarathustra in Persia, Gautama the Buddha in India, Confucius in China, the prophets in Israel, King Numa in Rome;[1] and the first philosophers – the Ionians, Dorians and Eleatics – in Hellas – all made their appearances pretty well simultaneously as reformers of the national religion' he wrote.[2] In 1870 Viktor von Strauss referred to the same set of facts as 'a strange movement of the spirit (which) passed through all civilized peoples'.[3] Karl Jaspers explored it further in his book *The Origin and Goal of History*.

The Western world, from about the sixth century right down to the present, has dated its calendar from the supposed birth year of Jesus of Nazareth. It saw that year as a central point which divided history into two halves. Even Hegel could say, 'All history goes towards and comes from Christ'. Since this axis of history is valid only on Christian premises, Jaspers looked for an axis which would be valid for the whole of what we have called the civilized world and he believed one could be found. 'It would seem that this axis of history is to be found in the period around 500 BC in the spiritual process that occurred between 800 and 200 BC. It is there that we meet with the most deepcut dividing line in history. Man, as we know him today, came into being. For short we may style this the "Axial Period".'[4]

The religions of the civilized world (referred to by Arnold Toynbee as the 'higher religions') either have their origin in the Axial Period (e.g. Judaism, Zoroastrianism, Hinduism, Buddhism, Jainism, Confucianism, Taoism) or are directly dependent upon those which do (e.g. Christianity, Islam, Sikhism). The limits of 800 to 200 BC set by Jaspers cannot be applied very rigidly but nothing of significance hangs upon those limits. Certainly when one thinks of all that the subsequent world owed to them, it is surprising to find what near contemporaries were Zarathustra, Mahavira, Gautama the Buddha, Confucius, Lao-tzu (or the author of the Tao Te Ching), Chuang Tzu and the Greek philosophers.

Whether we regard as pure coincidence the almost simultaneous appearance of these men in some five or six areas which were geographically isolated from each other, or whether we interpret it as evidence of some underlying spiritual force (as some have been inclined to do), the fact remains that this period stands out as a kind of watershed in the history of religion. In Greece, Palestine, Persia, northern India and northern China religion underwent a change. It was just as if man's religious apprehension of his world underwent a giant turn on its axis. Through a limited number of individuals, some of them known to us by name, the human race passed over a threshold in self-understanding, a threshold which was destined to have far-reaching consequences for the whole human race. Human self-consciousness, mental reflection and spirituality reached a new level. Man asked new and radical questions about himself, his world and the cultural traditions which he had inherited from the past. The threshold man passed over was irreversible. This did not mean that the religion of the pre-Axial period disappeared never to return. In actual fact much of the pre-Axial religion did survive and live on, just beneath the surface of the new level then reached. The threshold was irreversible in the sense that never again has the human race as a whole reverted to religion of the pre-Axial type and as time goes on this prospect becomes increasingly unthinkable.

Presently we shall describe and compare the characteristics of the two types of religion – pre-Axial and post-Axial. But before doing so we must draw attention to the fact that the Axial Period does not itself mark the origin of the civilized world. The Axial Period marks a threshold crossed *within* the history of civilization itself (or, if one prefers, within the several civilizations which then made up the civilized world).

Civilization (so far as the historical data allow us to determine) first arose in the fourth millennium BC in the river valleys of Mesopotamia and Egypt, and perhaps a little later in the Indus Valley and in China. We now know these civilizations developed remarkable technical skills and achieved a high level of sophistication. The advent of urban culture naturally meant changes to religious belief and practice. One could readily demonstrate that an important stage of development took place there in the total story of man's religious development. Robert Bellah has set it out admirably in his well-known essay on 'Religious Evolution'[5] where he refers to it as the change from Primitive Religion to Archaic Religion.

We shall not here describe the particular characteristics of this Archaic Religion of the earlier civilizations, for two reasons. The characteristics of the primal religions of man which we are now about to sketch also apply substantially to the religions of the early urban societies. It is true, however, that in the latter they occur in a more sophisticated form and, consequently, the contrast between them and the post-Axial religions is not so striking as that between the primal religions and the post-Axial religions. This fact leads to the second reason why we need not pause to give them special attention. None of the religions of the early civilizations survived the advent of the Axial Period. They may be regarded as stepping-stones to the religion of the post-Axial type and, as such, were left behind or superseded. The absence of any pure example of Archaic Religion at the advent of the modern world, with the possible exception of the Aztecs and Incas, made the contrast between the primal religions of the uncivilized world and the post-Axial religions of the civilized world all the more striking.

The first thing to be said about pre-Axial religion is that it had no name. We still have to refer to examples of it by reference to the people who practised it. We speak of the religion of the Sumerians, of the Romans, of the Maoris, etc. Pre-Axial man was not aware of possessing a religion. What we may choose to describe as his religion was such an integral part of his whole culture and way of life that it could not be divorced from it and objectified as an entity in itself. This phenomenon has sometimes led anthropologists to describe a few isolated tribes as religionless.

It is true that some primitive societies are not religious in ways which resemble religion of the post-Axial type. We have already noted that by the same narrow definition of religion some moderns describe themselves as non-religious. It is not only because of modern men but also because of some primitive men that we are forced to adopt the broader definition of religion enunciated in the last chapter. When we ask if pre-Axial man responded to the ultimate issues of his existence with a complex of beliefs, rituals, life-styles and social structures then the answer is always in the affirmative and it is by looking for these that we may isolate what is to be called his religion. For him, however, it was simply a total way of life which he had inherited from his ancestors reaching back to the mythical past.

Two important corollaries follow from this first observation about pre-Axial religion. The first is that for pre-Axial man religion was always ethnic in character. It could not be divorced from the tribe, city, or people who practised it. It expressed the identity of the group rather than that of the individual. The second is that, by the same token, the individual had absolutely no choice in his religion. He was born into it. It belonged to him like the colour of his skin. He was not free, in this respect, either to embrace it or to opt out of it.

Now we must turn to the world-view of pre-Axial man, for the way in which one responds to what is ultimate depends upon how one sees the world in which one lives. In one sense there were innumerable world-views, for the particulars varied from one society to another. But there are some broad and important aspects which they all shared. To pre-Axial man the world around him was pregnant with unseen powers, very varied in character, and both beneficent and hostile. These unseen forces permeated man's own world. He did not project them into a world divorced from his own. Being unseen, these forces had distinct advantages over him and he was at their mercy. It was in that sense that they transcended him. The world in which he lived, in fact, was *their* world and man did not really have a world of his own.

The world-view of pre-Axial man was consequently basically monistic. For him there was *one* word, alive in diverse ways with powers superior to himself, whether they were conceived as gods, spirits or impersonal forces. 'The most elementary forms of behaviour motivated by religious or magical factors are oriented to *this* world', wrote Max Weber.[6]

In this one world, in which there was so much to threaten his existence, pre-Axial man was chiefly concerned with the basic needs of food, protection and reproduction. His beliefs and rituals evolved around these – the perpetuation of the food supply, the warding off of evil powers, the phenomenon of birth and death, growth and decay. The religion of pre-Axial man developed in such a way as to relate him to the unseen forces in the natural world about him and may be loosely referred to as nature-religion.

The religion of pre-Axial man was pragmatic in character and not at all theoretical. He performed his rituals because, in his experience, they worked. He was not much interested in asking how or why they worked. Two of the great collections of the ancient practice of sacrifice, preserved today in the Brahmanas and in the Levitical Law of the Old Testament, are noteworthy for the fact that they embody no theory, or even hint, of why they should work but only of how they should be performed. As Durkheim has said, 'The religions of Antiquity are, above all, systems of rites, the essential object of which is to assure the regular working of the universe. For the wheat to spring up and yield an abundant harvest, the rivers to flow, and the stars to move in their appointed paths, the gods of the harvest, the gods of the rivers and the gods of the stars must subsist, and it is the rites which allow them to do so. If they ceased to take place on the established days, and in the prescribed manner, the life of the universe would come to an end'.[7]

Although pre-Axial man was not interested in how his rituals worked he was clear as to why they should be performed and this was expressed in the myths associated with the rituals. These were often narrated in the course of the performance of the respective rituals and told how they originated in the mythical past. Indeed all of the beliefs in which pre-Axial man verbally expressed his understanding of the ultimate issues of existence belong to the category we now clearly recognize as mythology. We see them as symbolic and imaginative creations of the human mind. For him they described reality.

The myths and rituals by which pre-Axial man related himself to the world were for him as old as the world itself. They had come down to him, unchanged, from that mythical time of origins – the beginning-time. They represented the unchangeable truth of the world and the continuance of the world depended upon his playing his part. This discouraged him from attempting any novel practices, which could have the effect of upsetting the balance or destroying the world order. There was thus an inbuilt conservatism in pre-Axial religion. Religion legitimated and preserved the *status quo*. Change was minimal and for the most part was to be avoided at all costs. Pre-Axial man was deeply convinced of the dire necessity to continue the ritual with attention devoted to the smallest detail. This conviction derived from the feeling response and was not based on any form of reasoning. Most of us have experienced, even in the modern world and especially during childhood, a non-rational reluctance to depart from an established routine for fear of the unfortunate consequences to which it might lead.

Finally, for pre-Axial man, religion was essentially something social. It was that on which the continuing life of the society (tribe, city or nation) depended and the life of the community took precedence over that of the individual. The individual who appeared to threaten the viability or identity of the community had to be liquidated for the sake of the latter. There was little future for the individual who would not conform. This factor, too, discouraged any change initiated from within. The innate potential in the individual for creative enquiry was permanently suppressed by a religious system which was committed to the *status quo*. The religious office of witch-doctor, medicine man, priest was dominant.

This sketch of the chief characteristics of pre-Axial religion does not pretend to be exhaustive but it will suffice for our purposes. In the light of the last-named it is all the more remarkable that the Axial Period occurred as it did. Here for the first time in history, and on a grand scale, men dared to be individualists and to ask radical questions about their cultural inheritance. They actively initiated change. The men who did so were still only a tiny minority. They lived sometimes as hermits or wandering ascetics. They were solitary thinkers. They introduced the religious role of prophet. Through these men the human race took a giant step forward in self-understanding and religion passed over an important threshold. The fact that it took centuries for the fruits of these pioneers to become widely disseminated and that pre-Axial religion still continued in some areas should not be allowed to blind us to the significance of that period itself. As Jaspers observed, 'What the individual achieves is by no means passed on to all. The gap between the peaks of human potentiality and the crowd became exceptionally great at that time. None the less, what the individual becomes indirectly changes all. The whole of humanity took a forward leap'.[8]

Through those solitary thinkers mankind passed over a threshold of reflection. It was not the beginning of thought. But thought operates at different levels. At the Axial Period man not only thought but became aware that he was a thinker. Human consciousness became conscious of itself. Self-reflection lifted man out of the tangible context in which he lived and enabled him to see it more objectively and to question it. He reached a new level of existence. In his reflection he transcended the world of space and time and had a taste of eternity. 'What is new about this age in all three areas of the world', wrote Jaspers, 'is that man becomes conscious of Being as a whole, of himself and his limitations . . . He asks radical questions. Face to face with the void he strives for liberation and redemption. By consciously recognizing his limits he sets himself the highest goals. He experiences absoluteness in the depths of selfhood and in the lucidity of transcendence.'[9]

Man's apprehension of things eternal and transcendent made him all the more aware of his limitations and of the finiteness of the world in which he lived. His reflections led him into a spiritual conflict which needed to be resolved. To rise above the tragic enigma he found in human existence – that is, to find salvation – he looked beyond his immediate world to another order of reality, another world.

He was no longer satisfied with the world of space and time. He was no longer satisfied when his bodily needs were satisfied. He looked for that which would satisfy his spirit – that of which he had newly become aware. He looked for that which is eternal. Since nothing in this world could be identified with what he sought he found it necessary to look beyond this world to another world which transcends space and time. The way in which this search produced results varied from one centre to another wherever the Axial change was experienced, but there were some features common to them all. As Jaspers says, 'In this age were born the fundamental categories within which we still think today and the beginnings of the world religions, by which human beings still live, were created'.[10]

Man's newly found capacity for reflection manifested itself most impressively in Greece, reaching a peak in the Age of Pericles, so much so that we still see Socrates, Plato and Aristotle, along with the pre-Socratics, as having laid the foundation of Western philosophy. The reign of mythology had come to an end. Whereas man had previously expressed his understanding of the world, and of his own place in it, in the form of myth, man now subjected his traditional myths to critical examination. He developed an understanding of himself and of his world at a more fundamental and non-mythological level. Greece produced thinkers, however, rather than religious founders. Philosophy *per se*, is not for popular assimilation as religion must be. Even Stoicism and Neo-Platonism, which were more clearly religious in function, became absorbed later into Christianity.

It was out of Israel, Persia, India and China that the chief post-Axial religions emerged, supplying for us in themselves and their derivatives the living religions of the civilized world which have survived to this day. In their founders – the Israelite prophets, Zarathustra, the Upanishadic seers,

Mahavira, the Buddha, Confucius, Lao-tzu – we also find ample evidence of critical reflection on past tradition, resulting in new formulations of the way in which man should respond in faith to the ultimate issues of existence. While there was certainly some continuity (as there always must be) with what had gone before, there was also an important element of discontinuity, and it was this which allowed for creative change to take place.

As we turn now to look at the post-Axial religions and see how they differed from the pre-Axial religions we must be alert to the dangers of the simplistic overview. Human history, human society and even the solitary individual are always more complex than any of the patterns or schemes into which we try to press them. Provided we allow for this caveat there are some useful observations which can be made about the post-Axial religions as a whole. As Jaspers notes, 'These paths are widely divergent in their conviction and dogma but common to all of them is man's reaching out beyond himself by growing aware of himself within the whole of Being and the fact that he can tread them only as an individual on his own'.[11]

In the Middle Eastern family of religions (Judaism, Christianity and Islam) polytheism gave way to monotheism. The one God is himself regarded as the only eternal reality. The tangible world lost its earlier sacred quality. The latter pertained to God alone. Neither images nor temples could any more contain, or be identified with, the eternal deity. Consequently there has been a strong iconoclastic component in Western religion. At the same time this gave man a new freedom to possess the earth and to use it. He acquired a new mastery over the earth because it had been desacralized, at least partially, and holiness was concentrated in a supra-earthly deity.

In India the eternal reality, conceived as Brahman, was also differentiated from the tangible world which consequently is *maya*. This means that the world is not itself eternal but is the mask of reality only. But since the spirit or *atman* of man may be identified with Brahman, man finds salvation in the process of realizing his identity with Brahman. Once again man saw his ultimate destiny in a reality beyond the tangible world.

The Buddha shared the basic Indian premises but was so taken up with the problem of human suffering that his programme of salvation took a different form. Ultimate Reality was conceived, not as the loving God and not as identity with Brahman, but as the final cessation of suffering in the blowing-out of the candle of desire. This leads to Nirvana or Sunyata (emptiness).

Confucius did not think any worthwhile purpose was served by asking radical questions for which there was no certain answer. He settled for a way of life which proved pragmatically satisfying if not intellectually complete. The Taoist, however, did go further in his search for the eternal and found it in the eternal Tao which is beyond speech and description.

In all these areas (for even Confucius found it necessary to order one's life by reference to the world of one's deceased ancestors) there was a reaching out to another world. Man's ultimate concern was conceived in terms of a spiritual, intangible, non-spacial, non-temporal world. A consequence of this was the devaluation of the physical world of space and time. It was destined for destruction. It was *maya*. It had to be transcended. There was also an accompanying devaluation of this-worldly human existence. It involves sin, evil, death, the burden of rebirth, suffering.

As Max Weber said, 'As otherworldly expectations become increasingly important . . . the problem of the world's imperfections press(es) into the foreground of thought. The more life here on earth comes to be regarded as a merely provisional form of existence, when compared with that beyond, the more the world comes to be viewed as something created by God *ex nihilo* and therefore subject to decline'.[12]

The first observation to be made about the Axial change is that the monistic world-view of pre-Axial man was replaced, to a greater or less extent, by a dualistic world-view where reality was conceived as consisting of two different and mutually exclusive worlds. There is the finite, tangible, physical and temporal world, in which we experience this life, with its accompanying conditions of suffering, evil and death. There is an infinite, invisible, non-physical and timeless world where perfect bliss is to be enjoyed in one of a variety of ways. Man finds himself living in the first but seeks a way of reaching for the second. Each of the new Axial religions offered to show him that way, in some cases claiming it to be the only way. The transition from a monistic to a dualistic world in the case of the Christian tradition was described by Durkheim thus, 'In a word, with Christianity, the world lost the confused unity which it possessed formerly, and split into two parts, two halves of very unequal value; there is on the one hand, the world of thought, consciousness, morality and religion, and on the other the world of inanimate matter, amoral and a-religious'.[13]

In contrast with pre-Axial man, who had been primarily concerned with the basic needs of food, protection and reproduction, post-Axial man fastened his attention on his spiritual needs. He became convinced that 'man does not live by bread alone' but needed to nourish his own spirit by communion with the world of the spirit. The dualistic world-view was thus mirrored in a dualistic view of man. Man is both body and spirit and the true self of man was conceived as a spiritual entity, not necessarily tied to the physical body with which it is always associated in this world. Religion consequently changed from a nature type to a salvation type. The religious aim was no longer to ensure the continuation of the natural order of the cosmos but to ensure, in another world, the ultimate salvation of the true self.

Man's new awareness of his spiritual potential had the effect of shifting the focal point of attention from the social group to the individual. Religion became more of an individual, personal affair. It became a matter of choice and required some active decision on the part of those who embraced it. Interpersonal responsibilities and social cohesion, while not neglected, became secondary to the primary goal of individual salvation and resulted from the sharing of the common faith.

The fact that there was something to be shared, something which could be embraced or rejected by an act of the will, meant that post-Axial religion expressed itself as an identifiable entity which, unlike pre-Axial religion, could be named. Although names like Buddhism, Hinduism, etc., are relatively modern, each of the post-Axial religions did use a term which pin-pointed the substance of the faith – the Law of Moses, the Gospel of Jesus Christ, Islam, the Dharma, etc. It was what could be accepted or rejected.

The capacity of post-Axial religion to become a definable body of beliefs, attitudes, rituals and codes of behaviour, all revolving round some permanent centre, such as the above names pointed to, meant that it could disengage itself from the ethnic context in which it originated. The religious tradition could travel from person to person, crossing over ethnic and national boundaries and becoming international. One did not embrace post-Axial religion simply because of an accident of birth. It was not necessary to be born into it. It was not tied to any race. It was for all men and not only for particular groups of men. As Toynbee noted, 'the appearance of a higher religion splits an integrated culture and finds social expression in an independent organization of its own and engages in missionary activity. It becomes universalist and wishes to communicate its message to all mankind'.[14]

The originators of post-Axial religion were prophets and authoritative teachers who, by their own epoch-making messages, introduced into the religious scene a new religious office, that of the prophet. The prophet commands attention because he is heard to speak, not on his own behalf, but on behalf of the ultimate source of truth. Only by means of such authority could men be disengaged from the iron grip of past tradition, and the inbuilt conservatism of pre-Axial religion be overcome. Before very long the post-Axial religions developed their own forms of conservatism. But a tradition which has once accepted the voice of the prophet also retains the potential to bring forth more prophets, even if usually of a lesser stature than the originating prophet. The office of prophet, though not necessarily referred to by that name, became a feature of the ongoing post-Axial religions, ready to counter the complementary office of the priest when the influence of the latter became too dominant. Post-Axial religions could never become as static as pre-Axial religion had been. Through the office of prophet, change could not only be tolerated but even be promoted from within the tradition itself.

In association with the role of the prophet, but also to be differentiated from it, we must also note in the post-Axial religions the place of the thinker, the theologian, the philosopher. This also was the legacy of the prophetic founders. Each of the higher religions developed its own tradition of philosophical reflection in which the religion in question was subjected to intellectual exploration, examination and self-criticism. This phenomenon not only differentiated these from pre-Axial religion but was to prove of great importance for future development and change.

Finally we must note that the originating founders, by

bringing new and authoritative teachings, were able to disengage religion from much of the mythology which pre-Axial religion had inherited from pre-historic times. Certainly new myths emerged, for religious faith cannot dispense with myth, if understood as a symbolic portrayal of ultimate truth. But the new myths were of a somewhat different order. In so far as these evolved round the historical figures of the founders they may be said to be historically-grounded myths in contrast with the earlier mythology which had much less obvious contact with the scene of human history.

Once again this is not an exhaustive list of the characteristics which distinguish the post-Axial religions from pre-Axial religion but they are sufficient to make the difference clear. It must be freely conceded that not all the higher religions display the above marks to the same degree. They are most clearly to be found in Buddhism, Christianity and Islam. Even in these the break with pre-Axial religion has never been absolute. Much of pre-Axial religion has lived on as folk-religion, either beneath the surface, or synthesized with the later tradition. When elements of this are pointed out, however, they are usually not claimed by authoritative exponents of the religion in question as belonging to the essential character of that faith and sometimes they have been emphatically disowned.

Judaism, Hinduism and Confucianism do not display the post-Axial characteristics as clearly as the above three. They have remained more ethnic in character, more monistic in world-view, more pragmatic and almost totally non-missionary. Yet Judaism formed the matrix for the emergence of Christianity and Islam while Hinduism did the same for Buddhism. These two appear to straddle the Axis rather than to find a place clearly on one side or the other. Justification for placing them in the post-Axial category is to be found not only in the fact that they have survived to the present day but even more in the fact that their derivative religions could not displace them. It is a feature of post-Axial religions that wherever they have spread they have displaced or overlaid the pre-Axial forms of religion they encountered. Judaism, however, firmly maintained its identity in both Christendom and the Islamic world. Buddhism could not displace the Hindu religion of the land of its birth but flourished in the Orient outside of India. But neither could Buddhism displace the Confucianism and Taoism of China.

Once the post-Axial religions had come to birth they began to radiate out from their respective points of origin, as circumstances permitted. The fact that they appealed to the needs of the human condition, and not just to those of a particular ethnic or geographical grouping, gave to each of them the capacity to become the religion of all mankind. If there had been only one post-Axial religion, perhaps by now it would have become the global religion. Because there were several, they were able to spread with maximum influence only as far as the geographical boundaries where they finally encountered each other. Buddhism, Islam and Christianity, for example, have all made strong efforts in turn to become the religion of India, but without success.

This sketch of the significance of the Axial Period and of the resulting post-Axial religions is admittedly an over-simplification. But in spite of the many objections that can be validly made on this score there still remains sufficient truth in the schema outlined to make it a worthwhile perspective for viewing the religious past. Jaspers summarized the Axial Period thus: 'The conception of the Axial Period furnishes the questions and standards with which to approach all preceding and subsequent developments. The outlines of the preceding civilizations dissolve. The peoples that bore them vanish from sight as they join in the movement of the Axial Period. The prehistoric peoples remain prehistoric until they merge into the historical movement that proceeds from the Axial Period, or die out. The Axial Period assimilates everything that remains. From it world history receives the only structure and unity that has endured – at least until our own time.'[15]

In this schema we have attempted to outline the basic changes which the manifestation of religion underwent during the Axial Period. What are often regarded as the higher religions – or the major religions of the world – such as Judaism, Christianity, Islam, Hinduism, Buddhism, Confucianism and Taoism, derive their distinctive character from what came to birth during that period. Each of these subsequently went through its own particular form of development. Each has its own, very complex history. There was a strong tendency for some of these at least to revert to religious forms which were pre-Axial rather than post-Axial in character. But there was no distinctively new religious development until the advent of the modern era, a movement which began with the disintegration of medieval Christendom. To understand the nature of this we must now turn.

CHAPTER 3

SOME SIGNIFICANT STEPS LEADING TO THE MODERN WORLD

❖

The modern world emerged out of the medieval world of Western Christendom by a series of steps, many of which were felt as social shocks. Although the watershed between the modern world and what preceded is most clearly to be found in the eighteenth century, we need to go back as far as the fourteenth century if we are not to overlook the earliest signs of the great changes which were destined to appear. In many ways medieval culture may be said to have peaked in the thirteenth century.

The unity and homogeneity of medieval Western Christendom has sometimes been unduly magnified by later generations, as they looked back with nostalgia to what they saw as the golden age of Christian civilization. Nevertheless medieval Europe was unified in a quite impressive way by a Christian-based culture which transcended differences of race, language and class. The twelfth and thirteenth centuries witnessed vigorous intellectual activity of a high order. It saw the foundation of the early European universities.

The Christian faith had little difficulty in attracting the attention, and retaining the allegiance of the best intellects of the time, at least in a general way. Theology was the Queen of the Sciences and all great thinkers of the age were well grounded in it. This fact was the culmination of an intellectual tradition which had started with the second-century Apologists, who being confident that Christianity could adequately counter all the intellectual objections posed by non-Christians, laid the foundations of the enterprise of Christian theology. To some extent it superseded the philosophical enterprise which had originated in Greece, but largely by absorbing it and baptizing it into the Christian mould. We noted in the last chapter that one of the features of post-Axial religion is that it either gave rise to, or became closely associated with, the philosophical pursuit.

Christian theology from the beginning affirmed the importance of both faith and reason even though it gave to faith a certain primacy, as evidenced in Augustine's dictum, 'I believe in order that I may understand'. This synthesis of religious faith with rational thought, of divine revelation with human reason, was more or less complete in the Western intellectual tradition by the time of Augustine. It became consolidated in the Scholasticism which developed between Augustine and Aquinas.

The first serious threat to this tradition came through the influence of the Muslim rationalist philosopher Averroës (1126-98) through whom, among others, the works of Aristotle came to be known and studied in Christian Europe. Aristotelianism caused real ferment but Albertus, followed by his student, the even greater Aquinas, largely restored the equilibrium of Christian thought by embracing this pre-Christian philosophy and harnessing it to serve Christian ends. Some see this Medieval Catholic Synthesis, as it has been called, as the logical and legitimate development of Christian thought, while others view it as the introduction of a new and suspect element.

Although Thomism established itself eventually as the authoritative Christian philosophy (remaining so for Roman Catholicism up to Vatican II), it was not without rivals. The Franciscans, in particular, were not so convinced by the Thomistic synthesis. One of them, Roger Bacon (c. 1214-92), was encouraged by his attraction to Aristotle to study the physical world in a way which was independent of theology. Some have even hailed him as the forerunner of modern science. Yet he was not really an original thinker even though his ideas were sufficiently novel to lead to his imprisonment.

We must turn to a much greater Franciscan of the following century if we are to find the first evidence of how and why the Thomistic synthesis would eventually prove to be unstable. He is William of Ockham (c. 1300-49), a vigorous and independent thinker, who was largely responsible for the spread of nominalism (also called conceptualism). The prevailing philosophy of the day (known as realism) maintained that what is eternally real is to be found in ideas and universal concepts, for these are not subject to change and decay. In direct opposition to this the nominalists contended that the only things which really exist are the particular things which exemplify the universal. Universals, they said, are simply names or concepts which have been constructed by the human mind after reflecting on the particular objects observed and apprehended through the senses.

The great philosophical debate then waged between realism and nominalism may strike the modern mind as very abstract and academic. Actually the opposition between these two ways of looking at reality is much more far-reaching than at first appears, and then perhaps even Ockham realized. Ockham was thus led to assert that man has no knowledge of God, even by intuition. It is faith alone, and not reason, which forms the basis for conviction and certainty in theological matters. He denied that there is any such thing as a Christian philosophy. In contrast with Aquinas he believed it to be impossible to give any cogent proofs of the existence of God. Ockham thus drove a wedge between philosophy and theology and destroyed the Thomistic synthesis. For him theology and philosophy are two quite separate intellectual disciplines. The first explores and expounds what has been divinely revealed and is to be apprehended only by faith. The second explores those aspects of reality which can be examined and understood by human reason.

Although Ockham did not draw the contrasts nearly as sharply as this brief sketch has done, even men of the fourteenth century sensed they were at the crossroads and that nominalism would lead in a quite different direction. It was referred to as the *via moderna* in contrast with the *via antiqua*. Certainly it was destined to be some centuries later before the divorce between theology and philosophy was to be anything like complete. And when it did come it was not simply through the increasing development of an overt nominalist philosophy, for the latter tended to become reabsorbed into the Scholastic tradition.

Nevertheless, later thinkers such as Luther and Feuerbach, whose teaching represents significant milestones on the road to modernity, did not hesitate to acknowledge that they stood in the nominalist tradition. Jacques Maritain, a twentieth-century neo-Thomist, went so far as to assert, 'Whether they be neo-Kantians, neo-positivists, idealists, Bergsonians, logistics, pragmatists or neo-Spinozists or neo-mysticists, one ancient sin works in the root of all modern philosophers – the old error of nominalism'.[1]

In the fourteenth century nominalism began to capture the universities. It had the effect in the long run of causing philosophy to become a lay, rather than always a clerical, pursuit. It was the forerunner of the later empirical philosophy and of the modern scientific method. As Copleston has justly said of it, 'the way was being prepared for a philosophy of nature which, while not necessarily anti-

Christian, emphasized nature as an intelligible totality governed by its own immanent laws'.[2] To take an example, Ockham rejected Aristotle's theory of motion as a quality impressed on the projectile by the agent and to some extent he anticipated the laws of inertia and momentum.

The teaching of Ockham was recognized in his own day as a threat to Christian orthodoxy. He was excommunicated, expelled from the Franciscan Order, and forced to flee to Bavaria. This led him to write polemics against the Pope. He and his contemporary, Marsilius of Padua (c. 1280-1343), became the two most outspoken critics of the papacy in the Middle Ages. Whereas Ockham helped to destroy the unity of the theologico-philosophical tradition, Marsilius heralded the breakdown of the organizational structure of Western society. The ecclesiastical edifice which embraced Christendom was also a synthesis, joining the community of faith with the power pyramid inherited from ancient Rome. This centred on the Papal Office, which had assumed the mantle of the former Roman Emperors, as the title of *Pontifex Maximus* bears witness.

In his *Defensor Pacis*, the most original essay on political theory to be written in the Middle Ages, Marsilius applied Aristotelian principles to the problems of government and heralded the concept of the modern secular state. He affirmed that the source of all law and political power resides in the people themselves, who consequently have the right to choose their own ruler. To make this possible the power of the Church must be limited to the area of morals and doctrine. Even here, this authority should not be vested in the absolute power of the Pope but in a general council, representative of all Christians both clerical and lay. The authority of the council was to take precedence over that of the Pope.

Marsilius foresaw, and taught as desirable, the transfer of power from the Church to the State. He thought that

Church affairs should be related to the State through a kind of government department. He can thus be seen as the herald of much which was to emerge at the Reformation, particularly where Erastianism[3] prevailed, but more generally in the greater participation of the laity in ecclesiastical government. The first printed edition of his book (1517) was actually used by Cranmer and Hooker, two of the architects of Anglicanism. Today many of his concerns seem quite commonplace, so much have we absorbed them into the contemporary scene.

From forerunners such as these we move to what has been known since the mid-nineteenth century as the Renaissance. The men of the Renaissance were little aware, at first, that they were taking steps towards a brave new world. On the contrary they looked back with deep admiration to the cultural heights reached by ancient Greece and Rome and wished to revive the flowering of the human spirit which had been present in that pre-Christian world. They were not blind admirers of antiquity, however; they wished to emulate rather than to imitate. Petrarch (1314-74), in calling for the study of antiquity, expressed the hope that men would be able 'to walk forward in the pure radiance of the past'.

The Renaissance was both the revival of interest in the human attainments of the past and the launching pad for the journey by Western man to the new world. Copleston observes that 'Even among writers who were devout Christians one can discern the conviction that a new age for man was beginning'.[4] Those modern Christian thinkers who, like Berdyaev, deplore what they see as the fruits of the Renaissance and those who, like many modern humanists, rejoice in the same, all agree that 'the Renaissance was the starting-point of modern times',[5] and that it is therefore 'one of the decisive moments in man's history'.[6] S. R. Hopper in discussing what he called *The Crisis of Faith* concluded that 'The premises of the modern period stem from the Renaissance', to which we owe 'the basic assumptions which have given rise to our passion for freedom, for reason, for investigation, for science, for modernity'.[7]

J. A. Mazzeo in his *Renaissance and Revolution* went so far as to say that 'the Renaissance was a revolution of consciousness', one 'which first took place in the minds of the cultural leaders of Europe before it transformed their institutions and culture'.[8] These cultural leaders were no longer exclusively clerical as had been the case in the Middle Ages. With the growth of urban society there emerged a literate laity, for whom the monastic life was too austere and other-worldly. They found that the classics spoke to the human condition in a way that the scholastic tradition did not. In some respects the Renaissance was a peaceful revolt against the clerical monopoly of learning and the Scholastic strait-jacket into which it had been placed. The ancient classical writers were discovered to have a more complete understanding of the whole range of human experience.

The Renaissance did not threaten Christian orthodoxy by producing a new philosophy or doctrine. It was primarily a change of attitude, a change of direction. The word which sums it up and which was already used at the Renaissance is humanism. Their use of the term had no atheistic implications as it does in modern humanism. Both forms of humanism, however, focus attention on human values. Medieval man had been characterized by the upward, other-worldly look, exemplified in the spires of the great Gothic cathedrals. Renaissance man, by contrast, began to look with new eyes at the natural world around him. It no longer appeared to him as the fallen world destined for divine destruction as he had been led to believe.

The Renaissance promoted a fresh interest in man himself. From about the sixth century onward the Augustinian view of man had triumphed over Pelagianism. Whereas Pelagius had affirmed the importance of human initiative and responsibility, Augustine saw the human species as a fallen race standing in such dire need of divine help that nothing much of any value could be expected from man in his unredeemed state. The Renaissance study of the cultural achievements of ancient men of letters, pagans though they were, gave the lie to this. If even pre-Christians could reach such levels and display such gifts, how much more might be achieved by Christians once they acknowledged, and put to positive use, the various natural gifts within man. Beginning from an appreciation of the elegance and clarity of the classical writers, the Renaissance humanists were led to discern a new dignity in man himself. Man discovered his potential freedom and his capacity for creativity. It was something of a Pelagian victory.

The untapped potential to be found in the human condition was admirably expounded by Pico della Mirandola (1463-94) in his *Oration on the Dignity of Man,* written when he was only twenty-four. He tells us that the reason why God made man at the close of creation was in order that we may come to know the laws of the universe, to love its beauty and to admire its greatness. He imagined God saying to Adam, 'I created thee as being neither heavenly nor earthly . . . that thou might be free to shape and overcome thyself. Thou mayest sink into a beast or be born anew to the divine likeness . . . To thee alone is given a growth and a development depending on thine own free will. Thou bearest in thee the germs of a universal life'.[9] Here for the first time we have a vision of the unfulfilled potentiality present in the human condition, yet one which can just as easily lead to the diabolical as to the god-like.

The humanists manifested a new sense of history. The medieval scholar had treated all books as if they belong to a timeless present, in much the same way as the fundamentalist Christian still does with the Bible and the Muslim with the Qur'an. The humanists were more aware of the ebb and flow of historical change. They saw themselves divided from the zenith reached in antiquity by the nadir of the Dark Ages. Although the modern historical consciousness was to develop much more fully in the nineteenth century, Renaissance man did come to appreciate, more than the medievalists had done, the unique significance of human events and the possibilities of historical change.

We may link with this growing awareness of historical change and of the role of man within it, the fact that a stronger sense of national identity was beginning to poke itself through the surface of the cultural unity of Christendom. A pluralistic Europe, composed of sovereign autonomous states, was beginning to emerge. Since this movement constituted a challenge to the temporal power of the papacy, the growth of nationalism was bound to assume a this-worldly and anti-ecclesiastical character. It was this movement which prevented the Reformers from constructing a unified, pan-European structure and forced Protestantism to become fragmented into national Churches.

The men of the Renaissance, stimulated by the wide range of the philosophical and scientific literature of the ancient world, began to take a new interest in the physical world. Nicholas of Cusa (c. 1400-64), as cardinal, mathematician, diagnostic physician, experimental scientist, theologian and philosopher, has been described as a model of 'Renaissance Man' because of the breadth of his interests and skills. Influenced by the Neo-Platonism of John Scotus Erigena and the mysticism of Meister Eckhart, he became convinced of the unity of all reality. He affirmed that all things are in God and God is in all. Such a view encouraged him to urge the increase of knowledge through empirical enquiry. He himself, for example, showed by the study of plant growth that plants absorb nourishment from the air.

In his famous doctrine of the 'co-incidence of opposites' he ascribed to God all extremes, including transcendence and immanence. He abhorred religious wars and believed that men of different religions should live in mutual tolerance. In a book with the title of *On the Peace of Faith* he expressed the hope of seeing a universal religion emerge. He even caught a vision of a kind of United Nations Organization.

Another man who exemplified to the highest degree the many-sidedness of Renaissance Man was Leonardo da Vinci (1452-1519). He scorned speculative book knowledge and the appeal to authority. 'Anyone who conducts an argument by appealing to Authority is not using his intelligence, he is just using his memory', he said.[10] Da Vinci saw the supreme value to be attributed to conviction based on first-hand evidence. He believed the eye to be the main gateway to knowledge. One must observe reality for what it is. He conceived the plan of describing in accurate pictorial form all objects observable in the world and he filled forty codices with his voluminous notes and sketches. His work formed the prototype of the modern scientific illustration. The skill of seeing reality for what it is, and not simply of seeing what one expects to find, leads to both art and science. The all-round mastery achieved by da Vinci is quite breath-taking.

Significant technological advances have always proved epoch-making in cultural change. The Renaissance, through men like da Vinci, prompted a new wave of technological inventions and two in particular must be mentioned. The first was Gutenberg's printing-press. Nothing could have better matched and aided the new love of the written word initiated by the Renaissance. By 1500 the presses of Europe had produced six million volumes. The spread of ideas experienced a sudden acceleration, with the consequent dialectic of stimulus and response. It has been claimed that if it had not been for the invention of printing the Reformation would never have become more than a parochial monkish quarrel.

The other significant invention was the building of a ship which was capable of traversing the vast oceans with comparative safety. The horizon of the Western world was quite rapidly extended by the voyages of discovery which followed. Not only did the known world rapidly increase in size but first-hand knowledge of strange cultures at greatly varying levels of development now came within the world-view of Western man. The effect was similar to what we might feel in this latter twentieth century if we suddenly made contact with intelligent life on another planet.

The various aspects of the Renaissance so far mentioned, humanism, the new sense of history, nationalism, technology, speed of communication, knowledge of strange cultures, all illustrate the new direction in which the Renaissance was taking Western man. His gaze was being diverted from the vertical to the horizontal. The increased attention being devoted to an enlarged this-world led to a decrease of interest in the unseen other-world. The Renaissance reversed the trend towards other-worldliness which had been in operation from Augustine until the High Middle Ages.

This did not mean that the Renaissance was in any conscious way anti-Christian. The men of the Renaissance were breaking out of the rigidity of Scholasticism but they did not question Christian foundations. Even though they could be severely critical of the Church, they were not iconoclasts. They sought reform by peaceful, conciliar methods, befitting gentlemen who cultivated the human virtues. When the Reformation did break out, quickly engendering confrontation, bitterness and violence, some of the leading humanists stood aloof from it. The Catholics charged them with having 'laid the egg that Luther hatched', while Protestants saw them as cowardly hypocrites who lacked the courage to follow their convictions to the logical end.

In this respect Erasmus (c. 1466-1536) is the obvious example. Regarded as the most learned man of his day he was the 'Prince of the Humanists'. His evangelical humanism led him into conflict with both Catholics and Reformers. He was extremely critical of much Church practice and of the fruitless debates of the Scholastic theologians. 'It has long been my cherished wish', he said, 'to cleanse the Lord's Temple of barbarous ignorance and to adorn it with treasures from afar, such as may kindle in generous hearts a warm love for the Scriptures.'[11] But though he was sympathetic with many of Luther's ideas he saw him as a dogmatic, aggressive theologian. In particular he found Luther's emphasis on justification by faith to be too anti-Pelagian. The humanists avoided extremes and looked for the temperate, balanced position. Thus, as Cassirer has said, 'The Renaissance strove for a religion of affirmation of the world and of the intellect, a religion which conceded to both their specific value, and which found the real proof and seal of divinity, not in the degradation and destruction of the world and the human intellect, but in their exaltation'.[12]

The Reformation has to be related to the historical, social and political circumstances in which it occurred. For too long Christians have looked back to it through ecclesiastical spectacles and have seen it either as the divinely inspired revival of apostolic Christianity (the Protestant view) or as sinful apostasy on a grand scale (the Roman Catholic view). In fact it was not really either. The Reformation spread as rapidly as it did because it was aided by, and indeed was the reflection of, deep and widespread changes then occurring in the social and political life of Europe. We are concerned here, however, with the changes taking place in the religious mind. In this respect it was a quite natural working out of some of the Renaissance trends. Luther, Calvin, Melanchthon and others owed much to the humanists.

As Renaissance men looked back to Antiquity as the golden age of human achievement, so the Reformers looked to the Apostolic Age as exemplifying Christian thought and practice in its pristine purity. The growing autonomy of the human spirit present in the Renaissance made men critical of the Church but was not yet strong enough to challenge ecclesiastical authority effectively. The Reformers believed they possessed in the Bible the revealed word of God. This was more than enough for the task of challenging priestly tradition. Yet the Reformers also displayed the beginnings of a critical study of the Scriptures. They showed this in their commentaries and they learned it from the humanists. Although this was largely submerged in the following two centuries it was destined to flower in the biblical criticism of the nineteenth century onwards.

In some respects the Reformers reflected the medieval mind just as much as did their Catholic adversaries. This is borne out by the rigid doctrinal structure of the Protestant Scholasticism which developed in the following century. But in other respects the Reformation had the effect of furthering what had surfaced at the Renaissance and of thus speeding the Western world on its road to modernity. Let us look at some of the ways in which this was so.

First, the unity of Western Christendom was shattered, irrevocably it would now seem. Of course there has never been a time when all Christians belonged to one harmonious structure. But within the limits of Western Europe Christianity had achieved an impressive homogeneity and unity. The relationship of Church and State mirrored the dualistic character of the medieval world-view. Life in the Church represented a foretaste of heaven. To die in communion with the Church was the surest way of being offered citizenship in the Holy City. The fragmentation of the ecclesiastical structure was thus silently heralding the eventual collapse of men's confidence in the reality of that other world to which it was believed to point.

But that was not all. In Christian belief there can be only one Church. Therefore either all professing Christians who did not belong to one's own ecclesiastical structure had to be regarded as outside of the one true Church (this was the Roman Catholic solution up until Vatican II), or else a distinction had to be made between the one true Church (the elect who are known only to God) and the various visible Church structures. The Protestants, particularly Calvin, opted for the second solution, drawing a distinction between the Church visible and the Church invisible. The true Church had now become invisible. This had the effect, in the long run, of revealing the various Church structures to be human in origin rather than divine. As fragmentation later increased and denominationalism has come to be accepted (in spite of the Ecumenical Movement) it has raised the question of whether a Christian needs to belong to any at all of the self-styled Churches, seeing that he need not belong to any particular one.

Once the unity of Christendom had become fragmented then the critical spirit, in which the prophetic component of Christianity had already expressed itself from time to time, could no longer be contained and prevented from manifesting itself in undesirable extremes. In the succeeding centuries, and particularly from the eighteenth century onwards, it is from the cracks opened up between the Catholic and Protestant segments that there has arisen the chief criticism of past tradition. The prophetic pioneers of the future way of looking at the world emerged from the periphery of the Churches.

Secondly we must note how the Reformers, somewhat unintentionally it would seem, undermined the reality of the other-world by some of the drastic measures they initiated. For example, in their total rejection of Purgatory (made on biblical grounds and for theological reasons) they annihilated in one fell swoop the particular sphere of the other-world on which the attention of the late medieval mind had been chiefly fastened. The abolition of Purgatory said, in effect, that death brings to an end man's options for determining his ultimate destiny. After death there is only the Final Judgment. This had the effect of emphasizing the finality of all actions performed in this world and of implying that some vital aspects of life belong to this world only.

The Reformers themselves, of course, quite openly upgraded the values to be found in this world in the way they promoted an industrious attitude to one's secular work, in the abandonment of clerical celibacy, and in the abolition of monasticism. The cloistered life of the religious orders had long given the impression that to profess Christianity to the full one should withdraw from the world. The Reformers not only believed the Christian was in no way disadvantaged by expressing his Christian obedience in the 'secular' world but they saw the world of human affairs, including trade economics and politics, as potentially redeemable.

No modifications of Christian faith and practice which have occurred near to our own time have been carried through so suddenly and so ruthlessly as the change which came to Christendom with the Reformation. It is all the more important for us to realize that the Reformers saw themselves as deeply committed Christians and servants of God. The break with the sacramental system on which personal salvation had previously been believed to depend and the sweeping away of the external trappings of Christian worship, were as traumatic as they were dramatic. The closure of the monasteries and convents by Henry VIII is the kind of act which, today, would be thought possible only in an anti-religious, Communist state, and not in one which believed itself to be whole-heartedly Christian.

It is little wonder that the Catholic defenders of the *status quo* judged the Reformation to be the rebellion of the human spirit against the divine will. They rightly sensed that the Reformation, if not checked, could be the end of Christianity in its orthodox form, even though they could not be wholly clear why this was so. The Reformers, on the other hand, did not foresee that the implications of such a principle as 'the priesthood of all believers' would still be working itself towards its logical conclusions four centuries later. It was to mean the increasing responsibility of the individual for his own spiritual fulfilment, a greater share in the government of the community, both civil and ecclesiastical, and the consequent lessening of the role of the ordained, professional ministry.

During the period 1500-1650 the consequences of the Renaissance were still working themselves out in Catholicism also. In a later chapter we shall refer to the significance of Copernicus and Galileo. Here we must mention Giordano Bruno (1548-1600), for his views, and the treatment he received, may both be seen in their respective ways as signs of things to come. He was a brilliant and courageous thinker who had been much influenced by Nicholas of Cusa. More than any Catholic of his time he had broken free from Aristotelianism. He asserted that one should not allow oneself to be governed by other men's opinions. The fact that he possessed a stubborn and provocative disposition was no doubt a factor which contributed to his final martyrdom at Rome at the hands of the Church. But the charges made against him also show that while his views could hardly be tolerated at that time by either Protestant or Catholic, they nevertheless marked him off as a man far ahead of his time. He is said to have denied the divinity of Christ, to have asserted the mythical character of some biblical material and to have taught the eternity of the universe. His conception of the universe implies that positions, directions and movement in the universe are all relative. Though commonplace today it was an offensive thought then.

Catholic intuition of where Protestantism was leading eventually caused Catholicism not only to protect itself against Protestant heresy, but to seal itself off from the influence of emerging modernity. This process reached its climax in the stance taken at the Council of Vatican I in 1870, and in the subsequent attempt to eliminate the Catholic Modernists. It meant that from the mid-seventeenth century until well into the twentieth century it was left mainly for non-Catholics to be pioneers of the New Way. The Reformation, by providing an overt religious expression to the Renaissance rediscovery of what man has it in him to achieve, led the Western world right up to the threshold of that door on the other side of which was to be found a whole new world.

CHAPTER 4

THE SECOND MAJOR THRESHOLD OF RELIGIOUS CHANGE

❖

There is widespread agreement that somewhere between 1600-1800 is to be found the watershed between the late medieval and the modern eras. 'Between the sixteenth and nineteenth centuries', wrote J. C. Livingstone, 'a revolution occurred in man's understanding of himself and his world which caused a sharp break with medieval civilization and ushered in the modern epoch.'[1] Paul Hazard actually specified the year 1715 as the 'critical year' of modern Western civilization. While it may be going too far to name an actual year, the period of 1650-1750, and variously referred to as the Age of Reason or the Enlightenment, may be regarded as the watershed we are looking for. In this chapter we shall be sketching the evidence to support the thesis that during this period Western man, in his religious thought and experience, crossed over some kind of threshold which divides the modern world from all which preceded it, a threshold comparable with, yet even more far-reaching than, that crossed at the Axial Period.

By 1600 Western Christendom had become permanently divided into Protestant and Catholic factions. Yet Europe was still solidly Christian, in the sense that all, in their own way, professed the Christian faith. The Reformation and the Counter-Reformation had both brought renewal to Church allegiance of the one kind or the other, but the Christian world-view was still shaped by the medieval mould. By the end of the eighteenth century, however, it was becoming evident that the real issue was something more serious than a Christian schism. Out of fragmented Christendom something was emerging which was destined to threaten the classical form of Christianity at its very foundations.

The Enlightenment was, in many respects, the natural continuation of trends which had appeared in the Renaissance and Reformation. The bitter conflict and continuing confrontation in which the Reformation had left Europe had the effect of submerging those trends for a time. But in the long run the schismatic form of institutional Christianity provided the very situation which stimulated those trends to come to the surface again. The leadership of thought passed from ecclesiastics to laymen, partly because the attention of the former (both Catholic and Protestant) tended to be fastened too exclusively upon one another. Continuing theological debate on the Reformation issues has eventually proved to be fruitless and stultifying. The vital issues for the future were appearing in other areas.

Laymen, standing as they did a little distance from the centre of the continuing ecclesiastical conflict, were in a better position to examine the cultural tradition in the cool light of reason. This, in fact, is what some of them did. The leading minds of the Enlightenment were neither priests nor theologians. Even the pioneers of modern biblical study (known later as historical and literary criticism) were not Protestant theologians in spite of the latter's dependence on the Bible; they were four non-theologians – the jurist Grotius, the philosophers Hobbes and Spinoza and the medical professor Jean Astruc. Neither were the leaders of the Enlightenment university academics, for the simple reason that to gain and hold a university post one had to subscribe to orthodox Christianity.[2] The non-clerical origin of new thought was destined to be a sign of modernity in comparison with the medieval situation. But though the men of the Enlightenment may have become unorthodox, they were not anti-Christian or irreligious. They believed in God, in man's immortality, in human freewill and the desirability of manifesting the Christian virtues.

What the men of the Enlightenment did was to question more and more the dogmatic superstructure of Christian doctrine (whether Catholic or Protestant), particularly that which rested on appeal to external authority, such as ecclesiastical tradition or written records of divine revelation. They were opposed to dogmatism, monasticism, celibacy and the dichotomy between the natural and the supernatural. They stood for human freedom, the freedom to enquire and question, the right to discover the truth for oneself, the right to pursue happiness, the toleration of all views, the equality of all men. In this way they spelled the end of scholasticism, the end of subservience to Aristotle, and, above all, the end of the medieval world-view.

First we must look at a few original thinkers who preceded the period of the Enlightenment proper. The French humanist Montaigne (1533-92) was the first modern thinker to realize the extent to which our beliefs are relative to our experience and our cultural environment, a fact of which we are today very conscious. It was the conflict between Catholic and Protestant which led him to reflect in this way. Since Catholic and Protestant cannot both be right, how can one be sure that either is right? He revived the attitude of the ancient Greek sceptics and argued that even if we appeal to sense data we only know how things 'appear' to us and not how they are in themselves. Hence we can be sure of nothing and are like the man who was trying to decide whether a picture of Socrates was a good likeness when he had never seen Socrates. Trying to know reality is like trying to clutch water and the only answer to such complete scepticism is faith. The view that basic religious truths must be accepted on faith, without proof or supporting evidence, is called fideism. Montaigne expounded the consequent human dilemma on religious questions as a choice between complete scepticism[3] and fideism. He himself chose the latter and remained a practising Catholic. But he had considerable influence on both French and English thought and was studied by Francis Bacon, Pascal and Descartes.

A good example of how new thought was to break free of ecclesiastical control and develop independently of Christian orthodoxy is provided by Hugo Grotius (1583-1645), Dutch lawyer and theologian. His chief theological work, *On the Truth of the Christian Religion* (1622), was intended as a practical handbook for missionaries. It tried to show the superiority of Christianity over all other faiths; it became valued by Christians of all persuasions and was clearly orthodox. But the book for which he is justly famous and which earned him the title of 'Father of International Law' is a legal work entitled *Peace and War*. In this he severed all connection between law and theology and drew the principle of justice from the eternal Law of Nature. This was a sign of things to come. New areas of thought and knowledge were to arise which lay outside the horizon of the medieval mind; because the Scholastic theologians had not established any authoritative precedent, these could be explored relatively freely without many noticing any apparent conflict with Christian orthodoxy.

Francis Bacon (1561-1626), a lawyer and leading parliamentarian, remained an orthodox member of the Church of England and yet he believed that a new age was opening up. Modern critics have shown that he was much influenced by Bernadino Telesio (1508-88), an Italian humanist who had become strongly critical of Aristotelianism. Bacon came to the view that the Renaissance humanists and the Protestant theologians were just as tied to the past as were the

Catholic Scholastics. He contended that scholars should wake up to the times in which they were living and take as much interest in modern history as in ancient history. He pleaded with them to abandon 'vain speculations' and pay more attention to the 'contemplation of nature and the observation of experience'. Already envisaging the rise of new sciences, he argued that invention had been too much the result of chance and not enough the fruit of intelligent enquiry. In sketching his schema of sciences for 'the advancement of learning' he separated theology from the other disciplines; without repudiating it, he confined it to faith, liturgy, manners and Church government. He even applied his empirical approach to the realm of morals, denying the existence of any absolute rules of conduct.

Thomas Hobbes (1588-1679) was a son of a clergyman and a one-time secretary to Bacon. His views scandalized both Presbyterians and Papists alike and he came to be associated with free-thought and atheism. His chief work, *Leviathan*, was primarily a political philosophy but more than half of it was devoted to religious matters. His philosophy belonged generally to the nominalist stream. Hobbes was anxious to defend what he called 'true religion' from the extreme forms of Protestantism as well as from Catholicism, for he saw both of these as obstacles to the policy of political absolutism which he advocated. But he left it unclear as to what this 'true religion' is and, indeed, he wanted to shift the issue to what is the *legal* religion. He suspected all supernaturalism of being superstitious and speculated that religion originated in the fear of ghosts and other invisible powers. He was one of the first to question whether Moses could have written the Pentateuch and he contended that the origin of the biblical books should be enquired into without reference to the traditions which had come down concerning them.

Now we must turn to the person who has been called the

first modern philosopher, René Descartes (1596-1650). More clearly and deliberately than anyone else, he enunciated the method by which modern man was to become emancipated from subjection to faulty traditions inherited from the past. Like Montaigne, he was greatly exercised by the problem of how one can be sure of anything at all. A mathematician at heart, he wanted to arrive at a body of knowledge which had all the certainty associated with mathematical proof. He observed that 'what makes our convictions is custom and example rather than any sort of assured knowledge'.[4]

Descartes not only abandoned appeal to external authority, including the Scholastic synthesis of Aristotelianism and revealed truth, but he questioned even the most ordinary convictions which everybody takes for granted. His method of doubt he set forth in his two most important books, *Discourse on Method* (1637), and *Meditations* (1642). He set himself four rules: (1) to accept as true nothing that he did not know to be evidently so, (2) to divide each difficulty into as many parts as possible in order the better to solve it, (3) to conduct his thoughts in an orderly fashion, starting with the simplest and rising to the most complex and (4) to make so complete an enumeration of the links in the argument and to review them so thoroughly that nothing could possibly be missed.[5]

His *Discourse on Method* is, in part, an autobiographical account of how he proceeded to put his rules into practice. Knowing that our senses can deceive us and that, even in logical argument, men may be fallible, he pretended that everything that had entered his mind was false. There remained one thing he could not possibly doubt. 'In the very act of thinking everything false, I was aware of myself as something real.'[6] In his now famous dictum, *cogito, ergo sum* (I think, therefore I am), Descartes believed he had found the firm foundation on which he could build an absolutely reliable system of knowledge. He was sure of his own existence – but what was *he?* Even though he could pretend he had no body, he could not possibly doubt that he was a substance whose whole essence consisted in thinking. 'Thus the self, or rather the soul', he concluded, 'by which I am what I am, is entirely distinct from the body, is indeed easier to know than the body, and would not cease to be what it is, even if there were no body.'[7]

By a process of reasoning Descartes then went on to show (as he thought) that from this certain beginning he could be wholly confident that there exists a perfect being, namely God, that God is good and does not deceive us, and that, since he has given us a strong inclination to believe in the existence of our bodies and of the tangible world, they also must exist. He was further led to conclude that the soul is immortal, since (in his view) it is entirely independent of the body and thus not subject to dying with it.

Descartes finally reached the point where he believed there was nothing which could not be satisfactorily explained by the principles he had discovered. On the one hand, therefore, he may be seen as the rationalist *par excellence*, but on the other hand he still reflected in many of his conclusions the medieval mould from which he was trying to escape. Later thinkers were indebted to him for the clarity with which he enunciated his method, even though they could not share his conclusions.

Descartes opened the door to modernity but he himself did not step through it. He lived and died a Catholic, showing himself more cautious in temperament than Bruno and even Galileo. In the year of the latter's condemnation, 1633, Descartes was just finishing his first scientific treatise; so he withheld publication for he did not wish to alienate the orthodox. He had no intention of undermining Christian truth; but he believed he had discovered the philosophy which should replace that of Aristotle. His Jesuit teachers refuted his teaching, however, and his writings were placed on the Index of Forbidden Books.[8]

Nowhere did Descartes betray his medieval mould more clearly than in the radical dualism of mind and body into which he continued to analyse the human condition. This dualism parallels that of the eternal world of spirit and the temporal world of matter, which together composed the medieval view of reality. Descartes never found a satisfactory way of explaining how mind and body can react upon each other, if in fact (as in his view) they are entirely independent. This problem has continued to lie at the root of the conflict between two alternative approaches to the understanding of reality. If, with the nominalists and materialists, one reduces all reality to what is physical, does it mean that mind, freewill, consciousness, etc., are deprived of reality? But if, with the medieval realists and the nineteenth-century idealists, one starts with mind, spirit and ideas, then how is one adequately to explain the physical world?

This conflict, as we shall later see, was to become critical in the nineteenth century. Then both sides made some appeal to the philosopher who tried to solve the problem inherent in the Cartesian dualism. He was Baruch Spinoza (1632-77). It is of some significance that he was Jewish (even though his views led to his expulsion from the synagogue while still in his twenties), because the dualism which he found repugnant may be said to have stemmed ultimately from the Platonic influence in Christian thought. Jewish tradition, by contrast, only mildly influenced by Hellenism, had always retained a much more positive attitude towards the material world.

Spinoza started, where Judaism started, with the concept of absolute unity. It had long been asserted in the Shema 'The Lord our God is one'.[9] But whereas traditional Judaism (and Christianity even more so) conceived God as set over against the world he had created. Spinoza was convinced that Ultimate Reality is one. It is ultimate reality or absolutely infinite substance, therefore, which is to be called God or Nature.

Though there can be only one substance (thought Spinoza) it possesses an infinite number of attributes. There are only two, however, which men can grasp – thought and extension. These are different ways of envisaging the one and the same reality. All that is known to exist – physical objects, living creatures, ideas, etc. – are modes of one or both of these attributes. Man participates in both attributes. Whereas Descartes would have said that man is a mind but possesses a body, Spinoza said that man is both a mind and a body: 'The mind and the body are one and the same thing.' As mind, man is a mode of the infinite attribute of thought. This means, in effect, that he participates in the mind of God. As body, man is a mode of the infinite attribute of extension. Though the attributes are to be distinguished from each other, they have no existence independent of the one reality of which they *are* the attributes. Man is thus an indivisible unity and a finite manifestation of the one infinite reality.

Being convinced of the unity of all reality, Spinoza was led to a position which, though materialistic, was yet thoroughly religious, for it made God all in all. Everything that is, is contained in God. Spinoza is regarded as the father of all modern pantheism. Certainly he departed drastically from traditional theism, there being no place in his system for a personal God who cares for his creatures and no place for immortal human souls. Man is a wholly finite creature, participating in a mystical universe, the infinite substance of which is God. There cannot be a world without God, but neither can God exist without the attributes mentioned above and these entail the existence of the world.

In his *Theologico-Political Treatise* Spinoza pioneered biblical criticism two centuries before it really began to flourish. He believed the Bible had to be studied and interpreted just like any other natural phenomenon. Whereas man had previously attempted to understand the nature of things in the light of the Bible, he saw the Bible having to be understood in the light of the nature of things as a whole. The Bible, as an historically conditioned object, could not be expected to contain the *absolute* truth. He believed it did contain *relative* truth and the way to discover this was to use the tools of empirical investigation. In this way he reached conclusions which foreshadowed those of later biblical scholarship.

Spinoza did not exert a great deal of immediate influence. So long as traditional theism was firmly entrenched his ideas could be tolerated by neither Jew nor Christian. Only when man's confidence in theism had come to be undermined was he rediscovered and used by such people as Hegel, Schleiermacher and Feuerbach. By then the dualistic approach to reality was ceasing to convince. The fact that modern religious thinkers like Buber, Tillich and Teilhard de Chardin are often charged with pantheism is an indication of the importance to be attached to Spinoza and to his concern to affirm cosmic unity.

One who did publicize Spinoza's thought more immediately, though in a somewhat distorted form, was Pierre Bayle (1647-1706). His most famous work, *Dictionnaire historique et critique* (1695-7), was not only the first of all the modern encyclopaedias but also 'constituted the real arsenal of all Enlightenment philosophy'.[10] The son of a French Calvinist pastor, Bayle became a Roman Catholic for a time before returning to Calvinism. The fact that his father and brothers died of religious persecution prompted him to publish a brilliant plea for religious toleration, which in his view should be extended to all, including Jews,

Muslims, Unitarians and atheists. His fellow-Christians said he was really an unbeliever who was bent on destroying the Christian faith by making it look ridiculous; yet he claimed to the day of his death to be a Calvinist Christian. He insisted that man's ultimate appeal for justifying his beliefs was his own conscience and believed that his own non-rationally based fideism had been the orthodox Christian position from Paul down to Calvin.

Bayle was the first modern to argue that morality is not necessarily dependent upon religious belief, nor is religious belief any guarantee of a highly moral life. He contended, not only that a society of atheists could well live morally circumspect lives but, that he could point to countless religious believers, biblical, Catholic and Protestant, who were quite immoral. A few decades later the German dramatist Lessing (1729-81), who was also strongly attracted to Spinoza's pantheism, likewise emphasized the primacy of the morally circumspect life. To separate morality from theistic religion was a highly scandalous thesis at that time; today it is widely accepted.

Atheism was still extremely rare in the seventeenth century. In any case its main purpose has been simply to protest against an unacceptable theism; it is too negative in itself ever to be the basis of a satisfactory philosophy of life. The basic belief most distinctive of the Enlightenment was neither atheism nor pantheism but deism. This is a form of reduced theism, which makes no appeal to divine revelation, but which can be arrived at (it was claimed) on the basis of reason and the study of nature. It has also been referred to, therefore, as natural religion.

The man who has been called the father of English deism is Lord Herbert of Cherbury (1583-1648). He was seeking a reliable path to the truth amid the confusing variety of religious belief and disbelief which then obtained within the divisions of Christendom, but he wished to avoid both absolute scepticism and an uncritical fideism. Believing that it is only by the use of reason that one is able to discern the truth amid the current diversity, he came to the conclusion that implanted in all men are certain Common Notions which are self-evident and which can be used to test the trustworthiness of the faculties. He referred to these as 'the true Catholic Church which has never erred'. In his book *De Veritate* (1624) he enunciated as follows these basic Notions which are supposedly implanted in us: (i) there is a supreme God, (ii) this sovereign God ought to be worshipped, (iii) moral virtue is the chief element in this worship, (iv) men have the duty to repent for their moral failures, (v) there is reward or punishment after this life. Of all the religions claiming to be revealed he believed Christianity came closest to these five basic principles of natural religion.

Herbert did not deny revelation but set out certain criteria by which the trustworthiness of revelation should be tested. Using these he concluded that even the precepts of the Decalogue are actually Common Notions which are implicit in every religion. In his book *De Religione Gentilium* (written earlier but not published until 1663) he showed he had some awareness of religion in India and North America as well as of Islam and of the religion of the ancient world. He tried to show that when one stripped away superstition and priestly embellishments from all religions one would find in each that true Catholic or Universal Church which 'alone reveals divine universal providence, or the wisdom of nature . . . And it is only through this church that salvation is possible'.[11]

Herbert exerted a strong influence on John Locke (1632-1704), the philosopher recognized as the father of English empiricism. This he expounded in his *Essay Concerning Human Understanding* (1690). Locke, however, rejected Herbert's idea of Common Notions and maintained, on the contrary, that the mind of an infant at birth is quite blank, a *tabula rasa*. All the ideas, concepts, thoughts, convictions, with which it is eventually filled, arise out of experience, that is, out of the sense impressions received and the subsequent reflection upon them. This experience, of course, must include all that one learns from one's parents, teachers and cultural environment.

Locke contended that whatever is claimed as divine revelation turns out on examination by human reason to rest on an empirical foundation. Should any non-empirical reality exist, it would remain for ever out of reach of the human mind. Consequently there can be no non-empirical basis for metaphysics. Locke thus demoted divine revelation from its pedestal of absolute authority and insisted that no proposition, even though said to be divinely revealed, can rightly claim our assent if it is in conflict with knowledge arrived at on empirical grounds. The traditional content of divine revelation must be subjected to reason. 'If anything shall be thought revelation which is contrary to the plain principles of reason and the evident knowledge the mind has of its own clear and distinct ideas', he wrote, 'there reason must be hearkened to, as a matter within its province.'[12] If reason is not listened to, then blind faith (or fideism) can lead to all the 'absurdities that fill almost all the religions which possess and divide mankind'.[13]

Once again we should note that it was conflict between Protestant and Catholic beliefs, supported by the growing knowledge of the non-Christian religions, which was leading men to search for a reliable criterion by which to sift the truth from falsehood. The men of the Enlightenment believed they had found such a criterion in reason and empirical evidence. 'Reason must be our last judge and guide in everything.'[14] Although traditional Christians long continued to be reluctant to subject Christian dogma to examination by these criteria, they had no hesitation in using them to prononuce the falsehood of non-Christian religion.

Even Locke did not always take his position to its logical conclusions. Like Descartes, Locke believed that we can affirm the existence of God by reflecting rationally on the data of empirical experience. 'Though God has given us no innate ideas of himself . . . yet having furnished us with those faculties our minds are endowed with, he hath not left himself without witness . . . to show, therefore, that we are capable of *knowing,* i.e. *being certain* that there is a God . . . we nccd go no further than *ourselves,* and that undoubted knowledge we have of our own existence.'[15]

As a reasonably loyal Anglican, Locke had no wish to undermine Christianity, and he even denied that he was a deist or a unitarian. In his *Reasonableness of Christianity as delivered in the Scriptures* (1695), he set out to show how Christianity could be defended on the basis of reason. Nevertheless, later readers have little difficulty in discerning the hidden presuppositions he still retained concerning the divine authority to be attributed to the Bible and which he had absorbed from his early Puritan upbringing. He amassed a great deal of biblical evidence to show that the one and only article of Christian faith is the affirmation that Jesus is the Messiah. He concluded that to believe this, to repent of one's sins, to try sincerely to obey the Saviour's commandments, are the fundamentals of the Christian faith. For Locke, they constitute the necessary and sufficient condition to make one a Christian; all other doctrines are secondary and incapable of conclusive proof.

Locke maintained that it was because men had strayed from this minimum definition that Europe had been plunged into religious strife. He became a vigorous advocate of toleration and the spirit of free enquiry. In his ideal Church there would be complete freedom for the expression of individual convictions. Human understanding, he contended, is too limited and subject to error to justify the imposition of one man's belief upon another. He believed that all men should enjoy religious liberty except atheists (because they did not feel bound by oath) and Roman Catholics (because they were required to give allegiance to foreign jurisdiction).

At the Reformation medieval Christendom had been challenged to discard its superstitions by the Protestantism which emerged from within it. Now Protestant orthodoxy itself was being challenged and by a movement of thought which had emerged from within it, this time, to discard, as superfluous, doctrines falsely ascribed to divine revelation. This movement never assumed an organizational identity as Protestantism had done. It was promoted by a variety of influential books which stimulated wide discussion and debate and which brought forth many sharp rejoinders from the defenders of orthodoxy. Its leaders, the deists, remained practising churchmen for the most part, but they were on the boundary between orthodoxy and new forms of belief. They stood for what they saw as the pure religion of nature, based on reason and not on revelation. In some respects they were only the tip of the iceberg, for the contemporary writers often referred to the scepticism of their age. The Cambridge Platonists[16] and the Latitudinarians[17] of the Church of England were also moving away from traditional orthodoxy even though they did not go as far as the deists and one of their number, John Tillotson (1630-94), even became Archbishop of Canterbury.

The questioning of orthodoxy was interestingly illustrated by the spiritual pilgrimage of John Toland (1670-1722). Born and bred as an Irish Roman Catholic, he became a Protestant at the age of 16, studied divinity with a view to ordination, and at the age of 25 wrote *Christianity Not Mysterious*. There he asserted 'that there is nothing in the Gospel contrary to reason nor above it',[18] that God himself is not beyond the comprehension of human reason and that the supernatural mysteries in Christianity were pagan intrusions encouraged for priestly advantage. His book is said to have launched the deistic controversy in earnest and, in Ireland, it was burned by order of Parliament. Toland became more extreme than most of the deists, writing many polemical pamphlets against the clergy. He finally became a pantheist and was actually the first to use this term. In his *Pantheisticon* (1720), he even composed a pantheistic liturgy, intended as a substitute for traditional Christian worship.

A similar pilgrimage is found in Matthew Tindal (1655-1733). For a short time he embraced Catholicism by choice, then returned to the Church of England and finally became a Christian deist. An able scholar, he wrote a defence of his rational approach to religion in refutation of priestly claims but was prosecuted for it, along with the publisher and printer. In 1709 his *A Defence of the Rights of the Christian Church* was burned by order of the House of Commons. Near the end of his life he wrote *Christianity as Old as the Creation* (1730), and this came to be regarded as the classic expression of deism. In it he contended that in all rational creatures there is a law of reason which is absolutely perfect, eternal and unchangeable; the purpose of the Christian Gospel is neither to add to this nor to take away from it but simply to free men from superstition. Everything of real worth in Christianity, therefore, is as old as creation. Whatever is obscure or unreasonable in so-called revelation is worthless superstition.

The most widely influential deist was Anthony Collins (1676-1729), a friend of Toland and Locke, a country gentleman and a local administrator. He was extremely well read and had gathered one of the largest private libraries of his day. In books and pamphlets, from his *Essay concerning the Use of Reason* (1707) to his *Discourse of the Grounds and Reasons of the Christian Religion* (1724), he maintained the supremacy of reason in the examination and acceptance of religious beliefs, bitterly attacked all clerical defenders of orthodoxy and himself defended the right to think freely. In his *Discourse of Freethinking* (1713), he maintained that innumerable great and good men of the past and present had really been free-thinkers and these included such people as Socrates, Origen, Erasmus, Descartes, Hobbes, Locke and Tillotson. In the modern world we take for granted the right to think freely and forget what it cost the men of the Enlightenment to fight for it. The fact that the term 'free-thinker' still has derogatory associations stems from the opprobrium which attached to the deists who created it.

There was much debate at the time as to whether the soul is a material substance, it being argued that physical matter could not possibly be capable of thought and consciousness. Collins, who was more of a materialist than Locke, contended that a system of physical particles may well have a quality which is more than the sum of the qualities of the separate parts. On this basis it was possible to conceive that physical matter, adequately organized to the necessary degree of complexity, could think.[19] There was consequently no need to maintain that God must add an immaterial soul to the physical human body. Yet Collins was not a complete materialist in that he believed in the existence of one immaterial spirit – God.

In his last book Collins undermined, perhaps unintentionally, the very foundations on which Locke had based his defence of Christianity. Locke, as we have seen, had reduced the essence of Christianity to the belief that Jesus is the Messiah. It still seemed self-evident to most people that this central truth of the New Testament was amply confirmed by the way it fulfilled the Old Testament prophecies. Collins showed up the weaknesses in this defence and, though his own arguments are not free from error, he forced Christians to reassess the defence of Christianity by appeal to prophecy.

Collins, nevertheless, remained a practising member of

the Church of England. He was more fortunate than Thomas Woolston, perhaps because he was a layman. Woolston (1670-1733) was an ordained clergyman who, in his *Discourses on the Miracles*[20] and other writings, maintained that the narratives of the Virgin Birth and the Resurrection of Jesus should be interpreted as allegories. This led him to be deprived of his Fellowship at Cambridge, whereupon he openly confessed deism. The Bishop of London had him prosecuted and gaoled, and he died in prison.

Deism had reached its peak in England before the middle of the eighteenth century. It is not at all surprising that deism should have come to birth in Protestant England and only later be transported to Catholic France for, as Peter Gay has observed, the Enlightenment began in the fertile intellectual climate of England, moved to France and then spread through Europe and as far as America. The works of Collins had a wide influence in France, Holland and even Germany. The chief example of French deism is to be found in Voltaire (1694-1778), who was influenced by Locke, Collins and Toland. He believed in the existence of God but denied this was capable of proof. He had some doubts as to whether there is any future life and he rejected the idea of post-mortem punishment on the grounds that correction can be the only moral basis for punishment.

France, of course, had already produced such people as Montaigne and Bayle as noted above. A further figure worthy of notice is Pierre Charron (1541-1603), a lawyer turned priest, whose work on the place of human wisdom is said to have paved the way for the advent of deism on French soil, as well as for the secularization of morals. Another priest, Richard Simon (1638-1712), became a pioneer in the field of biblical criticism. In his *Histoire Critique du Vieux Testament* (1678), he denied that Moses could have been the author of the Pentateuch (as Jew and Christian had long believed) on the grounds that these books often contained duplicate accounts of the same incident. This book led to his expulsion from his religious order. The irony of his unfortunate fate was that he had been prompted to undertake the critical study of the Bible, partly to counteract the influence of Spinoza, and partly to undermine the Protestant use of biblical authority to attack Catholicism.

When, in the seventeenth century, deism did take root in France, then, just because it was a predominantly Catholic country, it became more sharply polarized against the Church and its priesthood than had been the case in England. '*Écrasez l'infâme*' became the slogan of Voltaire. In addition, French deism moved further in the direction of materialism and atheism, as exemplified in the thought of Denis Diderot (1713-84). The great encyclopaedia on which he spent most of his life, and to which he contributed the articles on 'Christianity' and 'Faith', was based on a rationalist, humanist philosophy. 'I love that philosophy which raises up humanity', he said. There is an observation in his *Pensées philosophiques* (1746) which is strangely prophetic of some later comments by Dietrich Bonhoeffer. 'Men have banished divinity from their midst; they have relegated it to a sanctuary; the walls of a temple are the limits of its view; beyond these walls it does not exist. Madmen that you are, destroy these enclosures which obstruct your horizon; liberate God; see him where he actually is or else say that he does not exist at all.'[21] He sensed the collapse which was occurring in the dualistic world-view which, in over-emphasizing divine transcendence, had the effect of easing God out of the secular world. For modern man, Diderot contended, the only God to be recognized was the one conceived to be immanently present everywhere.

Diderot argued that no historical religion (or what we have called post-Axial religion) could afford to divorce itself from natural religion for it was only by appeal to reason, and to various aspects of natural religion, that each could defend itself against its rivals. This meant, in effect, that each already gave some kind of authority, if only secondary, to the underlying natural religion which is common to all men. He also made the point that historical religions like Judaism and Christianity, which claim to have historical origins, must also expect some day to perish. 'Everything that has a beginning will sometime have an end, and, vice versa, that which has never had a beginning (such as natural religion) can never perish.'[22]

Much more could be said of the Enlightenment (German representatives such as Reimarus and Lessing will be mentioned later in another connection, and the atheistic consequences of French deism will be taken up in Chapter 10), but sufficient exponents of the Age have been cited to illustrate the religious transition which was taking place. Let us now attempt a tentative summary of the reasons for regarding the Enlightenment as the transition to a radically new religious era. A fuller interpretation will be left until Chapter 13.

First of all, up until the Enlightenment Western man had looked to external seats of authority in religious matters and had been content to do so. When man submits to an authority external to himself, he may be described as heteronomous. After the Renaissance and the Reformation there was increasing difference of opinion as to where the earthly seat of external authority lay – the Church, the Bible or even the Classics. The Reformation, with partial success, had challenged the authority of the Church, but largely by appeal to the authority of the Bible. During the Enlightenment all external authorities were being challenged, and by appeal to the internal authority of human reason. Heteronomy was being replaced by autonomy – the condition in which final authority is believed to be seated in the inner self.

Immanuel Kant (whom we shall briefly discuss in the next chapter) lived through the end of the Age of the Enlightenment and he interpreted it thus: 'Enlightenment is man's exodus from his self-incurred tutelage. Tutelage is the inability to use one's understanding without the guidance of another person . . . "Dare to know" (*sapere aude*)! Have the courage to use your own understanding; this is the motto of the Enlightenment.'[23]

Of course it does not mean that only at the Enlightenment did men first begin to rely on their own understanding. Men had often been doing this earlier when they thought they were being loyal to a higher authority. For example, Christians had long believed they should submit to the authority of the Bible, but whenever they arrived at quite different interpretations of what the Bible meant they were, without sometimes realizing it, appealing to their own understanding. What was new at the Enlightenment was the increasing recognition, not only that this *was* the situation but that, by virtue of the condition in which man found himself, it *had to be* the situation. Man was now beginning to realize how much he was dependent on his own mental efforts for his understanding of reality. He sensed that this must always have been so but that this condition of man had been disguised by the fact that earlier men had believed (evidently mistakenly) that they had received divinely revealed knowledge and this naturally assumed an infallible status. Man was now being freed from what had previously held him in bondage, whether it was the Church, the Bible or simply the power of past tradition. This is why Kant likened the Enlightenment to the Mosaic Exodus from Egyptian slavery and to the reaching of adult responsibility after passing through adolescence. The Enlightenment marked the turning point in the coming of age of the human race.

The radical shift from heteronomy to autonomy had

important and serious consequences. It meant that all the traditional channels of authority – the Church, the Bible, the aristocracy and the traditional civil institutions – were to suffer from a process of slow erosion. This is still going on and is by no means near completion. Even the leading thinkers of the Enlightenment often unconsciously gave credence to the authority of the Bible in spite of the fact that, in their own eyes, they had abandoned appeal to divine revelation. The voice which speaks with authority to autonomous man is heard from within rather than from without. However much he may continue to value the voices which speak to him from without, it will be for the inherent value of what is spoken rather than because of the status of the speaker. The content of what he hears must possess the inherent power to win his conviction or else he will reject it no matter what source it comes from.

A further, and complementary, consequence was that no beliefs, including even those arrived at by the use of reason, are to be imposed unwillingly on others. It was recognized that truth is not something to be forced upon the human mind. Each person is to be left free, both to question the beliefs of another and to arrive at his own convictions for himself. The men of the Enlightenment stood for freedom of thought in the full and proper sense of that term. This made them adamant in their defence of toleration. The age of imposed dogma was over, in theory if not in practice.

In the Axial Period the questioning of inherited belief and practice had been undertaken by the isolated few. The most outstanding of them soon became acknowledged as the mediators of divine truth and their words and actions became permanently authoritative thereafter in the traditions which stemmed from them. In the transition to modernity, what had earlier been the privilege of the very few was to be shared by all who were willing to enter the new age. It is increasingly now the case that each human being is not only free to think for himself, but is being encouraged to do so. The consequences of this are still working themselves out.

It has led to the unfettered exploration of new ideas, the rapid expansion of the sciences and the subsequent knowledge explosion. It has led to universal education and to a type of education which encourages people to think for themselves rather than simply accept, in a second-hand way, the beliefs of the preceding generation. It has led to the questioning and undermining of the inherited social structures. It spelled the end of monarchies and the influence of the aristocratic classes. It heralded the dissolution of the hierarchical structure of the Church and of the class structure of society and the emergence of democratic self-rule in all areas of the community.

It led to a new respect for the individual human being regardless of the categories and stereotypes into which historical circumstances had placed him. Early consequences were the emancipation of the Jew from the ghetto and his admission to citizenship in Western Europe. Then came the abolition of slavery. Later again came a whole series of emancipations. More recently we have witnessed the war against discrimination on the grounds of colour, race or sex.

Even the established mores of society were not immune from the questioning. Long established standards of personal morality and social morality have been questioned and are undergoing change. New moralities of one kind or another are replacing the old. The shift from heteronomy to autonomy meant that instead of seeing himself as subservient to God, as law-maker, man was coming to see himself as the law-maker. Since the Enlightenment man has been gradually taking over functions formerly believed to be the divine prerogative.

The emancipation of man from his previously supposed divine tutelage has consequently been pregnant with danger for man's personal security and his future as a race. It is unlikely that the men of the Enlightenment foresaw all that it would lead to. That is what one would expect with man's coming of age. The young adult often becomes the supremely confident, self-assured know-all who believes he possesses the answers to all of life's problems. The men of the Enlightenment were supremely confident in the power of human reason. That confidence was soon to be undermined and it was this fact which brought the Age of Reason to an end. But when this happened, it did not mean a return to the former age of a simplistic faith in some external authority. As with the opening of Pandora's box, there was no going back to the situation which had obtained before the Enlightenment. It led to the post-Enlightenment or Modern Age, where man is increasingly aware of the lack of certainty and of the absence of eternal absolutes in any tangible form.

On this side of the Enlightenment man has found himself in a new kind of world. Like his mythical ancestors, Adam and Eve, man's eyes have been opened to a new awareness of the human condition. He now enjoys a greater freedom and a vaster range of options than he had ever known before; but he also shoulders a comparable burden of responsibilities for himself and his world, such as previously he did not know to exist. Man now has the potential for both good and evil on the grand scale.

Consequently, some look back to the Enlightenment as the disaster which has led to so many of our modern problems, while others see it as a great milestone in human progress. Many have not yet realized that we have entered this new age. The rise of various reactionary movements shows that some prefer to surrender the newly found freedom in return for the security once enjoyed (as it was thought) by heteronomous man. Whatever our judgment on the matter, the fact remains that, for good or evil, mankind has stepped over an irreversible threshold.

Now we must ask what all this means for religion? From the point of view of traditional, or pre-Enlightenment, Christianity, this has been judged to be a transition from belief to unbelief, from theism to atheism, from religion to irreligion. But is this the most adequate way of evaluating the Enlightenment? It is salutary to remember that from the point of view of the religion of ancient Rome the spread of Christianity was judged to be the spread of unbelief and even atheism, involving as it did the neglect of the Roman gods. Christians, on the other hand, saw it as the transition from paganism and superstition to true belief. In a similar way, from the point of view of Catholicism the Reformers were judged to be religious renegades and the promoters of religious apostasy. The Reformers, on the other hand, believed they alone stood for genuine religion and that those who chose to stay in the Catholic camp were in bondage to idolatry and superstition. Today we are able to look back on the Reformation as a schism in Christianity, in which neither Catholic nor Protestant could fully justify their exclusive claims to the possession of the whole truth.

We are now sufficiently distant in time from the Enlightenment to be able to view it with similar objectivity. Christian orthodoxy, whether Protestant or Catholic, has seen the men of the Enlightenment (and their successors) as non-Christians and pioneers of modern unbelief. But they, on the other hand, believed they stood for the true religion and that those who did not follow them remained in bondage to superstition. Their criticism of much to which they objected in the Church and its doctrines derived, in their own view, from righteous indignation, not dissimilar from that expressed by the ancient Israelite prophets. It is for such reasons that Cassirer questions whether we should consider the Enlightenment as a basically irreligious age. 'The strongest intellectual forces of the Enlightenment', he writes, 'do not lie in its rejection of belief but rather in the new form of faith which it proclaims, and in the new form of religion which it embodies.'[24]

Evidence for the assertion that the Enlightenment opened the door to a new religious era which would eventually produce its own religious forms, is what we shall explore in the chapters which follow, what determines whether or not these are genuinely religious forms, is not whether they are closely parallel to the traditional forms of religion (indeed for the most part they are not) but whether they express an ultimate concern on the part of man. If they do, then we can say that though the threshold we have been describing may mean, in the long run, the decay of the kind of religion which obtained in the pre-Enlightenment world, it does not mean the end of religion *per se*, but rather a new phase in man's religious quest.

In what follows we shall be looking particularly at the nineteenth century, examining the thought of some of the men who first realized that a threshold had been crossed over and who were looking for the new religious forms which should replace those which were now to be discarded as outmoded. In many respects these men may be said to have been the pioneers of the contemporary religious situation.

CHAPTER 5

FROM RELIGION TO PHILOSOPHY

❖

Before the end of the eighteenth century the Age of the Enlightenment was itself being superseded. The Protestant Reformers had challenged medieval Christianity by appeal to the Bible; the deists had challenged orthodox Protestantism by appeal to reason; now it was being found that not even reason was an infallible guide to the eternal verities. It could not provide the certain basis for even that reduced form of Christianity which the deists had called natural religion. Aquinas had been able to appeal to both reason and divine revelation; but confidence in both had now been undermined. The Age of Reason was giving way to the age of religious uncertainty. A void began to appear where the eternal truths once stood.

The way in which the deists' confidence in natural religion came to be undermined is best illustrated by the thought of David Hume (1711-76), sometimes hailed as the greatest British philosopher. Hume showed that it was impossible, on the basis of reason alone, to establish even the basic beliefs affirmed by the deists, such as God, miracles, the immortality of the soul. He virtually destroyed the rational basis for the Western metaphysical tradition and became the father of modern scepticism.

In an essay 'On the Immortality of the Soul' Hume argued that this traditional belief could not be established by the use of reason and was of doubtful validity. He drew attention to the observable correlation between soul (or mind) and body; in infancy both mind and body are immature, in manhood both are growing to maturity, in old age both show equal signs of decay. 'The organs of the one are all of them the organs of the other; the existence therefore, of the one must be dependent on the other.'[1] Since it is conceded that the souls of animals are mortal, where the same correlation is to be observed, why should the same not also be true of man, especially when there is no empirical evidence to suggest that an invisible entity survives the death of the body? In his *Treatise of Human Nature* (1739) Hume had actually gone further and concluded that the idea of a permanent self or personal identity is a fiction of the imagination since it is 'nothing but a bundle or collection of different perceptions, which succeed each other with an inconceivable rapidity, and are in a perpetual flux and movement'.[2] This is quite strangely close to the Buddhist doctrine of *anatta* (or no-self).

Although this does not mean that Hume was closely acquainted with Buddhist teaching, he nevertheless took cognizance of several non-Christian traditions and is regarded today as one of the founders of the modern study of religion. In *The Natural History of Religion* (1757) Hume discussed the origin of religion and tried to show that theism is neither the original, nor even the highest, form of religion. It was his conclusion that religion originates from human ignorance, is motivated by fear, and operates by the imaginative projection of human qualities on unknown causes.

Hume was himself neither a theist nor an atheist. Strictly speaking he was an agnostic, though that term was not coined until a century later. He acknowledged a whole area of mystery in which it is necessary to suspend judgment and avoid being dogmatic. 'The whole is a riddle, an enigma, an inexplicable mystery. Doubt, uncertainty, suspense of judgment appear the only result of our most accurate scrutiny, concerning this subject' is how he ended his investigation of religion and he himself made his 'escape into the calm, though obscure, regions of philosophy'.[3]

In his *Dialogues Concerning Natural Religion*[4] Hume discussed religion through three characters: Demea (who represented the Calvinist orthodoxy under which he had suffered in his youth), Cleanthes (spokesman for the natural religion of the deists) and Philo (the philosophical sceptic who substantially represented the views of Hume himself). Through Philo Hume contended that, since our ideas arise out of our experience and we have no direct experience of God, we are in no position to pontificate on the attributes and actions of God. Hume showed that the common argument for the existence of God, based on appeal to the design to be discerned in nature, was invalid, since it depended on an illegitimate use of the principle of analogy.

Though Hume repudiated both orthodox Christianity and the natural religion of the deists, he did not altogether reject religion *per se* and even hinted that he regarded his own philosophy as the 'true religion'. 'In proportion to my veneration of true religion, is my abhorrence of vulgar superstitions.'[5] But if 'the proper office of religion is to regulate the heart of men, humanize their conduct, infuse the spirit of temperance, order and obedience'[6] then the only true religion which Hume could acknowledge was 'the philosophical and rational kind'.[7] It was a religion which acknowledged no external absolutes, implied no participation in sacred ritual, claimed no knowledge of future rewards and punishments, and, by encouraging men to subject all truth claims to rational enquiry, left man to live with perpetual uncertainty. So Philo ended the *Dialogues* with the following two-edged comment which was rather typical of Hume: 'To be a philosophical Sceptic is . . . the first and most essential step towards being a sound, believing Christian.'[8]

The philosophical scepticism advanced by Hume cannot in itself form a viable religious philosophy but it nevertheless must become a permanent component of the religious awareness of mankind on this side of the Age of the Enlightenment. Scepticism provides a necessary safeguard against credulity, in a world where man now finds himself confronted by a great variety of conflicting faiths. On the other hand, Hume's scepticism highlights the real nature of faith. In Hume we see effectively brought to an end the marriage of faith and reason which had characterized Western Christian thought since the age of the second-century Apologists. Faith has now become divorced from reason and has been made to stand on its own feet, a point strikingly expressed by Kierkegaard[9] in his phrase 'leap of faith'.

Although, in retrospect, we can today see quite clearly the importance of Hume's scepticism as a key for understanding man's modern religious situation, his immediate influence in Britain was very small. His writings were largely ignored and 'natural religion' flourished for another century, the works[10] of William Paley (1743-1805) being particularly influential. Yet Hume anticipated many of the objections to traditional religion which were to become dominant in the religious scene in the next two centuries. His more immediate influence was in France and Germany, where his work served as a catalyst for the development of new religious thought. From this point onwards, and through the nineteenth century, Germany proved to be the main seedbed for the new religious foundations which the post-Enlightenment era awaited.

The first outline of these was supplied by Immanuel Kant (1724-1804), who, as a student, was much impressed by the new view of the universe, as well as by the scientific principles of Isaac Newton. At the age of 31 he wrote a *General Natural History and Theory of the Heavens*[11] which sketches the almost infinite dimensions of the physical universe in both space and time and which regards creation not as the work of a moment but as a process which 'will go on and on'. It is against the background of this new cosmology (to be discussed further in Chapter 9) that we must understand Kant's philosophy and religious thought. In his earlier days he spoke unhesitatingly of the divine Creator. Later he became more cautious. He openly confessed that it was the way in which Hume had attacked traditional metaphysics that 'first interrupted (his) dogmatic slumber, and gave (his) investigations in the field of speculative philosophy quite a new direction'.[12]

In his *Critique of Pure Reason* (1781) Kant showed how impossible it is, on the basis of reason, to show that God exists, that man has an immortal soul and that he possesses freewill. But Kant rejected Hume's scepticism. On the grounds that there are limits to the capacity of pure reason to deal adequately with certain important areas of human experience, Kant believed he could arrive at the essentials of religious faith by using another method. 'I have therefore found it necessary to deny *knowledge*', wrote Kant 'in order to make room for *faith*.'[13] In his *Critique of Practical Reason* Kant set out to provide a rational defence for faith by starting from the universal moral experience of 'the categorical imperative' and then reaching out to the 'postulates of practical reason', which appeared necessary to explain the fact of moral experience.

His argument is briefly like this, starting from his oft-quoted observation, 'Two things fill the mind with ever new and increasing admiration and awe, the oftener and the more steadily we reflect on them: *the starry heavens above and the moral law within*'.[14] In human experience we all know what it is to feel under a sense of obligation.

The fact that we experience a moral duty implies that we are free to fulfil that duty. 'I ought, therefore I can.' Though the fact of freewill cannot be proved on the basis of pure reason, yet on the basis of practical experience it is necessary to assume it. It becomes, therefore, the first 'postulate of practical reason'.

But since it is impossible within the limits of this mortal life to fulfil all the demands of the moral law within, and the achievement of moral perfection requires an endless duration of existence, then it becomes necessary to make the second postulate, namely, that the human soul is immortal and has the prospect of an endless post-mortem existence. Incidentally, this argument is similar to one used to support the Indian doctrine of *samsara* (the wheel of rebirth, or re-incarnation).

Further, if one is to harmonize satisfactorily the moral component in human experience with the natural world at large, a third postulate becomes necessary. This is the existence of a Supreme Being – God – who possesses all the moral values to an infinite degree: '. . . it is only from a morally perfect and at the same time all-powerful will and consequently only through harmony with this will, that we can hope to attain the *summum bonum* which the moral law makes it our duty to take as the object of our endeavours.'[15]

By means of his postulates of practical reason Kant thus tried to re-establish the basic religious beliefs which he had previously shown to be beyond the power of reason to prove. Because he set out from the premise of man's moral experience, Kant virtually turned religion into the recognition of a set of moral duties as divine commands. The Church is an ethical community. God had come to function as the Author of the moral order. Kant expounded his religious views in *Religion within the Bounds of Pure Reason* (1793), and showed that, as he saw it, there is no need for miracles, prayer or a personal redeemer and that the moral law serves no purpose beyond itself.

Orthodox Christians, not yet recognizing any need for new religious foundations, quite naturally rejected this reduction of God and of religion to moralism. Superficially it could be taken for a new version of deism, now based on moral experience instead of on reason. This ethical, as opposed to natural, theology did, however, exert considerable influence in the nineteenth century, providing what liberal Protestant theologians believed to be a viable philosophical basis for a new Christian theology. Yet Kant's ethical theology failed to fill the void beginning to appear in the post-Enlightenment age. In a witty history of German philosophy, Heinrich Heine likened the religious situation reached by Kant to one which necessitated 'bringing the sacraments to a dying god!'[16]

It fell to other philosophers, therefore, to attempt to build some of Kant's beliefs into a viable system of thought which could serve as the new religious form. It was Kant, after all, who had observed that the effect of the Enlightenment was to free philosophy from subservience to theology as its handmaid; in future, he said, philosophy would no longer bear theology's train, it would carry the torch ahead. This torch was carried forward by the German idealist philosophers, of whom the chief were Fichte, Schelling and Hegel, the last exerting by far the greatest influence.

These came on the scene at a very crucial time in the history of Western thought. Philosophy and theology had finally become divorced from one another. Religion could no longer fall back on the full support of reason. On the other hand, the Romantic movement was in full swing. It played down the place of reason and balanced it with a positive appreciation of human emotion and feeling. It encouraged free self-expression of the individual. This was a period of restless experiment. Romanticism had its roots in Nicholas of Cusa and the mystics, and more latterly in Rousseau. Religion, having lost the support of pure reason, found a new ally in the Romantic emphasis on feeling and imagination. Schleiermacher, the most creative German theologian acceptable within Lutheranism, made 'the feeling of dependence' the basis for a new theological approach. In his lectures *On Religion* (1799) he had tried to win back to Christian faith those whom he called 'the cultured despisers of religion'. The time had come for a revival of interest in Spinoza, for his monistic and pantheistic view of the whole of reality was a way of filling the void left by the now declining theism, dependent as it was, on the dichotomy of matter and spirit. Fichte and Schelling, each in his own way, attempted to synthesize Kant's moral order with Spinoza's mystical pantheism. After them Hegel developed the synthesis into an elaborate, all-embracing philosophical system, which was intended to supersede traditional religion and constitute its equivalent for the new age.

J. G. Fichte (1762-1814), like many of the seminal thinkers we are here dealing with, began with the study of theology before being attracted to Kant's philosophy. His own system of thought, which he himself regarded as being already implicit in Kant's own philosophy, has sometimes been labelled 'ethical pantheism'. This term itself suggests a synthesis drawn from both Kant and Spinoza, and the substance of it was in an essay he published in 1789 'On the Foundation of our Belief in a Divine Government of the Universe'. Fichte had clearly abandoned even the last deistic remnants of theism. He found no need to postulate, like Kant, the existence of a divine entity (God) to account for the fact of the moral order. For him 'the moral order is identical with God. We do not and cannot grasp any other God'.[17] Fichte was charged with atheism but maintained, in his defence, that true atheism consists in refusing to obey the voice of one's conscience. As Fichte saw it, the moral order is itself what is Divine and, when we do what duty prescribes without calculating the consequences, the Divine becomes alive and real in us. This is the complete faith by which men must live. Thus for Fichte, as also for Kant, the moral imperative was paramount.

F. W. J. Schelling (1775-1854) was less well-known in the English-speaking world, but is important for several reasons, one being his influence on Hegel who, though five years his senior, became his disciple for a time. The son of a Lutheran pastor, and himself destined for the ministry, Schelling met Hegel and Hölderlin at the Tübingen theological seminary and there they discussed Spinoza, Kant and Fichte. Schelling then turned to philosophy. He quickly became dissatisfied with Kant and Fichte and, in his later years, grew very critical of Hegel. He never constructed a philosophical system but his general position has been called a 'dynamic pantheism'.

Influenced by the ancient Neo-Platonists, by Bruno, by the Lutheran mystic Jakob Boehme (1575-1624) and by Spinoza, Schelling saw Nature as an infinite, unified, self-developing super-organism which was realizing itself in finite matter without ever becoming exhausted. That which makes the world into a living, dynamic system is an 'organizing principle' which he referred to as the 'world-soul'. It is this which comes to consciousness in and through human consciousness. He stressed the aliveness of Nature in contrast with Spinoza's rather lifeless and deterministic form of pantheism. When charged with pantheism, Schelling pointed out that even St Paul had spoken of God as one 'in whom we live and move and have our being'.[18] He was prepared to defend this form of pantheism (a form for which the term 'panentheism' is today preferred). Schelling's philosophy represented an exploration into new forms of religious thought, which influenced such people as Kierkegaard,

Schopenhauer and Nietzsche in the nineteenth century and Paul Tillich in the twentieth.[19] But we must now turn to the man who, drawing from Spinoza, Kant and Schelling, surpassed them all in the breadth of his influence.

G. W. F. Hegel (1770-1831) also began his career as a theological student but by the time of his graduation he had become disillusioned with traditional theology. He spent the next decade reflecting on the function of religion in human life and in society, searching (as we might now say) for the form of religion best fitted for the new era. His recognition of this need is reflected in his later words, 'It is surely not difficult to see that our time is a time of birth and transition to a new period. The spirit has broken with what was hitherto the world of its existence and imagination and is about to submerge all this in the past: it is at work giving itself a new form'.[20]

All of Hegel's early writings were theological: *A Life of Jesus* (1795); *A Positivity of the Christian Religion* (1796); *The Spirit of Christianity and its Fate* (1798). They were severely critical of orthodox Christianity. They deplored the fact that God was conceived as belonging so utterly to another world in which men have no share that, on behalf of this transcendent God, men fought, murdered and burned at the stake.[21] Although Hegel moved increasingly into the field of philosophy, his philosophy could be said to have remained a kind of theology. Indeed he believed that philosophy, of the kind he came to expound, had now to assume the role previously played by religion.

Hegel was able to distinguish clearly between religion in general and the particular forms in which it was manifested. He held the former in very high regard. 'All that has worth and dignity for man, all wherein he seeks happiness, his glory, and his pride finds its ultimate centre in religion, in the thought, the consciousness and the feeling of God.'[22] In the past, he asserted, it was religion which had unified man's world. But traditional Christianity was no longer able to do this because a rift had opened up between it and knowledge (or science). 'Science forms a universe of knowledge, to which God is not necessary, which lies outside of religion, and has absolutely nothing to do with it.'[23] But valuable though science is, it can say nothing about the Eternal. Therefore, argued Hegel, science and religion are both essential for man but they must be reconciled. Only philosophy can do this, reconciling in one system the finite and infinite, the temporal and eternal. But in doing so it becomes the new form of religion, superseding the old.

For Hegel the concept of God used by traditional theism had become too small for the greatly expanded world which man had now entered. He searched for a single concept, one basic Idea, which could be conceived as embracing all reality, and by reference to which one could do justice both to the new science and to the truth contained in the declining Christian theism. He believed he had found it in the German word *Geist*. This can mean both 'Mind' and 'Spirit' and was particularly useful just because it embraced elements of both. These two concepts reflected the two worlds of knowledge and religion (or science and faith) which he wished to reconcile.

Hegel, like Spinoza, saw the whole of reality as a rational unity. It is to be seen as the manifestation of *Geist*, from which it draws its laws and logical consistency. His starting point could have been expressed in these Hellenistic statements from the Fourth Gospel – 'In the beginning was the Logos . . . and the Logos was God', 'God is Spirit and they that worship Him must worship Him in spirit and in truth'.[24] Hegel's philosophy was intended to express most adequately the nature and structure of all reality and to make clear how each element in human experience and knowledge is related to the structure as a whole.

The unsatisfactory feature of traditional theism was that

it led to a duality, in which a Creator God is set over against the world which he had created and in which science now allowed him no place. So following Spinoza, but avoiding his materialistic tendencies, Hegel expounded a monism to which *Geist* is the key. He asserted, 'There cannot be a Divine Reason and a human, there cannot be a Divine Spirit and a human, which are *absolutely different*. Human reason . . . is the divine in man, and Spirit, in so far as it is the Spirit of God, is not a spirit beyond the stars, beyond the world . . . God is present, omnipresent, and exists as Spirit in all spirits . . . Religion is a product of the Divine Spirit.'[25] This monistic view of reality, promoted by Spinoza and Hegel, had occasionally surfaced in Christian mysticism without ever becoming dominant. We find Hegel quoting with approval the following words of the medieval mystic Meister Eckhart (c. 1260-1327), 'The eye with which God sees me is the eye with which I see him; my eye and his eye are one . . . If God were not, I would not be; if I were not, then he were not'.[26]

As Hegel saw it, he was not denying the God of theism but rather superseding the traditional imagery and concepts used for Ultimate Reality by the use of more adequate ones. God was no longer to be conceived as *a person* or even *a being*. 'He is no longer a Being above and beyond this world'. he said.[27] (This was a point which Fichte had already reached.) For Hegel, 'God is the One True Reality, and there is no other reality whatsoever'.[28] 'God is the absolute Substance'[29] and this substance 'is Spirit, the Absolute Spirit, the eternally undifferentiated Spirit, essentially at home with Himself'.[29] Hegel defined spirit as 'that which has its centre in itself' in contrast with matter which has its essence outside of itself. 'Spirit is self-contained essence.' It entails freedom and is 'none other than self-consciousness – consciousness of one's own being'.[30] Human self-consciousness is the manifestation of spirit in a finite form and is not to be thought of as apart from, but rather as being contained in, the God who is Absolute Spirit. So he was able to say that 'The idea which a man has of God corresponds with that which he has of himself . . . when a man knows truly about God, he knows truly about himself also'.[31] We shall later see how Feuerbach reversed the intention of this correlation.

Absolute Spirit, however, is not static, complete and finished but is dynamic and is in the process of realizing itself. This is the meaning of the existence of the world and of the course of human history. 'The power of spirit', he said, 'is only as great as its pouring out, its depth only as deep as it dares to extend and to lose itself in its self-expression.'[32] In this process of the self-realization of the absolute spirit, spirit has become estranged or alienated from itself. This is manifested chiefly in the human condition, where the human (or relative) spirit becomes alienated from Absolute Spirit.

Hegel frequently used the biblical story of Adam's Fall to illustrate this state of alienation. At a time when nearly all Christians were still treating this narrative as an historical event, Hegel took it to be a myth or parable, in which he found a 'deep philosophical meaning'. Paradise represents the life of animal-like innocence in which there was as yet no awareness of good and evil, and hence no suffering. It was a state prior to the emergence of the human condition. Hegel believed that 'Animals have the happy lot, if you like to call it so, of being supplied by Nature with what they need'.[33] But to become human, Adam (or man) had to have his eyes opened. In this way he became aware of good and evil and hence existed as a decision-making creature. The freedom which the creature needs before he can become human leads, however, to suffering. 'The greatness of man just consists in the fact that he eats his bread in the sweat of his brow . . . The sorrow of the natural life is essentially connected with the greatness of the character and destiny of man.'[33] Though man's history on earth has been attended by misery and suffering, this has been a necessary, if tragic, accompaniment of his being human. 'The Fall is therefore the Mythus of Man – in fact the very transition by which he becomes man.'[34]

The alienation of spirit from Spirit which is manifested in the human condition is not, however, the end of the matter. In the historical process through which Absolute Spirit achieves self-realization, alienation is succeeded by reconciliation. Again Hegel found this exemplified in the Judaeo-Christian tradition in general and in the notion of the Incarnation in particular. Alienation of spirit from spirit reached its climax in Western monotheism where we find self-conscious man estranged from his God. The Incarnation, i.e. the idea of Christ as both God and man, is the key to the end of alienation. Through the historical person of Jesus of Nazareth Christians have come to affirm both the humanity of God and the divinity of man, that is, that God and man have become one.

Hegel agreed with Christian orthodoxy that 'the death of Christ is the central point round which all else turns'[35] but for him 'Christ's death primarily means that Christ was the God-Man, the God who had at the same time human nature, even unto death'.[36] This enabled Hegel to say, 'God has died, God is dead',[37] and he noted elsewhere that this statement was already found in a Lutheran hymn. Although this phrase was to be made famous by Nietzsche[38] and more recently by the 'Death of God' theology of the sixties, Hegel was one of the first to use it.[39] But what did Hegel mean? Livingston interprets him as meaning that what he died in the death of the God-man, Jesus, was 'the existence of God as an individual standing over against us; the personal transcendent God of traditional theism'.[40]

As Hegel saw it, the death of God was real (frightful

though that thought may be) but it was also momentary. The death of God meant the end of the alienation of spirit from spirit, it meant the death of death. The narrative of the death of God had necessarily to be followed therefore by the resurrection. 'God comes to life again . . . This is the meaning of the resurrection and the ascension of Christ.'[41] Again we find that Hegel was among the first of modern thinkers to treat the Resurrection narratives of Jesus as symbolical. 'To consider the resurrection of Jesus as an event is to adopt the outlook of the historian and this has nothing to do with religion . . . As a human individual he lived, died on the cross and was buried.'[42] This is why 'The Resurrection is something which thus essentially belongs to faith'.[43]

The God who came to life again in the Resurrection of Christ did so in the Spirit which came upon his friends, enabling them to see and experience the true significance of the Incarnation, namely that, in Christ, God and man had become reconciled – had, in fact, become one. Christ had 'presented the eternal history of Spirit – a history which every man has to accomplish in himself, in order to exist as Spirit . . . The followers of Christ, who combine on this principle and live in the spiritual life as their aim, form the Church, which is the Kingdom of God'.[44] Prior to the Incarnation the spirit of man was alienated from the Divine Spirit: in the Incarnation reconciliation took place resulting in the self-realization of Absolute Spirit within the new Spiritual Community, the Church. 'God is Spirit, the Spirit of His Church in fact.'[45]

For Hegel all the religions of man had played their part in the self-realization of Spirit through the course of human history. In this way he was able to acknowledge the relative truth to be discerned in each of them. He believed there were three stages in the evolution of religion and these he likened to the human growth stages of childhood, adolescence and adulthood. The first stage is the religion of nature (he took Chinese religion as an example), the second is the religion of individual spirituality (to be found in Indian religion) and the third is the Absolute Religion. In this last the first two stages (which focused, in turn, on the world and the finite human spirit) are transcended and Spirit reaches complete freedom and self-consciousness.

The real significance of Christianity for Hegel was that it represents the Absolute Religion, the final stage of the evolution of religion. 'It is the Christian religion which is the perfect religion, the religion which represents the Being of Spirit in a realized form . . . In it . . . the infinite Spirit and the finite spirit are inseparably connected; it is their absolute identity which constitutes this religion and is its substance or content.'[46]

The finality, or absolute character of, the Christian religion was believed by Hegel to be exemplified in the doctrine of the Trinity, which thus succinctly portrays the divine history of spirit. First there was the Kingdom of the Father, the absolute, eternal Idea, who was before the creation of the world. In the act of creation this Idea moved out of its condition of universality and infinity into that which is finite and particular, namely, the physical world and finite spirit. This constitutes the Kingdom of the Son. In this phase mankind, being finite spirit, has the potential for eternity but is nevertheless alienated from eternity and, being finite, is subject to death. However, it belongs to the essential nature of God that he should reconcile to himself whatever is Other, or foreign to himself. To achieve this purpose it was necessary for one such as Jesus to appear as the God-Man to manifest 'the truth that the divine and human natures are not implicitly different'.[47] The historical Incarnation therefore marked the end of the Kingdom of the Son and ushered in the Kingdom of the Spirit, where is found 'the union of the two sides of the infinite antithesis

– God and the world'.[48]

This very brief sketch of Hegel's interpretation of Christianity, drawn from his *Early Theological Writings*, his *Philosophy of History* and his *Philosophy of Religion*, illustrates how he subjected traditional Christianity to a radical critique. He then proceeded, using what he took to be the essential truths of Christianity, to construct the new philosophical system which he believed the new age called for. This in its all-embracing completeness is found in his *Encyclopaedia of the Sciences*, supplemented by other works. On the one hand he claimed that Christianity was the absolute religion, the truest presentation of religion; on the other hand he claimed that religion (as known in the past) must be superseded by philosophy. 'At the present time', he said, 'it is philosophy which is not only orthodox, but orthodox *par excellence*: and it is it which maintains and preserves the principles which have always held good, the fundamental truths of Christianity.'[49]

Hegel tried to show that his philosophy was a legitimate, and indeed the true, form of Christianity by distinguishing between two kinds of faith. There is the faith which becomes identified with a certain content of belief and the faith which has no such content. The former refers to all the particulars in which historical Christianity had clothed itself – beliefs, doctrines, rites and even Scriptures. These were all relative to the time in which they appeared and were subject to change and reformulation. If Christian orthodoxy continued to demand faith of this kind it would no longer constitute 'the witness of God to Himself as Spirit in the Spirit'.[50]

For Hegel contended that just as Christ had promised his disciples that 'when the Spirit of truth comes, he will guide you into all the truth'[51] so 'true faith has no accidental content'.[52] He defined faith 'as being the witness of the Spirit to Spirit and this implies that no finite content has any place in it'.[53] Religion, he therefore concluded, 'should contain only eternal truths of the Spirit'.[54]

Tillich said, 'Hegel is in some sense the centre and the turning-point . . . of a world-historical movement which has directly or indirectly influenced our whole century'.[55] Why is this? Hegel captured the imagination of those who, like himself, either sensed, or were convinced, that men had entered a new, post-theistic age. Man needed a new vision or understanding of the nature of reality. Hegel attempted to supply that in his philosophical system which, by its completeness, would do for the new age what the *Summa* of Aquinas had done for the medieval age. It was much more ambitious and all-embracing than Kant's ethical theology. It was a synthesis which attempted to find a place for everything and, in particular, to bridge the growing rift between the new sciences and the religious vision of reality.

The strength of Hegel's system was that it avoided the incipient dualism inherent in theism, a dualism which had become evident during the Enlightenment. The world had come to be seen in independence of the God of theism; it could be explained more and more in terms of its own internal nature and processes and without reference to an external Creator. Theism had led to deism and this, in turn, could lead only to atheism. The alternative proposed by Hegel was a pantheistic monism, in which the unity of both the world and God is affirmed in an evolving, dialectical process. For Hegel, as Tillich says, 'The world is the process of the divine self-realization'.[56] For the first time in Western thought, God (or Ultimate Reality) was no longer being conceived as the unchangeable One, who is eternally the same. On the contrary, He who had traditionally been conceived as the Author of change had become identified with the process of change itself.

Yet Hegel's impressive synthetic system, influential though

it was, did not in itself become the new religious form. Even those most attracted to it also came to reject it, at least in part. Two defects may be briefly mentioned. Hegel gave the impression that the estrangement of spirit from Spirit had been overcome and the final synthetic consummation had been reached. This did not ring true to human experience, either for the individual (as Kierkegaard was quick to point out) or for society (where Marx found alienation more rampant than ever in the class war). In any case, if the Incarnation of the God-Man Jesus had itself constituted the overcoming of the alienation and the death of the theistic God, why was the real significance of this realized only nineteen centuries later? Moreover the very completeness of the system made it too good to be true, for paradoxically it meant that something vital had been left out, namely, the mystery, the enigmas, and the brokenness which continue to be felt in human experience and which form the very character of human existence. Kierkegaard's existentialism arose in direct response to Hegel's system.

Hegel's relationship to historical Christianity was ambivalent. An Italian philosopher, Benedetto Croce (1866-1952), said that Hegel was at once the most religious and the most irreligious of thinkers. This fact became reflected in the left and right wings into which Hegel's adherents quickly moved. The right-wing Hegelians, both in Germany and England, tried to adapt his system to support a liberal, but less radical, reformulation of Christianity. The left-wing, known as the 'Young Hegelians', were offended by the residue of Christian tradition still present in the master's system and they moved to even more radical positions, which became strongly critical of Hegel. Of these, Strauss drove a wedge between the mythical and historical elements in the Christian tradition, Feuerbach reversed the emphasis in Hegel's system and Marx applied Hegel's dialectical evolution of spirit to socio-economic history. To these men, in turn, we must now give some attention for, as Tillich has said, 'in these decades (1830-50) was prepared the historical destiny and the cultural self-expression of the Western world in the twentieth century'.[57] It is therefore not surprising to find in the last decade or so that both theologians and philosophers have been turning back to the study of Hegel with renewed interest.

CHAPTER 6

FROM RELIGIOUS TRADITION TO EITHER HISTORY OR MYTH

❖

An important consequence of the Enlightenment was the increasing attention given to the study of history, leading to a great improvement in the art of historiography. Traditions of the past, which had long been accepted without question on the basis of the authority of the transmitter, were subjected to doubt and critical investigation, often for the first time. The concern to find out 'just exactly what happened' has been an important characteristic of post-Enlightenment man. The historian enunciated a set of criteria by which he evaluated the extant evidence from the past and these were somewhat analogous to the methods being used by the empirical scientist. Subsequent experience has shown that the nineteenth-century historian was some times over-confident in what he hoped to achieve. It is now widely acknowledged that the task of the historian is not simply to uncover the 'bare facts' but to reconstruct as reliable a picture of the past as is possible on the evidence available. Post-Enlightenment man is concerned, however, to distinguish clearly, wherever he can, between reliable evidence (preferably from first-hand witnesses) and what must be placed in the categories of either legend or myth.

Such methodical sifting of the evidence could not but lead to a radical reassessment of religious traditions generally and of the biblical material in particular. Initially, both the critical historian and the defender of Christian orthodoxy were inclined to identify what was religiously valuable in the tradition with what was historically reliable. There was the temptation to think that the truth of Christianity could be proved or disproved, solely on historical grounds. The consequence was that material judged to be of little historical value was too quickly discarded as false. Only later did it come to be seen that traditions could have a religious value irrespective of their historicity. In particular, when the category of myth came to be clearly recognized, and the historical and mythical components separated from each other, it was realized that myth, far from being valueless, is of unique importance to religious faith. A key role was played in this development by David Strauss (1808-74), one of the 'Young Hegelians'.

We must go back a little earlier, however. Even during the Enlightenment the deists' rejection of supernatural miracles caused them to question the reliability of some of the biblical material. Yet they mostly assumed that each narrative pointed to an actual historical event and it was simply a matter of replacing the (false) supernatural interpretation by the (true) natural one. Much debate went on between the naturalists (or rationalists) and the supernaturalists (or traditionalists) on the basis of their commonly shared assumption. An early sign of something more revolutionary was the appearance in 1744 of an anonymous[1] work, entitled *The Resurrection of Jesus Considered*. It claimed that Christ's predictions of his own death were a forgery, that the narratives of Christ's Resurrection were incredible on internal grounds and that the diversity to be found in the various accounts showed evidence of fraud.

A critical and more thorough examination of all the Gospel material was performed by Reimarus (1694-1768), a Professor of Hebrew and Oriental Languages at Hamburg. He was known to be a typical deist, but not even his wife had suspected during his lifetime how unorthodox his views had become. These he wrote down in a manuscript entitled *Apology or Written Defence for the Rational Worshipper of God*. After his death, seven extracts from it were published by his friend, the dramatist and philosopher Lessing. 'The Wolfenbüttel Fragments', as they became known, produced such an outcry that further publication was forbidden.[2]

The chief criterion used by Reimarus in his examination of the Gospels was simply that of inner consistency. He argued that if the Bible is divinely inspired (as tradition had claimed) then it should be free from all contradiction. His researches revealed discrepancies in the Resurrection narratives of such a kind that they could not possibly be reconciled and he asserted that these would carry little or no weight in a court of law. He showed that the idea of a worldwide mission did not originate until quite some time after the death of Jesus. He pointed out that some of the most important tenets of Christian orthodoxy were not to be found in the recorded teaching of Jesus. He was the first modern scholar to bring to light the eschatological character of the New Testament writings. All these findings have, with some modifications, been confirmed by later scholarship. His chief error was to jump to the conclusion that the Apostles, faced with the disaster of Jesus's unexpected death after they had given up everything to follow him, proceeded to perpetrate a hoax – they stole the body of Jesus, waited fifty days and then announced the Resurrection. With the gift of hindsight we may now say that he was led into this blunder, not because he was too critical, but because he had not been critical enough. He had assumed the Gospels were closer in time to the Apostles than they are now believed to have been.

It was Strauss who saw where and how his predecessor had gone wrong. After a brilliant career as a theological student under F. C. Baur (1792-1860), another Hegelian, he was already outgrowing Christian orthodoxy by the time he graduated. It needs to be remembered that within the context of the modern world-view then emerging (see Chapter 9), the traditional Christian imagery (i.e. angels, heavenly throne, virgin birth, resurrection, ascension) was no longer so convincing when taken literally. Strauss had learned from Hegel how to make a distinction between religious imagery and philosophical concepts and to see them as alternative ways of expressing the same truth, even though, in Hegel's view, the philosophical mode was clearly superior. When, however, Strauss began his task of regular preaching, he encountered a problem which has tormented innumerable Christian preachers in modern times. He realized that what was for him simply religious imagery was actually the content of faith for many ordinary Christians. Since they would not understand the Christian faith if it were translated into philosophical concepts after the manner of Hegel, he continued to use the traditional imagery until he became finally persuaded that this was intellectually dishonest.

Strauss believed the time had come, openly to acknowledge the symbolic character of the traditional Christian imagery and to undertake the hermeneutical task of giving it fresh expression within the context of the modern world. In the doctoral dissertation he wrote in 1831 he argued that the imagery of the End-time (general resurrection, last judgment, etc.) must be seen not to relate to the distant future but to the eternal present. His dissertation is said to have shown the influence of Spinoza, Boehme and Schelling, as well, of course, as Hegel. At this stage he was 'a very religious man engaged in an intensely religious quest and struggle'.[3] He did not think of himself in any sense as a destroyer of the Christian faith, but rather as a rebuilder in the aftermath of devastation which had already taken place. He fully expected the results of his work to be welcomed by serious-minded people, for whom it would provide liberation from an outworn, and hence intolerable, dogmatism.

When Strauss returned to Tübingen as a young lecturer he set to work on the book which was to make him famous, *The Life of Jesus Critically Examined*. He painstakingly worked his way through all the Gospel material, from the infancy stories to the Resurrection narratives, dividing it up into appropriate sections. He treated each section in a dialectical way which was typically Hegelian. First he presented the traditional or supernaturalist assessment and this he followed with the rationalist or naturalist interpretations provided by the deists. Then he pitted one against the other in a way which showed up the inadequacies and even absurdities of both. Finally he presented what he believed to be the only adequate way of understanding the Gospel material. The cumulative effect of this approach was quite powerful.

When Strauss came on the scene the biblical debate between the supernaturalists and the naturalists had been going on for decades and he saw it to be fruitless. The way ahead was first of all to acknowledge the falsehood of certain premises, held by the orthodox and the deists alike, namely that the Gospels came directly from eye-witnesses. Strauss tried to free himself from all presuppositions and dogmatic considerations and to subject the Gospels to a strictly historical examination. 'If theologians regard this absence of presupposition from his work as unchristian', he writes in the preface, 'the author regards the believing propositions of theirs as unscientific.'[4]

The chief way in which Strauss superseded the supernaturalist-naturalist debate was by his resort to the category of myth with which to explain both the origin and the nature of many of the Gospel narratives. He was not the first to introduce the term and at that time it was common to use the Latin forms, *mythus, mythi*. We have already seen that Hegel referred to some biblical stories as myth. He was only one of several forerunners on whom Strauss depended. It was Strauss's distinctive and lasting achievement, however, to show firstly how necessary it is to distinguish between history and myth if one is to understand the Gospels adequately and secondly how important myth is for the expression of religious faith.

The positive value of myth in ancient religion was beginning to be recognized by the late eighteenth century. The founder of modern Old Testament study, J. G. Eichhorn (1752-1827), had said in 1779 that the myths of the ancient world are not simply fairy-stories or falsehoods but constitute an ancient form of philosophy, expressing the thoughts and history of a people in a sensuous form. G. L. Bauer, writing in 1799, considered it useful to distinguish between 'philosophical myths' (e.g. creation of the world) and 'historical myths' (stories about peoples and their founders). He proposed the following criteria for determining the presence of myth. A myth narrates events which (i) could have had no eye-witnesses, (ii) are caused by gods rather than by men or natural causes, (iii) are presented in a sensuous way, and (iv) do not now happen and cannot be readily conceived as actually happening. Thus theophanies, in which heavenly beings are said to appear and to converse with men, are not historical narratives but myths. Although he was extremely cautious in his references to the New Testament, Bauer placed all narratives referring to angels, the infancy stories of Jesus and the Transfiguration account into the category of myth.

In 1799 an anonymous writer contended that the real Jesus was quite different from the Gospel portraits since the early Christians had remoulded the stories they told about Jesus to make them conform to their own mental picture of the expected Messiah. This suggested that the

Old Testament could be a possible seedbed for the New Testament myths. An anonymous article in 1816 drew attention to the remarkable number of parallels to be found between Old Testament narratives and Gospel stories, e.g. Pharaoh's slaughter of the children at the birth of Moses and Herod's slaughter of the children at the birth of Jesus; the shining face of Moses on the mountain and the transfiguration of Jesus on the mountain.[5]

Drawing upon such suggestions, Strauss finally became convinced that the solution for the problems raised by the New Testament narratives for which neither the supernaturalist nor deist interpretations were satisfactory lay in what he called the mythical principle. 'The result, then, however surprising, of a general examination of the Biblical history, is that the Hebrew and Christian religions, like all others, have their *mythi*. And this result is confirmed, if we consider the inherent nature of religion, what essentially belongs to it and therefore must be common to all religions, and what on the other hand is peculiar and may differ in each. If religion be defined as the perception of truth, not in the form of an idea, which is the philosophical perception, but invested with imagery, it is easy to see that the mythical element can be wanting only when religion either falls short of, or goes beyond, its peculiar province, and that in the proper religious sphere it must necessarily exist.'[6]

Strauss not only categorized some of the key New Testament narratives as myth rather than history but he set out to explain how they could have developed in such a relatively short time. There are three chief factors which enabled him to do this. The first is that he recognized, more than his predecessors, that the Gospels were separated from the events to which they referred by a period of oral tradition, within which legends and myths were free to arise. He treated the Gospels as collections of stories which had circulated independently during that period before being selected and threaded into a continuous narrative by each evangelist. He believed Matthew's Gospel represented an earlier stage than the others in the development of the oral tradition. But even though the Fourth Gospel had long been the favourite one, Strauss's investigations forced him to conclude that it was inferior to the others as a source of historical evidence.

The second factor was his appeal to the Old Testament as the source of the themes, prototypes and general inspiration for the New Testament myths. There is no doubt that he overplayed this factor and tried to make it explain more than it can possibly do. But some at least of what he contended has not only been supported by later scholarship but receives confirmation from the New Testament itself when it reports how the first Christians 'searched the Scriptures' to find the answers to their problems. The process which Strauss stumbled upon is now seen to be all of a piece with the continuing formation of the Jewish Haggadah.[7]

Thirdly, and perhaps most importantly, Strauss recognized that the thought-forms of the first century were radically different from those of the modern world. The ancient mind was much more at home within a mythical world-view than is the modern mind. The supernaturalists and the rationalists, whose debate he was superseding, both assumed their own mode of thought was identical with that of the first century and consequently approached the material anachronistically. It was his Hegelian philosophy with its emphasis on the dialectical character of historical development which enabled Strauss to appreciate this factor.

Strauss concluded that the birth, infancy and childhood narratives of Jesus are largely mythical, that the Transfiguration, Resurrection and Ascension narratives are wholly mythical, that the miracle stories have a mythical component and that even the Passion story has been retold from the point of view of the mythical world-view of the early Church. He was particularly devastating with regard to the historical character of the Easter narratives. 'The proposition: a dead man has returned to life, is composed of two such contradictory elements, that whenever it is attempted to maintain the one, the other threatens to disappear. If he has really returned to life, it is natural to conclude that he was not really dead; if he was really dead, it is difficult to believe that he has really become living.'[8]

Strauss believed the only way to resolve this dilemma for the modern mind, and at the same time come to a correct understanding of how the Easter faith arose, is to transport oneself back into the 'situation and frame of mind into which the disciples of Jesus were thrown by his death'.[9] It was necessary for the disciples to resolve the contradiction between their conviction in the Messiahship of Jesus and the fact of his scandalous end. This they did by pondering the Scriptures once they had returned home to Galilee and begun to breathe freely again. There 'their faith in Jesus, which had been temporarily depressed, might once more expand with its former vigour. But here also, where no body lay in the grave to contradict bold suppositions, might gradually be formed the idea of the resurrection of Jesus; and when this conviction so elevated the courage and enthusiasm of his adherents that they ventured to proclaim it in the metropolis, it was no longer possible by the sight of the body of Jesus either to convict themselves, or to be convicted by others'.[10]

Although the author of Acts dates the first public announcement of the Resurrection of Jesus seven weeks after his death, Strauss pointed out there were dogmatic reasons for connecting it with the Feast of Pentecost as this was already associated with the giving of the Torah at Mount Sinai. He supposed, consequently, that the period in which the Easter faith came to birth may well have been longer than seven weeks. But 'once the idea of a resurrection of Jesus had been formed in this manner, the great event could not be allowed to have happened so simply, but must be surrounded and embellished with all the pomp which the Jewish imagination furnished'.[11]

Strauss's examination of the Gospel material still yielded a greater residue of historical data than his subsequent critics have often realized. He had no doubts that Jesus actually lived, was a disciple of John the Baptist, was baptized, called disciples, conducted a ministry in Galilee, came to regard himself as the Messiah, that the teaching attributed to him in the Synoptics is largely authentic, that he went to Jerusalem with a messianic plan, cleansed the Temple, predicted his return as the glorified Son of Man, had a farewell supper with his disciples and was arrested, tried, condemned and crucified. Some later New Testament scholars have been unwilling to confirm even as much as this as historical.

Strauss concluded his book with a short discussion of the implications of his work for dogmatic theology. He was fully aware that the results of his enquiry 'apparently annihilated the greatest and most valuable part of that which the Christian has been wont to believe concerning his Saviour Jesus' and that 'the boundless store of truth and life which for eighteen centuries has been the aliment of humanity, seems irretrievably dissipated'.[12] He now found it necessary 'to re-establish dogmatically that which has been destroyed critically'.[13]

Very briefly he sketched the reasons why the traditional Christology was no longer viable. The essential truth in it, however, could be salvaged, first by focusing attention upon the idea of Christ rather than on the historical figure of Jesus (the combination of these two having now become separable as a result of the critical work on the New

Testament), and secondly, by relating the doctrine of the Incarnation not simply to a single individual but to the human race as a whole. 'The history of the gospel is in fact the history of human nature conceived ideally, and exhibits to us in the life of an individual, what man ought to be, and, united with him by following his doctrine and example, can actually become.'[14]

By thinking of both God and man in terms of spirit (in Hegelian fashion) Strauss found a way in which he could reaffirm the Christian doctrine of the Incarnation, coming at it, as he said, 'by an inverted path'. God, as infinite spirit, is only real when he discloses himself or actualizes himself in finite spirits: and man, as finite spirit, is truly man only when he recognizes his divine potential. 'The true and real existence of spirit, therefore, is neither in God by himself, nor in man by himself, but in the God-man.'[15] Instead of seeing the Incarnation of God in Jesus of Nazareth as a unique historical event, Strauss saw it as a symbolic portrayal of the cosmic spiritual process which has been in operation from eternity and which is at once the humanization of God and the divinization of man. 'Humanity is the union of the two natures – God become man, the infinite manifesting itself in the finite and the finite spirit remembering its infinitude.'[16]

If God and man are really *one*, then man had to become aware of this in the course of his religious development at the point where he had become 'mature enough to receive as his religion the truth that God is man, and man of a divine race'.[17] It was this which took place in the rise of Christianity. In his expanded view of the Incarnation Strauss still affirmed the significance of the death and resurrection of the God-man. The death of Jesus, as the God-man, shows that the incarnation of God is real. Since this manifests and symbolizes the humanization of God, it must also be accompanied by the resurrection and ascension, which in turn symbolize the deification of man. The rise of the Easter faith came about when the true significance of Jesus as the God-man entered into the imagination and memory of the disciples, i.e. as 'the unity of the divine and human in him' becomes a part of the general consciousness.[17] Jesus had portrayed what all men must do, i.e. take up their cross, die and rise with him. The real truth of Christianity and the only viable Christology for the modern age, according to Strauss, is to see in Jesus the symbol of the race – 'It is Humanity that dies, rises and ascends into heaven'.[18]

Strauss was fully aware that this transformation of what was a supposed historical event into a spiritual philosophical idea constituted a radical transition in Christian thought. So he turned to the practical problem being faced by the Christian preacher in the new era. He saw four alternative paths:

(i) One could elevate the Church to the new point of view; but unfortunately the attempt would fail for the Church still lacked the necessary presuppositions.

(ii) One could return to the traditional point of view; but this eventually would be seen to be hypocrisy.

(iii) One could forsake the office of the Christian ministry; but this was not in the long-term interests of the Church in that it left the latter to move increasingly into a path of obscurantism.

(iv) The preacher could continue with the traditional forms but use every opportunity to show the real significance of, (say) the Easter faith, and to bring out its contemporary spiritual relevance. In so far as the orthodox preacher normally always drew a spiritual message from whatever historical text he expounded, he was already demonstrating that 'the history is not enough, it is not the whole truth, it must be transmuted from a past fact into a present one, from an event external to you, it must become your own intimate experience'.[19]

Strauss revealed not only genuine pastoral concern but also very real insight into a problem which has plagued the Christian Church in general and the preacher in particular, from his time right up until the present. He was anxious to affirm that, in his view, he was not undermining the Christian faith. On the contrary he asserted, 'The supernatural birth of Christ, his miracles, his resurrection and ascension remain eternal truths, whatever doubts may be cast on their reality as historical facts'.[20] But there was no easy way to avoid the inevitable confusion and controversy which would ensue from the fact that the new era required a radical transference of the eternal truths to a higher plane of understanding. Out of the inevitable collision between opposing points of view he believed that 'time will show whether by the one party or the other, the Church, Mankind, and Truth are best served'.[21]

The Life of Jesus Critically Examined is a most remarkable achievement to have come from a scholar in his twenties and in the age when it was written. Schweitzer described it as 'one of the most perfect things in the whole range of learned literature'.[22] When published in 1836 it brought forth a storm of protest. Pope Gregory XVI condemned it as 'demoniacal'. Far from being welcomed by the serious-minded, as Strauss expected, the book brought him into notoriety, cost him his post and prevented him from ever gaining another in either the ecclesiastical or academic fields. Yet the book was widely read and certainly appreciated by some. In 1846 it was translated into English by the novelist George Eliot and enjoyed a large sale.

In 1840-1 Strauss wrote a further lengthy work, intended to spell out in detail what he had only sketched at the end of his first book. This is indicated by the title *The Doctrine of the Christian Faith presented in its historical development and its struggle with modern scientific criticism* and it revealed his Hegelianism at all points. Although it never attracted as much attention as his *Life of Jesus*, it was judged by Schweitzer to be perhaps even greater and 'in depth of thought . . . to be classed with the most important contributions to theology'.[23] Orthodox Christians did not yet appreciate the point of what Strauss was trying to achieve, let alone tolerate the results. In the context of the new era which modern man had entered, Strauss contended that 'Religion is not concerned with supra-mundane beings and a divinely glorious future, but with present spiritual realities which appear as "moments" in the eternal being and becoming of Absolute Spirit'.[24] Following the lead of both Hegel and Schleiermacher who had already expressed extreme caution on the subject of personal immortality, Strauss rejected this belief entirely – 'The saying of Schleiermacher, "In the midst of finitude to be one with the Infinite, and to be eternal in a moment" is all that modern thought can say about immortality'.[25]

In 1864 Strauss published *A Life of Jesus for the German People*. Here, for the first time, he attempted to set forth in a positive, synthetic way the historical kernel he found in the Gospel records. He separated the historical and mythical components into each of two volumes, the first of which was an outline of the life of the historical Jesus. In this, as in the various editions of his *Life of Jesus*, he tended to keep changing his position, swithering, for example, between seeing Jesus as a human genius and as a deluded fanatic.

Of special interest is his more detailed explanation of how the Easter faith arose. He contended that the story of the empty tomb was a later myth, based on Isaiah 53:9, 'they made his grave with the wicked and with a rich man in his death'; and that the report that Jesus had risen after three days was based on the period which Jonah had spent in the belly of the fish, which the prophet himself had spoken of as 'the belly of Sheol'. Strauss saw little reason to doubt that the dead body of Jesus had simply been buried with those of the other condemned criminals and, since at least seven weeks and probably even longer elapsed before the resurrection of Jesus was publicly proclaimed, it was no longer possible for opponents to dispute it by producing any recognizable corpse.

But what caused the disciples to change from despair to enthusiasm? According to Strauss, it was a gradual, psychological process and is perfectly understandable. After the disciples returned to Galilee their earlier faith in Jesus began to revive. There they had no grave to contradict the fruits of their imagination. The general concept of resurrection was already well established. Once the idea of associating it with the destiny of the crucified Jesus had taken root in their imagination, it was but a short step to a vision of the risen Christ. 'In this way the faith in Jesus as the Messiah . . . was once again subjectively restored through the instrumentality of the mind, the power of the imagination. A living continuation was now ensured for all that new and profound religious life which had been present in Jesus and imparted by him to his followers . . . His whole life became veiled in a shining cloud, which continued to lift it even higher above the human sphere, but also alienated it more and more from the sphere of natural and historical truth.'[26]

Strauss's psychological explanation of the rise of the Easter faith is greatly superior to the hoax theory of Reimarus in that it did not make the Apostles guilty of deliberate deception. It could be argued, of course, that the Apostles were guilty of unconscious self-deception, but this argument can be applied by the non-believer, if he so wishes, to almost any kind of religious belief. Certainly the majority of Christians completely rejected Strauss's reconstruction of the rise of the Easter faith, and were not to know that it was destined to reappear in the twentieth century in a variety of fresh versions. They saw Strauss as one who had completely rejected the Christian faith and he became increasingly ostracized from both Church and academic circles. The personal disappointment this brought, coupled with the deep hurt over his broken marriage, probably contributed to the more negative character of his last work, *The Old Faith and the New*. It is not a good book even though it went through six large editions in six months, but it is worth looking at it for the way in which it illustrates, not only how his own thoughts were moving, but, more importantly, the general direction in which the unchurched masses of the Western world in the twentieth century were destined to proceed.

The title itself demonstrates how Strauss believed that modern man had passed over a threshold of change of such a kind that a radically new form of faith was required. 'I did not and do not want to disturb anyone's contentment or faith', he wrote in the preface, 'only where these have already been shattered will I point out the direction where, according to my conviction, a more solid ground is to be discovered. This ground, in my opinion, can be nothing other than that which we call the modern world-view, the laboriously attained result of continued scientific and historical research in contrast with that of Christian theology.'[27]

By this time he had read Feuerbach, Darwin, Haeckel and Schopenhauer. He had become a strong advocate of Darwinism though he regarded the theory as still very imperfect. He admitted to being a materialist like Feuerbach but believed the dispute between materialism (Feuerbach) and idealism (Hegel) was partly a quarrel of words: they were both opposed to the 'dualism which pervaded the conception of the world throughout the Christian era, dividing man into body and soul, his existence into time and eternity, and opposing an eternal Creator to a created and perishable universe'.[28] He contended that both could be regarded as monistic in that each endeavoured to derive the totality of phenomena from a single principle. Though Hegel started from ideas and idealistic forces and Feuerbach started from atoms and atomic forces, each of these modes soon led to the other.

First of all Strauss subjected the cardinal beliefs of traditional Christianity to a radical examination and showed why such doctrines as the Trinity, virgin birth, original sin, resurrection and immortality could, in his view, be no longer affirmed in the context of the modern world. Whereas the conception of the resurrection of the body had been acceptable in the ancient world to both Jew and Christian, it had become a stumbling block to orthodoxy itself in the modern world. He drew attention to the gulf which had now been opened up between the 'Christ of faith' and the 'Jesus of history', with all the problems which followed from this. He concluded that, to be honest and upright, it was necessary for men like himself to confess that they were no longer Christians.

Strauss maintained, however, that this does not mean that religion is necessarily obsolete in the modern world but only that it must be something different. In so far as religion is to be identified with belief in a personal God, the practice of prayer and belief in personal immortality (as traditionally it had been in the West), then the age of religion, in his view, was over. 'Religion is no longer with us what it was for our fathers but it does not follow it is extinct in us.'[29] The Cosmos in which man finds himself is not the work of a good Creator but is rather a laboratory of the reasonable and the good. The Cosmos is simultaneously both cause and effect, the outward and the inward together. Since it is arrogant for any individual man to oppose himself to the Cosmos from which he springs, it can be said that the same kind of devotion is due to the Cosmos as the traditional believer rendered to his God. But this kind of religion rests on an entirely different basis from that of the past.

Strauss took due cognizance of the way in which man's view of the Cosmos had expanded out of all comparison with what had obtained before the modern world. The Cosmos is the All, and nothing can exist outside of it. Our planet had a beginning and will one day come to an end. But there has never been a time when the Cosmos did not exist in some form. The Cosmos – the sum-total of all worlds in all stages of growth and decay – is constant in its absolute energy amid the everlasting change to which all particular things are subject.

Strauss did not expect his 'New Faith' to win immediate approval. Indeed, the reaction to his book was almost completely negative and even his few friends were silent. But he was confident that the vindication of his book would come in the end, even though he would not live to see it. It is certainly true that the majority of men in the Western world in this last quarter of the twentieth century would find it much more congenial than did Strauss's contemporaries. In his own progression of thought Strauss proved to be a rather striking prototype of the direction in which the popular religious mind has been moving even to the point where it finds itself today in a vague, indefinite and uncertain state.

Strauss was not a creative religious thinker. His greatness lies in the fact that his essential honesty caused him to penetrate into the nature of the changed situation into which post-Enlightenment man had moved. Because Strauss was led in the end to abandon his earlier allegiance to the 'Old Faith', at a time when few were ready to follow him, it caused him to be treated by Christian orthodoxy as one who had mounted a deliberate attack on Christianity and who could therefore be safely ignored as one who had gone sadly astray and become an enemy of the Christian faith. Even to this day he continues to be vilified by people who have never bothered to read his books. The partial neglect of Strauss in the latter half of the nineteenth century meant that much of what he had brought to light had to be rediscovered in later stages. Johannes Weiss, Albert Schweitzer and Rudolf Bultmann have each startled a too complacent orthodoxy in their own day just because Strauss, with all his faults (and they need not be overlooked), was not sufficiently appreciated and digested in his day.

At this distance we are in a better position to evaluate the lasting significance of Strauss more objectively. Perhaps Stephen Neill does not exaggerate when he refers to Strauss's *Life of Jesus* as a 'turning point in the history of the Christian faith'.[30] His work marks a watershed for the following reasons. First, he made it clear for all time how necessary it is to distinguish between history and myth, not only in the Gospel records, but also in the Christian doctrines based upon them. Previously these two components had formed an amalgam in the Gospel tradition. This had not really mattered within the context of the dualistic world-view which had previously obtained, for there the 'other-world' was just as real as 'this-world' and was conceived as being interlocked with it at certain decisive points. But as the expansion of 'this-world' was causing the 'other-world' to dissolve into unreality it was becoming essential to distinguish between narrative which related to 'this-world' (i.e. history), and narrative which related to the 'other-world' (i.e. myth). In the Creed, for example, the words 'crucified, dead and buried' belong to the first category while phrases 'rose again from the dead, ascended into heaven and sitteth on the right hand of the Father' belong to the second.

Secondly, although his *Life of Jesus* had the effect of intensifying the nineteenth-century 'quest for the historical

Jesus', Strauss himself called into question the degree to which Christianity (or any other religion) can appeal to history for a rational defence of the faith. He forced Christians to reflect more deeply on the way in which the essentials of Christian belief are related to the events of history. This question will be taken further in Chapter 12.

Thirdly, he brought out the essential relationship between religious faith and myth. Since his time, and continuing into the twentieth century, the positive value and significance of myth has been increasingly recognized. Martin Buber has referred to myth as 'man's creative answer to the unconditioned' and 'an eternal function of the soul'. Mircea Eliade has impressed on all students of religion the function and creative role of myth in all religious experience. He has claimed that myth will never disappear and that 'the understanding of the myth will one day be counted among the most useful discoveries of the twentieth century'.[31]

Finally Strauss saw the need for a radically new theology, one which took fully into account the 'this-worldliness' of the modern world-view. The traditional theology of divine transcendence needed to be replaced by a theology of divine immanence. One of his contemporaries, Ludwig Feuerbach, to whom we now turn, attempted to produce such a 'theology' in the decade which followed Strauss's epoch-making *Life of Jesus*.

CHAPTER 7

FROM THEOLOGY TO ANTHROPOLOGY

Ludwig Feuerbach (1804-72) may be regarded as one of the principal interpreters of the new age of religion into which post-Enlightenment man had entered. 'No philosopher of his time penetrated the contemporary theological situation as effectually as he, and few spoke with such pertinence', wrote Karl Barth.[1] Feuerbach came to influence such seminal, and yet quite diverse, thinkers as Marx, Kierkegaard, Nietzsche, Freud, Buber and Heidegger. Like Strauss, he tended to be dismissed too cheaply by the defenders of Christian orthodoxy and became overlooked in the later nineteenth century, only to be rediscovered in the twentieth. 'Feuerbach's critique of religion commands a new attention in our day, and its impact is pervasive', writes Manfred H. Vogel. 'Feuerbach's critique is based on a position that is closely akin to the spirit of our age.'[2]

Like Hegel and Strauss, Feuerbach also began his career as a theological student. But having moved from Heidelberg to Berlin in order to study under Schleiermacher he there came under the spell of Hegel and devoted himself thereafter to the pursuit of philosophy – a philosophy, however, which expounded a new kind of theology. As a young academic at Erlangen he delivered a lecture on 'Thoughts on Death and Immortality' in which he contended that the only immortality man can hope for lies in the culture to be handed down from generation to generation. He later said that this lecture contained the outline of what was to become his more developed philosophy. 'Man is not only a spiritual being', he said, 'he is also an earthly being, inseparable from the earth.'[3] His lecture was so controversial that it destroyed for him all chances of academic advancement and he spent his life as a private scholar.

Feuerbach started as an ardent 'Young Hegelian' but in 1839 underwent a radical change of position. He abandoned the idealist philosophy of Hegel and embraced the empirical approach which stems from medieval nominalism and which leads to materialism. Like Hegel he learned much from Spinoza. All three were convinced of the absolute unity of all reality. This means that, for them, the theistic picture of an eternal Creator standing over against the created world could no longer be tenable. But whereas Hegel affirmed the absolute unity by resolving the material into the spiritual, Feuerbach did so by resolving the spiritual into the material. Consequently, he could appeal to Spinoza even more enthusiastically than Hegel had done, calling him 'the Moses of modern free-thinkers and materialists'.[4] 'Spinoza hit the nail on the head', he said. 'God is an extended, that is, material being. He found, at least for his time, the true philosophic expression for the materialistic tendency of the modern era.'[5]

The three most important books of Feuerbach for our present purpose are: *The Essence of Christianity* (1841), *Principles of the Philosophy of the Future* (1843) and *Lectures on the Essence of Religion* (delivered in Heidelberg by student request in 1848). Although it was the first of these books which was most widely read we shall start with a brief look at the second, for in this his critique of Hegel is most explicit. He agreed with the general contention of Hegel that, in the era now entered, religion of the traditional kind must be superseded by philosophy. In his view, however, Hegel's philosophy was still basically theological. 'The Hegelian philosophy is the last magnificent attempt to restore Christianity, which was lost and wrecked, through philosophy, and, indeed to restore Christianity – as is generally done in the modern era – by identifying it with the negation of Christianity.'[6]

Feuerbach believed Spinoza was the only modern philosopher to provide the first elements of a critique of religion and theology and that, though Hegel had been influenced by him, he had moved in the wrong direction. Feuerbach took exactly the opposite direction. Because of this reversal Feuerbach is often said to have turned Hegel upside down (a feat sometimes wrongly attributed to Marx). Feuerbach maintained, however, that it was Hegel who had things upside down and that he was simply looking at truth the right way up. As Feuerbach said, 'The old world put the body on the head, the new puts the head on the body. The old world made spirit the parent of matter, the new makes matter parent of spirit'.[7]

What the reversal means in simple terms is this. Man had long argued that only spirit can give rise to spirit and that spirit must therefore be prior to matter. In transforming the traditional theology of a transcendent Creator God into the philosophy of Absolute Spirit, Hegel was still affirming that all reality originates and culminates in thought or spirit. Hegel's philosophy, Feuerbach asserted, was therefore to be seen as the rebirth, in German form, of ancient Neo-Platonism.[8] For Hegel, therefore, man is God coming to self-realization. Feuerbach, as a materialist, argued on the contrary that the basic stuff of which reality is composed is material, physical and non-spiritual. For him 'Thought proceeds from being, not being from thought'. Things material make possible, and give rise to, things spiritual. Feuerbach's God, instead of revealing himself in man, is the projection in human thought of the true nature of man. 'Thus, God is derived only from man, but not conversely . . . man from God.'[9] 'God is what man would like to be; he is man's own essence and goal conceived as a real being.'[10]

Feuerbach contended that what the modern age calls for is not the deification of man (as Hegel's philosophy propounded) but 'the humanization of God – the transformation and dissolution of theology into anthropology'.[11] ('Anthropology' here refers, as it originally did, to a doctrine of man and not to the modern scientific study of man.)

Just because Feuerbach started from materialistic premises it does not mean (as his critics have sometimes assumed) that he ignored, or treated lightly, the spiritual dimension of human existence. He simply denied that it is necessary to postulate, as theism does, an eternal spiritual source or world in order to explain the presence of the human spirit. He said it was only because the theist has too disparaging a view of nature and too lofty a view of spirit that he arrives at his dualistic view of reality.[12]

Feuerbach associated the human spirit with mind and the mind with the activity of the brain, a view consistent with the growing appreciation of the psychosomatic condition of man. He pointed out that it is only because 'the activity of the brain is the most hidden and imperceptible that men have come to conceive it as an absolutely disembodied inorganic abstract being to which has been given the name spirit'.[12] If the mind or spirit is seen to be dependent upon the physical organ of the brain and cannot operate in separation from the physical body, then it can be argued that it derives from nature. Feuerbach fully conceded that the mind or spirit is the highest and noblest aspect of man, giving rise to ideas, thoughts, science, philosophy and religion. But these are all human products. They have a reality, once they have been formulated and expressed, but it is a reality derived from man, their creator; they have no ontological reality of their own, such as Plato's forms were believed to have.

The ideas and thoughts in which man expresses his spirituality are not the creation of any one individual however. When Feuerbach spoke of the human spirit he was thinking of corporate man, Man, man in community. 'The essence of man is contained only in the community and unity of man with man', he said, 'it is a unity, however, which rests only on the reality of the distinction between I and Thou.'[13] (Martin Buber, who is most widely known for his little classic *I and Thou,* acknowledged that in his youth he was given a decisive impetus by Feuerbach.)[14] In contrast with Hegel, Feuerbach claimed that 'The true dialectic is not a monologue of a solitary thinker with himself; it is a dialogue between I and thou'.[15] He even suggested (perhaps unconvincingly) that this is the reason why the Christian concept of God came to be expressed in the form of the Trinity. The reason why Feuerbach attached such vital importance to the communal character of man is that it is only through dialogue that the individual grows in the confidence that his senses are not deceiving him and then, on the basis of shared sense experiences, comes to a clearer understanding of himself and his world. 'Only through communication and conversation between man and man do the ideas arise. Not alone, but only with others, does one reach notions and reasons in general. Two human beings are needed for the generation of man – of the spiritual as well as of the physical man; the community of man with man is the first principle and criterion of truth and generality.'[16]

It is clear from this beginning that Feuerbach judged all religion to be the product of man, and not the result of a divine revelation. In spite of this fact he assigned to religion the place of highest importance. He asserted that all of his writings had only one theme, viz. religion, on the grounds that religion is the very foundation of human life, ethics and culture. It is religion, more even than reason, which distinguishes the human species from other animals. 'The brutes have no religion', he said.[17] He believed religion to be essential to man for in it man comes to terms with his finiteness and finds his true place in the natural scheme of things. 'He who has an aim, an aim which is itself true and essential, has, *eo ipso*, a religion.'[18]

Religion, however, like all other human products, is subject to change. He recognized that his own time was witnessing such change in a quite radical way. 'What yesterday was still religion is no longer such today; and what today is atheism tomorrow will be religion.'[19] As we have already seen in Chapter 1, when religion is undergoing radical change we have difficulties in defining it. This fact led Feuerbach to speak of religion in an ambivalent way which is at first confusing. Sometimes he used the word 'religion' to refer to the theistic tradition which was to be superseded. At such times he spoke of religion as false and idolatrous and he heralded the end of religion. At other times he used the word in a broader sense, to mean the expression of man's self-knowledge. On these occasions he saw himself as the exponent of the true religion; he said his aim was not to abolish religion but to perfect it. He saw himself as a kind of second Luther, expounding a new form of Christianity – a new religion, the true religion, the religion of man. In true religion, as he saw it, man recognizes his dependence on nature and the necessity for him to live in harmony with nature. The earlier nature-religions, however, had made too much of nature, while the theistic religions had made too little of it. 'Man's true task', he said, 'is to take things as they are, to make *no more* and also *no less* of them than they are.'[20]

Feuerbach's main critique of theism, as we shall see, was to reduce the concept of God to a mental image conceived and projected by the mind of man. Atheistic though this may appear, Feuerbach was no ordinary atheist and refused to acknowledge the label for himself. He contended that the debate about whether God exists had already been disposed of during the Enlightenment and he did not wish to waste time fighting old battles. The time had now come, he said, when 'It is equally meaningless to say "there is a God" and "there is no God" '.[21] He was much more concerned with the explanation of how belief in God had arisen in the first place and to differentiate between the right and wrong ways of interpreting that belief.

It was this aim which led him to divide *The Essence of Christianity* into two parts: in the first part he expounded 'the true or anthropological essence of religion' and in the second he dealt with 'the false or theological essence of religion'. It was not his intention simply to demolish the traditional religious beliefs; he wished, rather, to bring to light the truth he believed they clothed. 'I by no means say: God is nothing, the Trinity is nothing . . . I only show that they are not *that* which the illusions of theology make them.'[22]

First of all, then, how did men come to be using the concept of God? The theologian, appealing to divine revelation as testified to in Bible and Church, replies that men know of God because he chose to reveal himself to them. Hegel could have replied that since it is God who is coming to self-realization in man, it is still really God who has created the term to refer to himself.

But Feuerbach, starting with man, replies that the concept of God has been mentally constructed by man in his search for self-knowledge and that, into this concept, man has projected all that he aspires to be. 'Man makes a god of what he is not but would like to be; that is his god.'[23] Whereas the Bible says that God made man in his own image, the real truth is (asserts Feuerbach) that man has made God in his own image. 'The personality of God is nothing else than the projected personality of man.'[24]

Feuerbach's answer to the question of the origin of the God-symbol could be seen as the end-product of the nominalist (and later the materialist) position, in which

Feuerbach openly acknowledged himself to stand. The nominalist (see Chapter 3) saw universals as human constructs which have no ontological reality. The term 'god' originated as a universal in polytheistic religion. The monotheist had already denied ontological reality to all of these gods except one and the consequence of this is that the term God acquired the status of a proper name. But this fact, argued Feuerbach, does not give the term any more ontological reality than it previously did. 'To ask whether there is a God', said Feuerbach, 'is to ask whether the universal has an existence of its own.'[25] Therefore God, like the gods, remains an idea in the mind of man.

Once the concept of God is seen to have arisen in this way, then, argued Feuerbach, the true significance of belief in God can be seen for what it is. Belief in God is simply belief in the essential significance and potential of the human species. 'The belief in God is nothing but the belief in the absolute reality and significance of the human nature.'[26] Theology, as the study of God, turns out to be an exercise in human self-understanding. Theology, in actual fact, is anthropology in disguise.

All the moral qualities to which he aspires, such as justice, love, compassion, forgiveness, etc., man projects into his concept of God as divine attributes. All the abilities which he would like to possess, such as power, knowledge, ubiquity, durability, etc., man projects into God and magnifies them infinitely. There they become the divine attributes of omnipotence, omniscience, omnipresence, eternity, respectively. 'God is thy highest idea', said Feuerbach, 'the supreme effort of thy understanding, thy highest power of thought.'[27] Feuerbach drew attention to the fact that the proponents of the Ontological Argument for the existence of God, in defining God as 'he than whom nothing higher can be conceived', were unwittingly giving support to his contention. He quoted Kant as saying, 'Fundamentally we cannot conceive God otherwise than by attributing to him without limit all the real qualities which we find in ourselves'.[27] He even appealed to a saying of Luther that 'the way in which God appears to a man depends on that man's frame of mind; as you think and believe, so you have him. If in your heart you paint him merciful or angry . . . that is how you will have him'.[28] Feuerbach interpreted this to mean, 'God is as I imagine him to be . . . in short God is a product of fantasy, and because fantasy is the essential form or organ of poetry, it may be said that religion is poetry and God is a poetic being'.[28] Feuerbach concluded that the concept of God is wholly the product of the human imagination and the reality of the qualities to be found in him are derived from the reality of the human condition, of human self-awareness and human understanding. 'The personality of God is the personality of man freed from all the conditions and limitations of Nature.'[29]

Feuerbach later pointed out that in *The Essence of Christianity* he had been dealing only with the moral and personal attributes of God and that there is another angle to the traditional concept of God. In so far as God is conceived as the creative cause of nature, minerals, the stars, etc., he is also the 'deified, personified essence of nature'. Into this imaginary concept of God, therefore, man has projected both elements of himself and elements of the world of nature. God is conceived as both a form of understanding the human self and a form of understanding the world. Feuerbach extended his earlier equation now to read: theology is really anthropology plus physiology (i.e. God is the essence of man plus the essence of nature).

Feuerbach fully conceded that his analysis of how the God-concept arose and came to be conceived could be regarded as a-theism, for it followed that 'there is no God, no abstract disembodied being distinct from nature and man, who decides the fate of the world and of mankind as he pleases'.[30] But he believed there was something much more important to do than simply draw this atheistic conclusion and that was to bring out the positive content in the now outmoded theistic belief. The positive truth it contained consisted in its being a form of human self-understanding. Once this is recognized it is found that the traditional belief in God is not simply false but has very tragically distorted man's understanding of himself; it has had the effect of disuniting actual (or existential) man from his true (or essential) self.

The God who originated as the projection of all that is best and truest in the human condition (contended Feuerbach) came in the theist's imagination to be set over against man, as the antithesis of his actual self. As the concept of God embraced more and more of what man aspires to be (but is not), the more man found himself to be the polar opposite of his God. God is infinite, man is finite: God is perfect, man is imperfect: God is immortal, man is mortal: God is almighty, man is weak and powerless: God is the sum of all the positive realities, man embraces all the negations. Man thus becomes separated from his God by an unbridgeable gulf for which he, in his sinful guilt, must bear the blame. The holier God is conceived to be, the more sinful does man feel himself to be. There is an inverse correlation between God's perfection and man's imperfection. 'The conception of the morally perfect being' has the effect, said Feuerbach, of 'throwing me into disunion with myself; for while it proclaims to me what I ought to be, it also tells me to my face, without any flattery, what I am not.'[31]

Feuerbach's analysis of the rise of God-belief is equally applicable to the development of the two-world view of reality. As God represents actual man projected into perfected form, so heaven represents the actual world projected into perfection. The potential which originally this world was seen to possess is posited in another world and becomes eternally divorced from this world by the same gulf as that which separates God from man. There is no way, thereafter, in which this world can ever realize its full potential. It remains lost for ever and man's salvation consists in his being delivered by divine grace from this world and translated into another world.

The phenomenon of human misery and suffering in this world was attributed by traditional Christianity to the sinful state of mankind. We have already seen that Hegel translated this belief into his own doctrine of alienation – the alienation of finite spirit from Absolute Spirit. Feuerbach, in turn, translated this into the alienation of man's actual self from his true self. Whereas Hegel saw man as God in a state of alienation from himself, Feuerbach insisted that the true state of affairs is that God is the essence of man in a state of alienation from his actual self.

Moreover, traditional Christianity not alone reflects the alienation of man from his true nature, but in its practices continues to perpetuate it. 'The cultus itself consists in nothing else than in the continual renewal of the origin of religion – a solemnizing of the critical discrimination between the divine and the non-divine.'[32] For example, argued Feuerbach, 'Prayer is the self-division of man into two beings – a dialogue of man with himself, with his heart'.[33]

How is the state of alienation to be overcome? It might have been sufficient for Feuerbach to say that when one comes to a right understanding of the rise and significance of God-belief, then the alienation of actual man from his true self will be overcome. But Feuerbach went further than that. Just as Christianity had found the solution to man's sin in the doctrine of the Incarnation, and just as Hegel had fastened on the Incarnation as the event which should spell the end of theism, so Feuerbach also produced a subtle reinterpretation of the Incarnation in order to support his thesis.

First we must note that Feuerbach (evidently following Strauss) drew a clear distinction between the Jesus of history and the Christ of faith. He did not deny there was an historical Jesus, but when this Jesus became transformed by devout imagination into a god-like figure he ceased to be an historical person. So the Gospel portraits of Jesus were not simply those of an historical figure. Like Strauss, Feuerbach denied that the historical Jesus was born of a virgin, was God, was a wonder-worker, raised men from the dead, and was himself raised physically from the dead. The elements in the Gospel accounts, which had originated in devout imagination and which Strauss had categorized as myth, Feuerbach referred to as 'religious facts', to be distinguished from historical facts. In his terms the resurrection of Jesus was not an historical fact but a 'religious fact' and it was a great misunderstanding of religion to 'attempt to trace religious facts, that exist only in faith, back to historical facts'.[34]

Although the historical Jesus had clearly been the starting point for the emergence of the Christ of faith, it was the latter, and not the former, who was the subject of the doctrine of the Incarnation. Feuerbach contended that the reason why the idea of the Incarnation of God in human form was even tenable was because 'Man was already in God, was already God himself, before God became man, i.e. showed himself as man'.[35] The descent of God in human form had necessarily been preceded by the exaltation of man into the form of God. But further, the real truth in the doctrine of the Incarnation is that the theistic process of objectifying man as God has been reversed, with the effect that man's self-alienation has been cancelled out and overcome. Thus Feuerbach rather ingeniously declared the real significance of the Incarnation to be the fact that it spelled the end of theistic religion, along with its alienating consequences.

Moreover, said Feuerbach, in proclaiming that it was out

of love for man that God sent his only-begotten son, Christianity itself proclaims the supremacy of love over the concept of God. Love has conquered all the inadequacies in theism. It is just as if God has renunciated his divinity out of love. For if one were to ask whether it is Love or God who has overcome man's state of alienation, then the answer to be given is clearly 'Love; for God as God has not saved us, but Love, which transcends the difference between the divine and human personality. As God has renounced himself out of love, so we, out of love, should renounce God; for if we do not sacrifice God to love, we sacrifice love to God and . . . we have the God . . . of religious fanaticism'.[36]

Christianity, of course, has always affirmed that God loves and the New Testament even says that God *is* love. Important though love is, however, it has been regarded as an attribute of God. This is false, said Feuerbach, and the real truth is that theism made love an attribute of God because it recognized love's own intrinsic value. Love *is* God and apart from love there is no God. If the theist complains that when God is sacrificed to love we end with atheism, Feuerbach retorts that the alternative is to sacrifice love to God, that this ends in fanaticism and that there is no question which is preferable.

Feuerbach contended that, when the Christian doctrine of the Incarnation is interpreted anthropologically, it enables man to be reconciled to his *alter ego*. It results in the religion of man in which man finds his true and proper place. His place, however, is that of a finite creature. Since Feuerbach affirmed the indissoluble unity of the human individual it meant that for him the activity of the human spirit, or self-consciousness is subject to death, just like the body, since it is dependent upon the physical body. 'I know that I am a finite mortal being and that I shall one day cease to be', he said. 'But I find this *very natural* and am therefore perfectly reconciled to the fact.'[37]

Feuerbach made two important points about the traditional doctrine of personal immortality. In the last two centuries it has been common for Christians to defend this doctrine by appealing to the nature of God. They argue, for example, that a God who loves his children must ensure that they somehow survive death in order to enjoy eternal fellowship with him, and, consequently, if there is no immortality, then there is no God. Feuerbach agreed with theists that belief in a personal God and belief in personal immortality stand or fall together and he regarded the two beliefs as being essentially one, like the two sides of the one coin. 'God is heaven spiritualized', he said, 'while heaven is God materialized or reduced to the forms of the senses.'[38]

Secondly, he observed that when the doctrine of personal immortality is interpreted anthropologically it is seen to contain an important meaning. 'Faith in a future life is therefore only faith in the *true* life of the present . . . faith in a future life is not faith in another unknown life; but in the truth and infinitude and consequently in the perpetuity, of that life which already here below is regarded as the authentic life. As God is nothing else than the nature of man purified . . . so the future life is nothing else than the present life freed from that which appears a limitation or an evil.'[39] Thus we may say that Feuerbach interpreted the belief in immortality to be a symbolic way of affirming the significant and eternal values which are seen to be potentially present in this finite existence. The traditional doctrine of immortality lifts them out of this world and objectifies them into an eternal, timeless world. Unfortunately this undercuts man's expectations that this world will ever be changed for the better. The overcoming of alienation not only reunites actual man with his essential self, but it restores to the actual world its true potential.

Feuerbach was often accused of being negative. Certainly he appeared to be destroying the positive beliefs of traditional Christianity. His counterclaim was that it is theism which is really negative, for it encourages a negative view of nature, of the world and of man. Since theism is prepared to sacrifice the reality of this life and of this world to a being who is the product of human imagination, then the negation of this God is actually the reaffirmation of man (argued Feuerbach) and the negation of the next world (which is an imaginary one) is actually the reaffirmation of this world.

Feuerbach's counterattack struck a very responsive chord. It prepared the way for Marx's much more trenchant criticism of nineteenth-century Christianity in that, in the modern world then emerging, Christianity most frequently appeared as the bastion of reactionary forces, protecting the *status quo* and putting obstacles in the way of man's social and material betterment. Other-worldly Christianity taught men to put their hope in the world to come and to bear patiently the suffering and injustice of this world. 'Most genuine Christians have declared that earthly good draws man away from God', complained Feuerbach, 'whereas adversity, suffering, afflictions lead him back to God.'[40] The more empty and unsatisfying life became, the more the Christian was being encouraged to pin his hopes on a future world of bliss. It accentuated a vicious circle. 'The impoverishing of the real world and the enriching of God is one act. Only the poor man has a rich God.'[41] Traditional Christianity, contended Feuerbach, was having the effect of paralysing all human effort for the improvement of this world.

Feuerbach believed not only that the age of traditional Christianity was past but that it had to be speedily replaced for man's own good if there were to be any real emancipation from the growing conditions of material want and injustice. In Feuerbach's view man still needed a religion but it had to be a new religion, one which did justice to the changed situation in which man found himself, one which took seriously man's creaturely, mortal existence, one which fully valued both man and his world – the natural world, the only truly existing world. So he ended the first and main part of *The Essence of Christianity* thus: 'Our most essential task is now fulfilled. We have reduced the supermundane, supernatural, and superhuman nature of God to the elements of human nature as its fundamental elements. Our process of analysis has brought us again to the position with which we set out. The beginning, middle and end of religion is MAN.'[42]

Feuerbach was writing before Darwinism and before the historical study of religions had properly begun, yet he vaguely discerned three main stages in the religious development of mankind and these are not unlike the three phases being referred to in this book. First he spoke of the childhood stage of mankind in which religion originated to meet man's primitive needs in an age of great ignorance and inexperience. In a later period came religions like Christianity. These introduced a critical element, reforming and spiritualizing the earlier religious forms and adapting them to a more advanced stage of human development. Morality now came to play a much greater role and the concept of God was enlarged to embody moral values to an infinite degree.

A third phase, thought Feuerbach, was just beginning. 'We are living in a situation where religion and culture are in conflict; our task is to do away with the contradictions between the two. This is the indispensable condition for the rebirth of mankind and the only condition for the appearance of a new mankind and for the coming of a new era. Without it all political and social reforms are meaningless and futile. A new era also requires a new view of the first elements and foundations of human existence; it requires – if we wish to retain the word – a *new religion*.'[43]

The distinctive features of the new religion required by

modern man, according to Feuerbach, are to be discovered not in some eternal source external to man but within man himself. 'Henceforth man should seek the ground of his existence, the goal of his thinking, the cure of his ills and suffering *in himself*, rather than *outside himself* like the pagan or *above himself* like the Christian.'[44]

Feuerbach believed he was expounding this new religion and he ended his Heidelberg lectures with a call to embrace what he called the religion of man: 'We must replace the love of God by the love of man as the only true religion . . . the belief in God by the belief in man, i.e., that the fate of mankind depends not on being outside it and above it but on mankind itself . . . My wish is to transform friends of God into friends of man, believers into thinkers, devotees of prayer into devotees of work, candidates for the hereafter into students of this world, Christians who, by their own profession and admission are half-animal, half-angel, into men, into whole men.'[44]

Feuerbach, like many others in the nineteenth century, was unjustifiably optimistic about the capacity of man to handle readily and adequately the heavy responsibilities which the modern era has placed upon him. He can be easily criticized as shallow. His religion of man is too simplistic, and lacks that transcendent component, without which no religion can come to life. Feuerbach somehow lost sight of the mystery of life and of the enigmas of human existence. Yet his critique of traditional Christianity was devastatingly penetrating. He undercut the theistic foundations of Christianity, he revealed the earthliness of man and he challenged modern man to recognize that the responsibility for the future destiny of the human race lies squarely on his shoulders. Modern man has become increasingly aware of these things in this last quarter of the twentieth century.

CHAPTER 8

TO A RELIGION WITHOUT GOD?

❖

The name of Karl Marx (1818-83) has become much more widely known in the twentieth century than those of Strauss, Feuerbach or even Hegel. Yet, as another 'Young Hegelian', he stood on the shoulders of his predecessors. The three we have just dealt with in the preceding chapters all believed that the post-Enlightenment world called for radically new forms of religion, yet no such new religious traditions have become attached to their names. The irony of the situation is that Marx, who had no intention of founding a religion and who called for the abolition of religion in all its forms, is the very one whose name is today a household term and whose memory is honoured by a significant section of mankind with overtones of reverence.

Many would prefer to say he did not so much found a religion as expound an ideology. His ideology is nevertheless studied, taught and defended with all the passionate zeal which men displayed in the post-Axial age for their religion, particularly in the monotheistic traditions. Consequently it has been common in recent years to refer to Marxism as, at least, a kind of religion. In his introduction to the writings of Marx and Engels *On Religion*, Reinhold Niebuhr wrote, 'Marx, as an empiricist, would have been just another learned man. As an apocalyptic dogmatist, he became the founder of a new religion, whose writings would be quoted as parts of a new sacred canon'.[1]

Marx was born into a middle-class Jewish family during

the early period of Jewish emancipation, itself a direct result of the Enlightenment. Marx's father, a liberally-minded Jew already influenced by the ideas of Voltaire and Rousseau, converted to Protestantism in order to aid his advancement in the legal profession. This entailed the Christian baptism of Karl at the age of six and his subsequent confirmation in the Lutheran Church. The fact that his father found it socially expedient to abandon the Jewish tradition of his forebears undoubtedly contributed to the militancy of Marx's later atheism and to his insistence that the State should be free from all religious affiliation. 'The political emancipation of the Jew, the Christian, the religious man in general', he said, 'is the emancipation of the state from Judaism, from Christianity, from religion in general.'[2]

Having tasted the fruits of Jewish emancipation, Marx was never tempted to return to the faith of his rabbinical Jewish ancestors. The only way he could revolt against the bourgeois Christian society in which he was brought up was to adopt an atheistic, secular stance. His first steps in this direction were not unlike the way in which many a young adolescent in the modern era has come to question and then abandon the faith of his earlier years. His earlier youthful faith and his later rejection of it are reflected in the following. Writing on the choice of a profession at the age of seventeen he said, 'To man . . . the Deity gave a general aim, that of ennobling mankind and himself, but he left it to man to seek the means by which this aim can be achieved . . . religion itself teaches us that the ideal Being whom all strive to copy sacrificed himself for the sake of mankind, and who would dare to set at nought such judgments'.[3] But in a letter written to his father two years later he confessed, 'A curtain had fallen, my holy of holies was rent asunder, and new gods had to be installed . . . If previously the gods had dwelt above the earth, now they became its centre'.[4]

Unlike Hegel, Strauss and Feuerbach, all of whom began with a theological education, Marx studied law, philosophy and history. During an illness he 'got to know Hegel from beginning to end'.[5] Then he became intimately acquainted with the Young Hegelians in Berlin. He regarded Hegel as the Aristotle of the modern age and referred to him in his doctoral dissertation as a 'giant thinker'. All through his life his thought was expressed in an Hegelian framework, e.g. his vision of history as one in which the present imperfect society must inevitably be led to, and replaced by, a completely harmonious and integrated world. Yet Marx was never a pure Hegelian, for he quickly became dissatisfied with philosophical idealism and found it necessary to seek 'the idea in reality itself'.[6]

Marx's transition from idealism to materialism was greatly assisted by Feuerbach, whose *Essence of Christianity* was published soon after Marx had completed his doctoral dissertation. This is how Engels, forty years later, described the occasion, 'Then came Feuerbach's *Essence of Christianity* . . . One must oneself have experienced the liberating effect of this book to get an idea of it. Enthusiasm was general; we all became at once Feuerbachians. How enthusiastically Marx greeted the new conception and how much – in spite of all critical reservations – he was influenced by it one may read in *The Holy Family*'.[7] Marx himself asserted that 'there is no other road to truth and freedom for you (speculative theologians and philosophers) than the road through the "brook of fire" (*Feuer-bach*). Feuerbach is the *purgatory* of our time'.[8]

Feuerbach not only spurred Marx on in his movement towards materialism but he also helped Marx to see that there remained considerable truth in Hegelianism provided it was turned the right way up. So Hegel remained for Marx the 'giant thinker'. 'Compared with Hegel, Feuerbach is very poor', he wrote in 1865. 'All the same he was epoch-making *after* Hegel.'[9] Feuerbach, by his explanation of the rise of theistic religion, had shown Marx the way in which the criticism of religion should begin and since for Marx, the 'criticism of religion is the premise of all criticism',[10] Feuerbach's influence on the early Marx was clearly vital.

Marx quickly became critical of Feuerbach on the grounds that the latter's reduction of theology to the religion of man did not go far enough. He believed Feuerbach was correct in seeing the concept of God as the projection of man's own aspirations but that he had not adequately explained what had caused mankind to make the projection in the first place. 'Feuerbach starts out from the fact of self-alienation, the duplication of the world into a religious, imaginary world and a real one. His work consists in the dissolution of the religious world into its secular basis. He overlooks the fact that after this work is completed the chief thing still remains to be done. For the fact that the secular foundation detaches itself from itself and establishes itself in the clouds as an independent realm is really only to be explained by the self-cleavage and self-contradictoriness of this secular basis.'[11]

We must now look at the way in which Marx interpreted the origin and significance of man's self-alienation, for there is an important thread of continuity, marked by stages of transition, running back from Marx to Feuerbach, to Hegel and ultimately to the Christian doctrine of original sin. We have already discussed how Hegel interpreted the Garden of Eden myth and introduced the term alienation. We have noted how Feuerbach changed Hegel's self-alienation of spirit into his own doctrine of the self-alienation of man. Marx complained that Feuerbach's materialist philosophy had not yet been liberated from its theological roots and that Feuerbach had simply substituted 'human nature' for 'Absolute Spirit'. Marx contended that the alienation between actual man and essential man (projected as God) was itself a projection of the self-alienation of man which already existed in human society. This, claimed Marx, was the real, and completely non-theological, truth about alienation.

Hegel had already indicated, in the context of his own philosophical system, that alienation had resulted from the creative urge of Spirit in pouring itself out in self-expression. Feuerbach, in turn, had claimed that the conception of God as the ultimate Creator was itself a projection of man's creative ability. Marx fastened on to the capacity of man to create and produce, as the key to the origin of alienation present in human society. But whereas Hegel had been thinking of creativity in terms of spirit, thought or mental labour, Marx thought of creativity as the activity of the manual labourer or craftsman. He asserted that neither Hegel nor Feuerbach had adequately understood the importance of manual labour in the development of the human personality and as a creative expression of life. Further, whatever a man creates with his hands belongs wholly to him and is, in a sense, a part of him. In the modern industrialized society, however, the labourer quickly becomes divorced from the created fruits of his labour. He is deprived of them and has only his labour to offer. The divorce of man from the fruits of his labour constitutes the root cause of man's state of alienation.

One of the many influences which came to bear upon Marx during his formative period was that of Moses Hess, an older member of the Young Hegelians, and known to his fellows as the 'Communist rabbi'. Hess, well-versed in the socialistic thought emanating from France, and a convinced Feuerbachian, identified the state of alienation with the economic conditions by which the worker was being exploited. 'Money is the product of mutually alienated men', he said, 'it is externalized man.'[12] Marx was much impressed by Hess at the time and came to regard the accumulation of money as the tangible expression of alienation or estrangement. 'Money is the jealous god of Israel before whom no other god may stand. Money debases all the gods of mankind and turns them into commodities. Money is the universal and self-constituted *value* of things. It has therefore deprived the entire world – both the world of man and of nature – of its specific value. Money is the estranged essence of man's work and existence; this alien essence dominates him and he worships it.'[13]

If alienation were simply a matter of man being divorced from the fruits of his labour (transformed in turn into money), the solution would lie in the just redistribution of accumulated wealth. This was the kind of Communism which Hess was advocating. But Marx believed that alienation was a kind of cancerous growth, the roots of which went much deeper than could be adequately dealt with by such a programme. In his view, as soon as man became alienated from the fruits of his labour, he became alienated also from his spiritual essence, from his fellow-men and from the whole world of nature.

As he traced the spread of this cancer step by step, Marx was not unaware of its parallel with the Christian doctrine of sin. 'Theology explains the origin of evil by the fall of man, i.e., it assumes as a fact in the form of history what it should explain. We shall start from a present-day economic fact. The worker becomes poorer the more wealth he produces . . . *The devaluation* of the human world grows in direct proportion to the *increase in value* of the world of things . . . the worker is related to the *product of his labour* as to an *alien* object . . . the more the worker exerts himself in his work, the more powerful the alien, objective world becomes which he brings into being over against himself, the poorer he and his inner world become, and the less they belong to him. It is the same in religion. The more man puts into God, the less he retains within himself.'[14] The last point, of course, he had learned from Feuerbach.

Marx then went on to explain how the worker experienced this alienation in the factory situation where 'the worker feels himself only when he is not working . . . He is at home when he is not working, and not at home when he is working. His labour is therefore not voluntary but forced, it is *forced labour* . . . the external character of labour for the worker is demonstrated by the fact that it belongs not to him but to another, and that in it he belongs not to himself but to another. Just as in religion the spontaneous activity of the human imagination . . . detaches itself from the individual and reappears as the alien activity of a god or a devil, so the activity of the worker is not his own spontaneous activity. It belongs to another, it is the loss of his self'.[15] Again we note the application of the Feuerbachian thesis.

The Christian doctrine of sin traced man's corrupt condition to the first act of disobedience on the part of our primeval parents and then proceeded to show that man's separation from God also means that man stands in a broken relationship with the world of nature, with his fellow-man and with himself. Similarly Marx proceeded to claim that the initial alienation of man from the fruits of his labour leads to the alienation of man 'from his own body, from nature as it exists outside of him, from his spiritual essence, his *human* essence'[16] and finally from his species. It gives rise, he said, to the condition in which man is estranged from man.

Marx then went on to ask, 'If the product of labour is alien to men and confronts me as an alien power, to whom does it then belong?'[17] It does not belong to the gods and it does not belong to nature. It can only belong 'to a man other than the worker', viz. 'the capitalist – or whatever other word one chooses for the master of labour'.[18] The effect of alienation, therefore, is to break man's natural relationship with the fruits of his labour and to replace it with an unnatural relationship, that of employee and employer, of worker and capitalist. 'Every self-estrangement of man from himself and nature is manifested in the relationship he sets up between other men and himself and nature.'[19] Just as in the religious world the fact of sin causes the layman to be dependent on the priest, said Marx, so in the everyday world the worker becomes slavishly dependent upon the property-owner, private property itself having been created by the alienation of labour. 'Private property thus derives', he said, 'from an analysis of the concept of alienated labour, i.e., alienated man, estranged labour, estranged life, estranged man.'[20]

The final consequence of alienation, in Marx's view, was the polarization of human society into the struggle between two classes. So the *Communist Manifesto* of 1848, which he largely wrote, begins with the words, 'the history of all hitherto existing society is the history of class struggles'.[21] It then briefly mentions that in former centuries the class struggle was between patricians and plebeians, freemen and slaves, feudal lords and serfs, etc., but in the modern industrialized world it is the struggle between the Bourgeoisie and the Proletariat. The Bourgeoisie referred to the capitalist owners of the means of production, while the Proletariat encompassed the wage-earners, who, having no means of production of their own, were reduced to selling their labour in order to exist.

In Marx's later writings the word alienation disappeared. Its place came largely to be taken by the phrase 'class struggle'. Instead of analysing the human condition as the state in which man is disjoined from his true self (Feuerbach), or as the state in which man is disjoined from the fruits of his labour (the early Marx), the later Marx saw the human race divided into two great corporate selves which, in *Capital*, he even personified by names. The greedy, exploiting, despotic class he called 'My Lord Capital' and the exploited, tormented, enslaved class he named the 'Collective Worker'. The 'class struggle' is the final Marxist version of the concept of alienation or estrangement, which can be traced back through Feuerbach and Hegel to the Christian doctrine of the Fall, in each case being used to explain the root cause of human suffering and the broken character of the human condition.

We can now appreciate more fully why Marx could not be satisfied with the simple Communism he learned from Hess. Marx disdainfully dismissed such slogans as 'the fair and equitable distribution of wealth' and 'a fair day's wage for a fair day's work'. These, in his view, did not get to the root of the problem. Marx was gripped by a soteriological concern – of the kind to be found in every genuine religion to date. He saw mankind embroiled in a class struggle which dehumanized it and from which it must be delivered.

We can also clearly see why Marx became so quickly dissatisfied with Feuerbach, his criticism being set out in his *Theses on Feuerbach,*[22] written in 1845. Feuerbach had implied that the solution to the problem of man's self-alienation was a philosophical, rather than a practical, one, viz. that man had only to come to the true (i.e., the humanistic) understanding of theistic Christianity and he would be delivered from the alienation it had initiated. For Marx this was just talk, and worse, it was theological talk. It is not sufficient to have the right view, he said; one must act. 'The philosophers have only *interpreted* the world, in various ways; the point however, is to *change* it.'[23]

How is the world to be changed? How is man to be delivered from the dehumanization which takes place in the succession of class struggles? It was in finding a practical answer to these questions that Marx moved from philosophy to myth, from a supposed scientific analysis of the economic condition of man to soteriological beliefs of a religious character. Marx looked for the instrument of change, or what is referred to in Christian terminology as the Saviour. He found it in the proletariat and this new component made his system of belief different from all earlier forms of Communism.

Tucker[24] has claimed that Marx was particularly influenced in his adoption of the term 'proletariat' by Lorenz von Stein. The latter was a staunch monarchist and a right-wing Hegelian, who had used the term to refer to the growing section of defiant, destitute workers who were already becoming rebellious against their lot. But whereas Stein viewed their presence with alarm, seeing them as a potential threat to the stability of society, Marx found in them the very sign of hope he was looking for.

Whatever the origin of the term 'proletariat', it came to assume an essential place in Marx's thought and established itself as an indispensable part of Communist terminology. Marx believed it was impossible for one of the existing classes of society to achieve the looked-for emancipation of man. It required the rise of a new class which would have concentrated in itself all the evils of society. It would be raised up, not by particular wrongs, but by the fact of universal suffering. It would be raised up because of the 'total loss of humanity' and its redemption would bring about 'the total redemption of humanity'. It would be the class which would spell the end of the class struggle and the dissolution of all classes. This was to be the role of the proletariat. 'When the proletariat proclaims the dissolution of the existing world order, it is only declaring the secret of its own existence, for it is the actual dissolution of that order.'[25]

As many have since pointed out, the analogies between the emerging Marxist myth of the proletariat and the Christian myth of the Saviour Jesus Christ are quite remarkable, even though it is doubtful if Marx was ever aware of them. As Christians applied to Jesus (if Jesus had not already applied them to himself) the earlier images of the Suffering Servant and the corporate Son of Man and saw Jesus as the one who, in his crucifixion, suffered because of all the sins of mankind, so Marx conceived the proletariat as bearing, in their most intense form, the evils accruing from the class struggle. As Jesus Christ was believed to have risen victoriously over sin and death, shortly to usher in a new social order, the Kingdom of God, so the proletariat would rise victoriously against the oppressor, break the chains which had previously kept the oppressed classes enslaved and then usher in the new social order, the classless society. As not all, at first, recognized the Christ for the Saviour that he was, and as even the Kingdom of God was to be likened to leaven, hidden in the flour, so the proletariat, as yet, had only a secret existence, and could not be openly identified with any existing class.

The more Marx looked in hope to the rise of the proletariat, the more he mistook the wish for the reality. The more myth replaced philosophical analysis, the closer became the parallels between Christian foundations and Marxist foundations. Both of these faiths came to birth in eschatological settings. In each case there was some empirical evidence to support the feeling that men were living at the end of an age and that the breaking in of a new age was imminent. In both periods there was an air of change and impending doom. The ancient Jews had suffered successively at the hands of the Babylonians, Persians, Greeks and Romans; they had come to think in terms of Armageddon, the last great conflict between the children of light and the children of darkness. The moderns thought in terms of revolution. Ever since 1789 some men had feared, and others had hoped for, further revolutions. Talk and plans of revolution were already much in the air when it became an essential part of Marx's eschatology. He became convinced that, for the successful emancipation of man, revolution was absolutely necessary, 'not only because the ruling class cannot be overthrown in any other way, but also because the class overthrowing it can only in a revolution succeed in ridding itself of all the muck of the ages and become fitted to found society anew'.[26]

As Jesus is reported to have come into Galilee proclaiming, 'The appointed time has come and the Kingdom of God is close to hand. Change your mental outlook and believe the good news',[27] so Marx heralded the imminent revolution. In 1844 he wrote of the certainty of its coming in words reminiscent of ancient apocalyptic, 'When all the inner conditions are met, the day of the German resurrection will be heralded by the crowing of the Gallic cock'.[28] In 1848 when Marx hurriedly wrote *The Communist Manifesto,* he fully believed the time had already come and the revolution could be triggered off by his clarion call, 'Let the ruling classes tremble at a Communistic revolution. The proletarians have nothing to lose but their chains. They have a world to win. WORKING MEN OF ALL COUNTRIES, UNITE!'[29] Even though it did not eventuate immediately, Marx remained expectant, just as the early Christians continued to expect, through two generations and more, the Second Coming of Jesus. In 1857 Marx wrote to Engels, 'I am working like mad all through the nights at putting my economic studies together so that I may at least have the outlines clear before the deluge comes'.[30] So convinced did Marx remain of the certainty and imminence of the coming world revolution that he feared the final upheaval would arrive before he had finished writing *Capital,* which would explain why it had to come. Yet, by that time, the social unrest of earlier years had already begun to quieten down, for working conditions (which in Marx's view should have got worse and worse) had steadily begun to improve; but Marx did not seem to notice. He was by that stage completely gripped by the myth he had helped to create.

It appears, however, from the parallels we have already been drawing, that Marx did not create *de novo* the soteriological myth which now bears his name. It is rather the case that he was reshaping, in a form suitable to the post-Enlightenment age, the Judaeo-Christian myth which had long embraced and motivated the Western world. It is unlikely that he was aware of this to any great degree. He had probably absorbed something of it in his early years, both from the Jewish heritage of his family, and from the Lutheran grounding in Bible and Christian doctrine he had received in the course of his formal education. It is reported that in later life he once told his wife that instead of going to church she would be better off to stay at home and read the Old Testament prophets. If this means that he was familiar with and appreciative of them, we should not overlook the fact that it was partly from their proclamation of the coming 'Day of the Lord' that the later Judaeo-Christian eschatology had evolved.

Marx's reshaping of the ancient myth must have been mostly unconscious. It was present of course, though in an already transformed state, in the Hegelian system. The bare outlines of it could have formed part of his understanding of reality before he ever began his monumental study of economic history. If this was the case, the psychological process by which the myth came to birth in his developing convictions is in no essential way different from what has happened in the minds of other great creative religious thinkers.

Eliade has suggested that both the Marxist myth, and also the Judaeo-Christian myth which it seems so clearly to reflect, are to be related in turn to the great eschatological myths of the ancient Middle Eastern world where the soteriological role was played by the innocent poor, 'whose sufferings are invoked to change the ontological status of the world. In fact, Marx's classless society, and the consequent disappearance of all historical tensions, find their most exact precedent in the myth of the Golden Age which, according to a number of traditions, lies at the beginning and the end of History. Marx has enriched this myth with a truly Messianic Judaeo-Christian ideology; on the one hand, by the prophetic and soteriological function he ascribes to the proletariat; and, on the other, by the final struggle between Good and Evil, which may well be compared with the apocalyptic conflict between Christ and Antichrist, ending in the decisive victory of the former. It is indeed significant that Marx turns to his own account the Judaeo-Christian eschatological hopes of an absolute goal of history'.[31]

We are not here concerned, of course, with the question of whether the Marxist ideology is true or false but solely with the issue of how it is to be related to the Judaeo-Christian tradition which preceded it and to what extent it may be regarded as a new form of religion, whose successful spread in the twentieth century has been made possible by the fact that it was peculiarly suited to the world-view of post-Enlightenment man. We have tried to show, by tracing its progress through Hegel, Strauss and Feuerbach, that the Marxist ideology retained many of the essential components of the Judaeo-Christian tradition, though stripped of its theistic, supernatural and other-worldly elements. Marxism, in other words, was a thoroughly secularized form of the ancient soteriological myth. Marx himself rather prophetically, though unintentionally, conceded this when he said that the truly democratic state 'can discard religion because in it *the human foundation of religion is realized in a secular way*'.[32]

One is left in no doubt, of course, as to where Marx stood on the subject of religion. He passionately sought its abolition, not just because, in his view, it was untrue, but because he saw it as an evil which stood in the way of the emancipation of man. Hegel, Strauss and Feuerbach, each in their own way, thought religion could, and should, be transcended or reformulated. Marx believed it should be rooted out completely, for its continuance provided distressed and suffering mankind with an illusory outlet and thus prevented it from taking the steps which would lead to the necessary revolution. It was in the context of this belief that he made his most famous statement on the subject – 'Religious distress is at the same time the expression of real distress and the protest against real distress. Religion is the sigh of the oppressed creature, the heart of a heartless world . . . It is the opium of the people. The abolition of religion as the illusory happiness of the people is required for their real happiness'.[33]

It is important to remember that the religion which Marx hoped to see abolished was that which was still prevalent in his own day, the classical forms of Judaism and Christianity, each (and especially the latter) expressed in theistic, supernaturalist and other-worldly forms. For Marx these forms constituted the *sine qua non* of any religion. But they are also the very things which were being questioned and undermined during the Enlightenment and which people like Hegel, Strauss and Feuerbach were trying to replace by non-theistic, naturalist and this-worldly forms. Since Marx's own time Christianity has not only become considerably more this-worldly and humanistic in its emphases but, in the aftermath of the philosophical critique of theism, has been exploring new ways of speaking of God. A contemporary Marxist, for example, has written, 'Twentieth-century theologians have worked out new and more dynamic models for thinking about God, so that often we Marxists no longer know whether we are still atheists or not in this regard'.[34]

In the mid-nineteenth century it appeared self-evident, both to Marx and to non-Marxists, that the Marxist ideology, by virtue of its atheism, was non-religious. Today this is no longer so. Indeed a century and more after the birth of Marxism, we are more struck by the parallels it displays with the Judaeo-Christian tradition than by any absolute contrast. Marx's protest against the religion of his day does not appear nearly so irreligious today as it did then. On the contrary, it may even be regarded as a modern example of that iconoclasm which originated with the prophets of Israel and which became a distinctive feature of Judaism, Christianity and Islam, surfacing from time to time in various movements of radical reform. This prophetic protest could not tolerate anything that smacked of idolatry, that is, the identification of tangible forms with the ultimate reality to which they were supposed only to point. Christianity, for example, was continuing to identify ultimate reality with an other-worldly God in a dualistic world-view which the Enlightenment had now made to look outmoded; it continued to identify the will of that God for this world with a permanently class-structured society, as exemplified in the popular children's hymn, 'The rich man in his castle, the poor man at his gate; God made them, high or lowly, and ordered their estate'.[35]

Just as one does not need to be a Muslim in order to acknowledge the truly prophetic role of Muhammad, so one does not need to be a Marxist in order to concede to Marx a place among the prophets. His critique of the Judaeo-Christian tradition was a fresh manifestation, though this time in a non-theistic form, of the prophetic zeal and the this-worldly human concern which had long been present in the Judaeo-Christian tradition, however much it had tended to be overlaid by other-worldliness. It is impossible to conceive the rise of Marxism except from within a civilization shaped by that tradition.

There is something to be said for the thesis that, because of the *a priori* character of religious convictions, a living religion can be only successfully displaced by another religion, and one which is more powerful in its existential appeal. Alternatively, we may say that whatever has, as one of its chief aims, the passion to undermine and abolish a religious tradition, *ipso facto*, begins to assume the properties of religion, since religion originates in a conscientious concern for the things which really matter.

Although Hegel's philosophy of spirit, Strauss's 'new faith' and Feuerbach's 'religion of man' may be seen as providing much telling criticism of the traditional religion of the West, and prepared some of the guidelines for a viable religion in the new age, and may be regarded as early expositions of much modern humanism, they nevertheless lacked some positive components necessary for genuine religion. Humanism, for example, though widespread today at a superficial level, is somewhat vague, powerless and lacking in the capacity to stir the imagination. Like streams which flow into the desert and disappear in the sand, it tends to ebb away and leave a religious vacuum.

The positive components in Marxism which gave it a capacity to become one of the new forms of religion in the post-Enlightenment world are briefly these. First it does acknowledge a transcendent element. Though Marx rejected the personal God of theism, he believed firmly that history was on his side because it operated according to an eternal principle – that of dialectical materialism. This was his version of Yahweh, the Lord of history. Just as both Jew and Christian believed that the will of Yahweh must ultimately prevail, so Marx believed that nothing men might choose to do could permanently prevent this principle from leading mankind to the classless society.

Secondly, Marxism displays a soteriological concern. The life of man in this world is not as it should be. Mankind needs to be emancipated, delivered, saved from its present sufferings and enslavement, occasioned by the class war.

The instrument of that salvation – the proletariat – is hailed as being already present.

Thirdly, Marxism provides a living hope in its eschatological myth, which encourages its devotees to expect that the revolution is imminent and the new social order is just around the corner. Incidentally, this expectation of a new kind of world which, by the cataclysm of revolution, will replace this present corrupt world, is much closer to the primitive Christian eschatology than is the other-worldly eschatology which came to prevail in classical Christianity.

Fourthly, Marxism offers a practical programme, enabling its devotees actively to participate in the process of social change and to bring the day of consummation nearer, by co-operating with, indeed serving, that eternal principle which ultimately determines the course of history.

These are some of the reasons why Marxism may be regarded as one of the major 'religious' traditions operating in the world today and why it has caught the imagination, and won the allegiance, of modern man on such a global scale, particularly in those areas where men have been most acutely aware of the need of social change. Marxism is taking a variety of forms in the twentieth century, just as Christianity, in its much longer history, has assumed a multiplicity of forms. It is not self-evident that either Russian Marxism or Chinese Marxism is what Marx had in mind any more than it can be claimed that medieval Christianity is what Jesus had in mind. Marxism, moreover, is today having to face up to problems of internal division and problems of re-interpretation, all of which are similar to those faced by Christianity from the second century onwards.[36]

The future of Marxism can be no more accurately predicted than the future of the classical religious traditions of man. The spread of Marxism around the world at the present time, however, means that Marx must now be numbered with Moses, the Buddha, Confucius, Jesus and Muhammad as among the great religious founders. But there is this difference. These others founded religions of the post-Axial period, while Marx is the founder of a religion of the post-Enlightenment era, yet one which has much in common with the Judaeo-Christian tradition. It is not the only religion to have emerged in the post-Enlightenment era, but in its form and in the breadth of its appeal, it is a particularly interesting illustration of the new religious form called for in the new religious era. It is non-theistic, naturalistic, humanistic, global in outreach, future-orientated, yet affirming an ultimate, transcendent reality which is immanent in human history.

CHAPTER 9

THE IMPACT OF SCIENCE ON RELIGION

❖

In sketching the transition to the modern religious era, and in looking for the new formulations of religion which have been taking shape on this side of the transition, our attention has been chiefly fastened on philosophy and closely related thought. In the popular mind, however, it is science, rather than philosophy, which has been held responsible for the undermining of traditional religion. This impression is understandable for it was through the open clash between science and religion in the nineteenth century that many became aware for the first time that Christianity was being threatened at its foundations and that a new religious situation was opening up. It has been necessary to deal with the new philosophy first, however, for not only was it philosophical enquiry which first threatened the traditional form of Christianity but it was modern philosophy which also provided the intellectual basis for the rise of modern science.

In turning now to the rise of modern science we must backtrack in time initially in order to understand clearly what was so new and distinctive about science in its modern form, that it should have played such an important role in the transition to the modern era. Etymologically, of course, *science* simply means *knowledge* and man had believed for a very long time that he possessed knowledge, and knowledge of such a kind that he had every confidence in it.

When we use the word 'science' in the modern context we are referring to a special kind of knowledge. Science refers to a particular method of enquiring into the nature of the physical world and to the body of conclusions arrived at by the use of that method. Consequently the more precise term 'empirical science' is to be preferred and is intended even when the looser term science is used. The method which characterizes empirical science involves measurement and precise observation, the postulation of theories to explain events, processes and observable phenomena in the natural world, followed by the testing of those theories by experiment and further measurement.

Until the advent of empirical science in the last 400 years man had a readily accessible method for testing the 'knowledge' passed on to him by his cultural tradition and he usually accepted it on the authority of those who transmitted it to him, such as the ancients, scholars, the Church or the Bible. For a long time, therefore, what passed for knowledge was a relatively static body of beliefs (sound or otherwise), opinions and even superstition, existing in a kind of amalgam in which it was difficult to separate the true from the false. Certainly man could appeal to logic to question the truth-claims of conflicting statements. Moreover, since philosophers commonly thought that the natural world had a rational basis, it seemed plausible to assume that the rational faculty of man should be able to penetrate to the basic truth about the world without any external aid. The confidence which thinking men placed in their rational faculty led to the creation of speculative systems which, though aesthetically attractive and logically consistent, did not always have any demonstrable relationship to the phenomenal world. Such speculative systems of thought, including even Aristotelianism, could therefore often persist for very long periods.

What was so new and important about modern science

was that it provided a method for testing the truth of inherited knowledge, as well as for increasing the body of reliable knowledge. It partly replaced, and partly supplemented, the use of speculative reason. The method itself, and the knowledge to which it led, evolved slowly at first and later accelerated, resulting in the modern knowledge explosion. In its early stages it incorporated into itself the faculty for careful observation so well displayed by Leonardo da Vinci, the capacity to doubt promoted by Descartes, Galileo's urge to experiment, and the mathematics of men like Newton. In the course of time science manifested itself in an ever-increasing number of independent sciences, devoted to the scientific study of ever more specialized areas.

While this has been happening, more and more inherited beliefs (including some which were basic to traditional religion) have been successively questioned, challenged, shown to be false or inadequate, and finally abandoned. We can usefully isolate three main areas in which this has occurred and the change in each of them has been referred to by some as a Copernican revolution after Copernicus (1473-1543), the man who is commonly associated with the first. These three revolutions of thought, initiated by science, have dealt respectively with our view of the universe, our understanding of the origin of life (including that of man) and our understanding of man's inner life. In this chapter the first two will be outlined and the third will be left to Chapter 11.

Although it was Copernicus who pioneered the cosmological revolution, by expounding a view of the universe in which the earth was no longer at the centre, it is Galileo (1564-1642) who is usually taken to be the father of modern science. Building on the work of several forerunners, he was the first to combine rational theory with accurate observation and experimentation, these being, as we have seen, the basic essentials of the scientific method.

Of special importance is the fact that Galileo pioneered a new way of asking questions about natural phenomena. From Aristotle until the late Middle Ages men looked for the reason which would explain a particular event or phenomenon in the purpose it was believed to fulfil. For example, Aristotle explained the falling of free objects to the ground by saying that, in view of the end reached, the object must have within it an inherent or natural capacity to fulfil this purpose. Thus the causes of natural events were thought to be discoverable by looking at the end achieved. Medieval man, like ancient man, looked therefore for what he called teleological or final causes. This seemed eminently reasonable within the context of a world-view in which all nature and history were thought to be undergirded by the power of a purposeful God into whose coherent divine plan it all fitted.

Galileo stopped looking for final causes and searched for what we call efficient causes. This means that he looked not to the end result but simply to what preceded the event. This step, simple as it may now appear, had far-reaching consequences, especially when it became linked with careful observation and experimentation. It also points to an important and vital distinction between religion and empirical science. It will be suggested later that questions of ultimate purpose are basically religious questions. Men of science have increasingly come to acknowledge that questions of purpose lie outside the scope of empirical science. This does not mean that they are not real questions and, so far as human existence is concerned, may be quite vital questions. It simply means that they must be grappled with in some other, non-scientific way. The transference of attention from final causes to efficient causes was essential for the rise of modern science and it has enabled science to throw tremendous light on both the past and present. At the same time it shows why the scientific pursuit, however much it has come into conflict with traditional religious beliefs, cannot *per se* usurp the role of religion for, of the two, only the latter can address itself to questions of ultimate purpose.

The new cosmology opened up by Copernicus, and confirmed in part by Galileo's use of the telescope, introduced Western man to a quite new way of looking at the world as a whole. Most people today believe they have long become adjusted to it and even wonder what all the stir was about when it was first propounded. The reason is that the new cosmology was much more far-reaching in its implications than was often at first realized and this could be sensed, if not always clearly understood. Indeed, man is still adjusting himself to the implications.

We may sketch the change this way. Man had long felt his world to be substantially flat; we may legitimately call it a two-dimensional world. Though he could see the sky and the heavenly bodies, they were not really part of *his* world but belonged to the gods and higher powers. Even Christians regularly prayed, 'Our Father who is in heaven . . .' What the new cosmology eventually did was to add a third dimension to man's world by incorporating that heavenly space and turning *his* world into a vaster, three-dimensional world of space. Peter Gay put it this way, 'Newton alone grasped what dozens of brilliant researchers before him had glimpsed only in part; that heaven and earth were a single system governed by the same laws'.[1] To grasp the now universally acknowledged connection between falling objects, the movement of the tides and the orbits of heavenly bodies and to propose that these movements, previously thought to be unrelated, could be adequately explained by appeal to one principle – gravitation – was a brilliant, imaginative breakthrough into a three-dimensional cosmos. We may say, in retrospect, that the planetary laws of John Kepler (1571-1630) and the gravitational law of Isaac Newton (1642-1727) had the effect of desacralizing the heavens. These, and later astronomic research, brought within the empirical reach of man what had previously been associated with the divine alone.

It did not immediately cause men to disbelieve in God, though Kepler was somewhat pantheistic and Newton was far from orthodox. The implications were more subtle and slower to penetrate. What the new cosmology entailed was the fact that man could no longer draw so readily on spacial imagery in order to conceive the dwelling-place of God. God's heaven now had to be conceived in wholly spiritual terms, for the visible heaven, and indeed space in all directions, had been swallowed up by the expanding physical world in which man found himself. For Christians, heaven was not only the dwelling-place of God but the eternal home of the blessed departed. The imagery with which this had been described now slowly came to be recognized as wholly dependent upon human imagination. It was not simply another two-dimensional world just as real as earth itself, yet separated from it by the vertical or spacial dimension. Previously it had appeared so to be.

Then there is the fact that the central affirmations of the Christian Creed have long been expressed in terms drawn from the conceptual framework of the now outmoded two-dimensional world of ancient man. The Son of God was said to *have come down from heaven* to be incarnate in Jesus of Nazareth, to *have descended into the underworld*, to *have risen from the dead*, to *have ascended into heaven*. While man saw himself living in a two-dimensional world the vertical dimension could be convincingly used to describe the supreme act of divine intervention for man's salvation. When the third dimension became absorbed into man's empirical world, the traditional language about the Son of God could no longer be taken in any literal sense.

One reason why the way to understand the Resurrection of Jesus has remained a matter of keen debate even in the twentieth century is that the implications of the Copernican revolution are still catching up with us.

The new cosmology further entailed that God could no longer be so readily conceived as One who had created, and who continued to control, *the world from the outside*. There no longer appeared to be any *outside* to the universe. God now had to be conceived as *internal* to the world which he had made, co-terminous with it, permeating it, and working through the so-called laws of nature rather than in conflict with them.

Even this approach had its problems. The laws of nature, which scientists of the time believed they were discovering, were beginning to be fitted into a system which, if ever completed, would make the universe look like a working mechanical model which runs its course because of its own inherent structure. Newton believed there were still some gaps which could only be explained by appealing to the presence of divine control. But Laplace took the mathematical analysis of planetary motion further and when Napoleon asked him why, in his large book on the system of the universe, he had made no mention of its Creator, he made his famous reply, 'I had no need of that hypothesis'. Men like Hume, Kant and Hegel were clearly aware that a gulf was opening up between science and traditional religious thought. The scientific explanation of the movement of the heavenly bodies (and later extended to the whole of the natural world) was displacing the theistic explanation. In science there is no place for God, as conceived by past tradition. Theism faced a dilemma; either it had to move towards pantheism or else it had to be reduced to deism, which in turn readily dissolves into atheism. Today each of these alternative moves has attracted a wide following.

During the Enlightenment however, the main move, as we have seen, was towards deism. The first Copernican revolution had not, at that stage, shown up any serious conflict between religion and science. On the contrary, science was being hailed as a welcome support of the Christian tradition. The Royal Society included many clergymen in its early days, for the leisurely life of a country parson provided an ideal opportunity for a scholarly man to pursue his scientific enquiries. The Earl of Bridgewater (1756-1829) bequeathed a large sum to the Royal Society for the publishing of scientific treatises which made clear how the 'power, wisdom and goodness of God' was manifested in the created world. It gave rise to books such as *Insect-Theology* and *Water-Theology* which showed how the new scientific findings revealed the foresight and divine plan of the Creator.

It was not until the second Copernican revolution was taking place in the nineteenth century that science and religion appeared to come into open conflict. Although the debate centred on the incompatibility of the opening chapters of Genesis with Darwin's theory of biological evolution, the reason for calling it a Copernican revolution of thought is more complex than that. Darwin could never have produced a theory of evolution which was at all convincing if he had not been able to draw upon the findings of the then new science of geology. It was geology which first revolutionized man's idea of the span of geological time.

Biblical tradition had long conditioned the Western mind to think that the universe was only about 6000 years old. Bishop Ussher (1581-1656) had, on the basis of biblical evidence, calculated the date of Creation and the beginning of time to be 4004 BC.[2] Similarly Jewish tradition had long set Creation at a date 3760 years before the beginning of the Christian era. In the early nineteenth century this relatively short time span was shown to be quite inadequate even with reference to the earth, let alone to the universe, and this was largely as a result of the emerging science of geology. This in turn was an indirect consequence of the new cosmology. The attention of medieval man had been chiefly focused on the knowledge of heavenly or eternal things, the only access to which was believed to be through revelation and human reason. Since, in the new cosmology, heaven and earth were seen as one system and the planet earth, of all the innumerable objects in space, was itself the most accessible object for study, men began to ask what sort of object this planet is, for the answer clearly has a bearing on the nature of the universe as a whole. The study of the earth's surface in general and of the fossils found in the upper strata in particular, soon led to an expanded view of geological time.

Because of the biblical tradition, Western man had been accustomed to believe that the main features of the earth's surface had resulted either from the original act of Creation or from cataclysmic changes, such as the Deluge, which God had subsequently wrought. The presence of fossils, when first found, was interpreted as the remains of creatures which had not survived the Deluge. This way of explaining the features of the earth's surface (called catastrophism) came to be challenged by a new geological theory known as uniformitarianism. This originated with James Hutton (1726-97), but it was Charles Lyell (1797-1875), often called the father of geology, who was really responsible for making the theory fully convincing. It maintains that all present phenomena observable on the earth's surface can be adequately explained in terms of physical forces still seen to be operating.

Just as Newton had extended the operation of natural law out into heavenly space, so Lyell extended it back into time. It was no longer necessary to postulate catastrophic changes wrought by divine intervention. Natural forces still at work were quite sufficient to explain all the observable facts, provided the time span of the earth's existence was vastly extended. Instead of thousands of years, one had to think in terms of millions of years, and finally in thousands of millions. The variety found in the fossils provided valuable supporting evidence.

We may put it this way. The first Copernican revolution had the effect of adding a third dimension to man's empirical world by incorporating heavenly space; geology, in effect, now added a fourth dimension – the dimension of geological time. Of course man had always been aware of time, in terms of days and years, even to the extent of contemplating a span of 6000 years. But there is so great a quantitative difference between 6000 and 6,000,000,000 years that it introduces something like a new quality to time. Geology has shown that the previously accepted time span of the earth must be multiplied approximately by the order of a million. Just as the new cosmology had enveloped heavenly space, so the new dimension of geological time now enveloped that special time of divine Creation, which had long been thought to have occurred so relatively recently.

Just as the enlarged view of cosmic space prompted men to look at the earth in a new light, so the enlarged view of geological time caused men to look at the phenomenon of planetary life in a new light. Parallel to the geological theory of uniformitarianism there emerged the theory of the slow evolution of all the forms of life with which this planet has been inhabited either in the past or present. This questioned and challenged the belief of Western man (held not only because of biblical teaching but also because of what seemed to be common sense) that the many biological species must always have existed independently, and from the time they had been created so by God.

The idea of the biological evolution of all species from a common source seemed absurd to most people when it was first proposed and some people still so regard it. Although it will be for ever associated with the name of Charles Darwin (1809-92), the idea itself preceded him by at least two generations. It had been suggested in a general way in the eighteenth century by Diderot and Buffon. It had been held with strong conviction by Erasmus Darwin, the grandfather of Charles. It had been set forth as theory by Linnaeus in 1809. It had been expounded in 1844 in a book entitled *Vestiges of the Natural History of Creation* (published anonymously, but later shown to have been written by Robert Chambers (1802-71), the well-known Scottish publisher).

Before the theory could even appear feasible, it was necessary to conceive it to be in operation over a much vaster time scale than had previously been thought possible. The concept of geological time met this condition. (It has been more recently contended that life has been evolving on this planet for at least 3,000,000,000 years.) The second requirement was a single basic principle (of a kind comparable to the force of gravity discerned by Newton) which could be conceived as operating throughout the whole period down to the present. It was this which Darwin supplied with his notion of natural selection. Like Newton he made the necessary breakthrough by seeing the vital connection between several sets of data.

Darwin's world journeys as a naturalist enabled him to observe how related, but slightly different, species were grouped together in adjacent geographical areas. Then he read the *Essay on the Principle of Population* by Thomas Malthus (1766-1834). This tried to show that, since the human population increases in geometrical progression while the food supply increases in arithmetical progression, the surplus population must inevitably die through war, disease or famine thus leaving the population levels relatively constant. Adding this conclusion to the observable fact that each generation displays new variations of inherited characteristics, Darwin came to recognize by 1838 that he had the necessary ingredients for a theory of evolution by natural selection. By this principle, successive generations will maintain, and even improve on, those characteristics which enabled their parents to survive to maturity.

Although Darwin's original theory has undergone modification and development (e.g. modern mutation theory recognizes mutations, though very rare events, to be essential for evolution), yet it was his initial breakthrough which led to all later success in this field.

Whereas the implications of the cosmological revolution for the Christian tradition unfolded themselves only slowly to the Western mind, those of the biological revolution came to be realized almost immediately. This was not just because the theory was in complete conflict with the biblical tradition of the origins of life, though that was certainly a factor. Men also saw that it had far-reaching implications for the doctrine of God and the Christian view of man. Darwin actually avoided the subject of man in *The Origin of Species* (1859), except to say that 'light would be thrown on the origins of man'. In 1871, however, he applied the theory of evolution to human origins in *The Descent of Man*. Others were doing likewise. Ernst Haeckel (1834-1919) had become the vigorous champion of Darwinism in Germany, and had traced the whole evolutionary process from matter to man in *The Natural History of Creation* (1868), and then *The Evolution of Man* (1874).

To gauge the impact of Darwinism on Christianity it is important not to look at it in isolation. As we have already seen in earlier chapters, it was not the only factor threatening to undermine the foundations of Christianity, nor was it the only way in which science was making an impact on Christian thought in the nineteenth century. At the same time as Darwinism was spreading, the scientific tools of historical and literary criticism were being used to study the Bible itself. These were bringing to light the human, as opposed to the divine, origins of the Bible. As we have already seen it was becoming necessary to distinguish between history, legend and myth in the narratives of the sacred text. The scientific study of the Bible was proving a greater cause for alarm within the Christian Churches than the theory of evolution for it was being promoted by the Church's own scholars whereas the latter could still be, and frequently was, dismissed as the unproven hypothesis of a few misguided scientists.

This fact is well borne out by the furore which broke out in 1860 following the publication of *Essays and Reviews* by a group of Oxford scholars. It caused much more of an upset than had *The Origin of Species*, published the year before. Several of the contributors, including a future Archbishop of Canterbury, showed strong Hegelian influences. The general content of the *Essays* is today so commonplace that it is of no great interest to the general reader. Yet it was attacked by both the High Church and the Evangelical wings of the Anglican Communion, and two of the contributors were found guilty of denying the inspiration of Scripture and were suspended, only later to be reinstated by a successful appeal to the Privy Council. Even then, a petition, signed by 11,000 clergymen and 137,000 laymen, protested against the action of the Privy Council.

The scientific study of the Bible, whose beginnings in the Enlightenment we have already noted, constituted a revolution in itself, because it radically altered the ground on which the Bible can be legitimately understood and interpreted. In Protestantism this revolution mainly occurred in the latter half of the nineteenth century while in Catholicism it was delayed until the middle of the twentieth century. Unfortunately it has led to a gulf between the theologically educated and the laity, one which the clergy have often found it difficult to bridge and, because of this, many devout Christian laymen have been left in ignorance of the fact that such a revolution has ever taken place.

Benjamin Jowett[3] in his essay on 'The Interpretation of Scripture' in *Essays and Reviews* advocated, as a modern necessity, the interpreting of the Bible by the same canons of criticism as any other book and he deplored the tendency, even then being shown by many clergy, of withholding the results of biblical study lest the sensitive minds of the faithful be upset. The continuing tensions in English Christianity were reflected in a further symposium of essays by Anglican scholars which appeared in 1889, entitled *Lux Mundi*. Most offence seems to have been given by the editor, Charles Gore[4] who, in his essay on 'The Holy Spirit and Inspiration' used the term 'myth' in connection with some biblical material. He declared myth is 'not a falsehood; it is a product of mental activity, as instructive and rich as any later product, but its characteristic is that it is not yet distinguished into history, poetry and philosophy'.[5]

In the impact of science on religion Darwinism and biblical criticism rendered each other mutual support. This is further reflected in the fact that since the middle of the nineteenth century Christians have tended to accept either both biblical criticism and evolution or neither. There is still a solid section of conservative Protestants who reject both, even though biblical criticism has become an accepted fact in the theological world and evolutionary theory in one form or another has become universally accepted in the biological sciences of the Western world. The strength of conservative Christian resistance illustrates how keenly it has been felt that the new scientific world-view opened up in the nineteenth century completely undermined the premises on which the Christian tradition was believed to depend.

Only in the middle of the twentieth century did the Roman Catholic Church begin to relax, though quite cautiously at first, its previous steadfast resistance to both biblical criticism and the theory of evolution. In an Encyclical issued in 1945 Pope Pius XII acknowledged that the conditions for the pursuit of biblical study had greatly changed in the previous fifty years and he encouraged Catholic scholars to use the new methods, provided certain stringent safeguards were observed. In 1950, in the Encyclical *Humani Generis,* official mention was made for the first time of the theory of evolution. 'The Teaching of the Church leaves the doctrine of Evolution an open question, as long as it confines its speculations to the development, from other living matter already in existence, of the human body . . . Christians cannot lend their support to a theory which involves the existence, after Adam's time, of some earthly race of men, truly so called, who were not descended ultimately from him.'[6] Thus, while the Encyclical partly opened the door to Catholic acceptance of the possibility of evolution, it fell far short of what evolutionists such as Teilhard de Chardin were hoping for. Any theory of evolution acceptable to the Catholic Church had to be reconcilable with the view that all men are genetically descended from an historical Adam. Needless to say this is quite unacceptable to the scientific proponents of evolution.

It must be remembered, on the other hand, that by the end of the nineteenth century the more liberal section of Protestantism had come to accept both the theory of evolution and the scientific study of the Bible. J. R. Illingworth wrote in *Lux Mundi,* 'the last few years have witnessed the gradual acceptance by Christian thinkers of the great scientific generalization of our age . . . the Theory of Evolution'.[7] This meant that a new kind of division was opening up in the Christian world, one which had the capacity to cut right across the earlier denominational divisions. It was not so much a clear-cut rift as a very wide spectrum of opinion. So apart from local controversies and minor schisms, it did not express itself in any organizational way. The question was whether, and if so how, the Christian tradition could accommodate itself to the expanding world of science. The question had been made particularly acute by the doctrine of evolution but this was only one part of a larger and more complex challenge to traditional Christian thought. There were some who were actually saying that science had destroyed the whole surviving structure of Christian theology and compelled its reconstruction from the ground up.

Mrs Humphrey Ward expressed the deep tension then being felt in the Christian world in the form of a novel, *Robert Elsmere* (1888), which became a best-seller. She later said of it, 'I wanted to show how a man of sensitive and noble character, born for religion, comes to throw off the orthodoxies of his day and moment, and to go out into the wilderness where all is experiment, and spiritual life begins again. And with him I wished to contrast a type no less fine of the traditional and guided mind – and to imagine the clash of two such tendencies of thought, as it might affect all practical life, and especially the life of two people who loved each other'.[8]

In the widening spectrum of belief which the impact of science on religion was causing to open up there were three main positions being adopted. We have already referred to those who have steadfastly rejected all science which has come into conflict with basic Christian beliefs in their traditional form. At the other extreme there have been those who, agreeing with these that science and religion are incompatible, now regard as outmoded, religion in general and Christianity in particular. This position is well portrayed by Ernst Haeckel. In his best-seller, *The Riddle of the Universe* (1901), he spoke disparagingly of orthodox Christianity, acknowledged himself to be walking in the footsteps of Bruno, Spinoza and Strauss and declared his God to be the pantheistic one who could be described as the Spirit of Truth, Beauty and Goodness.

Between these two extremes there has been a body of liberal-minded thinking Christians who, feeling themselves torn between the claims of science and the values in the Christian tradition, attempted to find the way which would do justice to both. Of these we may take Aubrey Moore (1848-90) as a very clear spokesman. Equally at home in theology and the sciences, as were quite a number at that time, Moore welcomed the impact of empirical science. 'Science', he wrote in *Lux Mundi*, 'had pushed the deist's God farther and farther away, and at the moment, when it seemed as if He would be thrust out altogether, Darwinism appeared, and, under the disguise of a foe, did the work of a friend. It has conferred upon philosophy and religion an inestimable benefit by shewing us that we must choose between two alternatives. Either God is everywhere present in nature, or He is nowhere. He cannot be here and not there . . . In nature everything must be His work or nothing . . . It seems as if, in the providence of God, the mission of modern science was to bring home to our unmetaphysical ways of thinking the great truth of the Divine immanence in creation, which is no less essential to the Christian idea of God, than to a philosophical view of nature. And it comes to us almost like a new truth, which we cannot at once fit in with the old.'[9]

Those theologians who, like Moore, welcomed the findings of the rapidly developing sciences, were not unaware that they were conceding a great deal. They acknowledged science had given to modern man a radically new world-view, a new view of the cosmos as a whole, and a new view of man's place within it. They acknowledged that the Judaeo-Christian tradition could no longer speak with its former authority about the structure of the natural world, but that, in that area, man must listen with respect to the findings of science. But having conceded all this, including the fact that it entailed the re-thinking of Christian beliefs from the ground up, they went on to affirm that science too had its limits. This needed to be said, for in the first flush of victorious advance some scientists were inclined to give the impression that they could speak with authority on all subjects, and that science would provide answers to all of life's problems. This attitude engendered the widespread pseudo-religion of scientism which still operates at a popular level in Western society and by which the phrase 'Science teaches . . .' has tended to bring to all sorts of statements an air of infallibility which is quite inconsistent with science itself.

Although we yet have to trace the rise of the human sciences – particularly sociology and psychology – and discuss their impact on traditional religion, we can here point out that the apparent clash between religion and science which was evident in the nineteenth century has been replaced in the twentieth century by a much more open and fluid relationship. There is no longer any reason for regarding religion and science as mutually irreconcilable. They are rather seen as fulfilling complementary roles in relation to each other, even though we have yet to learn the most adequate ways of understanding this relationship.

It may be briefly sketched like this. It is the function of the physical sciences to help us understand the nature of the universe, including all life on this planet and ourselves as part of it. Science helps us to form for ourselves the most adequate cosmology. It provides the physical framework of our world-view. It attempts to answer the questions of the what and the how, recognizing however, that it can never speak with an infallible voice, for however confident it may be of its findings, they are always open to revision in the light of new data. Science is a continuing and open-ended pursuit, but it is one on which modern man has now become dependent for his understanding of the natural world.

Within the framework of the picture of the natural world unfolded by these sciences, it is the function of religion to open up for us and help us to respond to, the questions of meaning and purpose, as they apply particularly to human existence. Is there any meaning at all to human existence and, if so, what is it? Are there any essential, or even worthwhile goals in life which, if we strive for them, offer some kind of fulfilment of our human potential? The kind of answers we give to such questions, constitute the broad framework of our religion. Science, however much it may contribute to the formation of our world-view, cannot *per se* answer these basic religious questions. It must remain neutral on the question of values, purpose and meaning. Science is a pursuit which cannot even provide its own direction. Whenever a scientist has to make a choice with regard to which area of research should receive his priority, he has to doff his scientific hat and put on another, for he is making decisions on the basis, not of scientific findings, but of value convictions of a broadly religious character.

There is no doubt that the advent of modern science, like modern philosophy, has made a very great impact on religion and has actually undermined many of the basic forms of traditional Judaeo-Christianity. Instead of abolishing or replacing religion, however, it has had the effect of promoting its transition to a new phase. Science, like modern philosophy, emerged out of the Judaeo-Christian matrix (a point we shall take up further in Chapter 14). Just as the Judaeo-Christian tradition needed time to come to terms with its most radical prophets in the past, so in this late twentieth century the religion of modern man is slowly learning how to come to terms with science, but it may be in new forms which are not immediately recognizable as the continuation of the classical forms of religion.

The religion of post-Enlightenment man must openly recognize the continuing role of science, with both its strengths and its limits. It will acknowledge that neither science nor religion can speak with absolute certainty, even in their respective areas of concern. The day of assumed religious certainty is over. Far from being diametrically opposed, science and religion are mutually dependent on each other and have a surprising amount in common. They both depend ultimately on *a priori* convictions. This means that they must both walk forward in faith. They both depend, in part, on the creative power of the human imagination. They are both, in their respective spheres of interest, trying to discern patterns behind the superficial chaos of reality, the scientist doing it in the many areas of the physical world, the religious pilgrim in the art of living. Both seek the truth, both seek light in darkness. The scientist has his sudden flash of insight and puts it to the test. Religious man has his moments of revelation and tests them in life itself. The scientist creates his models and religious man expounds his deepest convictions in the form of myths.

It has not been the intention here to sketch how religion has responded to the impact of science by exploring, as it is doing, radically new ways of thinking about God, man, salvation and human destiny. This is a continuing process and is giving rise to ever greater diversity of thought. It has been our concern simply to show that the advent of modern science is one of the chief factors in making the modern world what it is and in differentiating it from all that went before. Because of this, religion in the post-Enlightenment age must differ in some essential respects from all former religious traditions, both primal and post-Axial.

CHAPTER 10

A NEW QUEEN OF THE SCIENCES?

❖

For the impact on religion of the second Copernican revolution we looked mainly to Britain, just as for the emergence of new religious thought of the post-Enlightenment period we had earlier looked mainly to Germany. For the rise of what we may tentatively call the science of human society, we must now turn our attention to France. Though the Enlightenment may be said to have begun in Britain, it reached its fullest flowering in France. The French Revolution was no isolated episode; it marked the birthpangs of the new social awareness and the determination to express it in a new social order, for which the Enlightenment had been the gestation period. The slogan 'Liberty, Equality, Fraternity' was to prove no passing fad but in fact points to a great deal which has been happening in the human scene since 1789, not only in France, but increasingly throughout the world.

It was during the Enlightenment that, in France more than anywhere else in Europe, there came to the surface the first examples of that total rejection of traditional religion which has become such a distinctive feature of the post-Enlightenment period everywhere. The religion of nature (or deism) proved to be only a transitional stage between theism and atheism. The swing from supernaturalism to naturalism, i.e., from God to man, was accompanied by the growth of materialism and socialism. It also meant the questioning and challenging of the inherited class stratification and established social orders. These had long been regarded as unalterable on the grounds that they had been divinely ordained. As theism and the plausibility of appeal to divine revelation receded into the background, man and human society came increasingly into the centre of the picture. The study of God which, as theology, had long reigned as the 'queen of the sciences' was destined to yield the throne to the study of human society. The new discipline of sociology came to birth. We shall look at some of the significant steps by which this came about.

Back in 1747 there had been published what became a notorious little book entitled *Man a Machine*. The author, Julien Offroy de La Mettrie (1709-51), was a physician, who based his materialist philosophy of man both on the medical science of the day and on the experience of a personal illness. He contended that all mental activity is dependent on organic changes in the brain and nervous system and, as a consequence, it is unnecessary to postulate the concept of an immortal, immaterial soul. He conceded that a Supreme Being may exist but, if so, he believed the fact to be of incidental interest only and that He need not be thought of as the primary source of human morality. What we take for moral laws, he contended, are human creations and conventions which have arisen out of physical, psychological and social needs. His book may have had many faults but it was an early sign of the pyschosomatic, materialistic and socialistic view of man which has been increasingly challenging the traditional view. Indeed, he foresaw that wherever the action of a criminal could be traced to psychological disorder, it would be necessary to reappraise the question of moral responsibility.

The first man of the French Enlightenment openly to declare himself an atheist was Baron D'Holbach (1723-89). He was a man of considerable learning, who did much to spread the influence of the English deists both by translating their works and by writing his own. He contributed more than 400 articles to Diderot's *Encyclopaedia*. Moreover his personal influence spread through Europe because of his practice, lasting nearly 40 years, of holding Sunday and Thursday dinners at his stately homes. Besides the regular coterie who engaged there in stimulating conversation, he invited leading thinkers from all over Europe, such as David Hume, Horace Walpole, Adam Smith, Cesare Beccaria and Benjamin Franklin.

D'Holbach was himself influenced by Bayle, Hobbes, Locke and Hume but he became more radical than any of their other disciples and carried the deist attack on supernatural religion to its logical conclusion. He was militantly anti-clerical and desired to see the destruction, not only of Catholicism but, of all religion – and this in the interest of truth and morality! He asserted that the facts of Christ's life were not sufficiently supported by historical evidence to warrant full acceptance, and that the Bible contained so many inconsistencies that it was unworthy of a divine author. Religion as a whole, he contended, was the product of human ignorance and fear and was deliberately perpetuated by the priesthood because of the power which it placed in their hands. Foreshadowing Marx's famous dictum he wrote, 'Religion is the art of intoxicating people with religious fervour to prevent them from being cognizant of their troubles, heaped upon them by those who governed. With the aid of supernatural powers which constantly threaten, one forces them to suffer in silence the miseries inflicted by terrestrial powers; they are made to believe that if they are unhappy in this world, they will be happier in the next'.[1]

D'Holbach asserted that the concept of Hell as a place in which there is no forgiveness and no possibility of moral improvement was morally reprehensible and incompatible with the concept of a loving almighty God. The doctrine of original sin was to him the work of the devil. If God was omnipotent, why did he allow Adam and Eve to fall into sin in the first place? If he was the epitome of forgiveness and justice, why did the Church portray him in such a vindic tive role? So he attacked religion at its very base – belief in God – and contended that the whole concept of God is utterly ridiculous. 'Ask anyone if he believes in God. He will be surprised that you can doubt it. Then ask him what he means by the word God . . . you will notice immediately how unable he is to attach any concrete idea to the word he repeats continuously.'[2]

He proposed that, instead of God, men should worship Nature or the Universe. 'O Nature! Sovereign of all beings! And you, her adorable daughters, virtue, reason and truth! Be ever our only divinities' – he wrote.[3] The natural universe, which to him was the whole of reality, he regarded as composed solely of molecules of matter which circulated in a continuous process of motion, often involving the transformation into new forms. Anything which men claimed to be supernatural was simply a natural process about which men had as yet insufficient knowledge to understand it for what it was.

Deists, including even Voltaire, feared that the decay of all religion would undermine and destroy all morality. D'Holbach, on the other hand, asserted that the record of religion showed that it was already morally corrupt and that it was possible to construct and defend a code of ethics based upon human nature. Such a code, moreover, would ultimately prove to be universal to the whole human race, whereas the traditional codes, currently associated with particular religions, differed from one another and were relative only to particular cultures. 'True morality has only one criterion by which to judge the mistakes of man; the most serious are those which harm society the most.'[4] He went so far as to claim that the future preservation of society depended on the ability of men to overcome their blind and dogmatic prejudices and arrive at an intelligent understanding of their mutual moral responsibilities.

Like other men of the Enlightenment D'Holbach stood for toleration and freedom of worship. In spite of his own disbelief in God and his antagonism to all forms of religion, he recognized the importance of religious beliefs for the majority of people and was strongly opposed to the use of force to change men's convictions, however superstitious and unenlightened they might appear to be. 'It is tyrannical to despoil a citizen of his goods; it is even more tyrannical and cruel to deprive him of his opinions on God, who is often more dear to him than his property or his very safety.'[5] Thus he was an apostle of freedom and toleration, and these, he believed, should be guaranteed by just and reasonable laws.

The titles of some of D'Holbach's books clearly indicate their thrust – *Christianity unveiled or an examination of the principles and effects of the Christian religion*, *Universal Morality or the Duties of man founded on Nature*, *Good Sense or Natural Ideas opposed to Supernatural*. His most important work was *System of Nature or the Laws of the Physical and the Natural World*. When this was translated into English in 1859 it was given the title *The Atheist's Text-book*.

The ideas of D'Holbach which we have just briefly sketched have today lost all their novelty for they are freely held in one form or another by many in the Western world. When he wrote them they were new and dangerous, and for this reason he usually wrote under pseudonyms. Hume is reported to have said at one of D'Holbach's dinner parties that he had never met a genuine atheist, only to be told by his host that he was then in the presence of some fifteen of them. The fact that prevailing beliefs have changed so much in 200 years is itself a clear indication of how D'Holbach heralded one of the dominant religious (or irreligious?) trends in the modern world. In spirit, therefore, D'Holbach belonged to the post-Enlightenment period rather than to the age of transition itself. Voltaire more properly represents the latter for he was severely critical of the Church but had no wish to go to D'Holbach's atheistic extremes.

The only alternative to the complete rejection of all religion, either in France or in Germany, was the transition to quite a new type of religion. It was Saint-Simon (1760-1825), an early French socialist, who was one of the first Frenchmen to move in this direction. Although he was not a very systematic thinker, many of his insights and ideas were to be used by his successors. In his book *The New Christianity* (1825), he maintained that the most fundamental principle in Christianity is that men should treat one another as brothers. He urged priests to disregard their dogmas and devote themselves to the social betterment of the depressed classes. He felt himself called to work for a new kind of society, a new expression of Christianity, one which saw man in a new and more positive light. In the future Utopian society he envisaged, there would be universal education, a Parliament of Industry, and a Church of Science and Art where scientists took over the former priestly role. He foresaw the rapid spread of industrialization and was confident that science and technology would solve most human problems.

Many of Saint-Simon's ideas were later developed and systematized by a young man who served for two years as his secretary, Auguste Comte (1798-1857). (Because their association ended in a bitter quarrel, Comte consistently denied the source of some of his ideas.) While still in his thirties, Comte produced his massive six-volume work,

Course on the Positive Philosophy, finishing it in 1842, the year after Feuerbach's *Essence of Christianity*. When looked at in its historical context, it still appears quite a remarkable work. Comte contended that during the previous two centuries human thought had passed through an intellectual revolution of a kind which meant that mankind was entering a new era, one in which men would live their lives and solve their problems by the light of what he chose to call 'the positive philosophy'.

Comte had been influenced by a book written by the Marquis de Condorcet (1743-94), entitled *Sketch for a Historical Picture of the Progress of the Human Mind*. It discerned nine epochs in the intellectual progress of the human race from primitive barbarism to the Enlightenment. Comte's own study of human history from the earliest civilizations down to his own time led him to the conclusion that human thought developed according to a clearly discernible pattern and that this was reflected in each branch of knowledge. He called this pattern 'the law of the three stages'. It states that the human mind passes successively through three stages of philosophical reflection and, as a consequence, each area of our knowledge passes through three successive states: the theological or fictitious, the metaphysical or abstract, and, finally, the scientific or positive.

In the theological stage, Comte contended, men had tried to explain and understand the world in which they lived by interpreting all changing phenomena as the acts of unseen supernatural agents. But man's inventive mind eventually grew dissatisfied with the gods he had invented and he began to look for principles, eternal essences and abstract forces which he assumed to be inherent in the various types of phenomena. It was in this way that man progressed to the metaphysical stage, though this, thought Comte, was in reality simply a modification of the first stage. The third or positive stage is that in which the human mind recognizes at last that it is impossible ever to reach ultimate absolutes; man therefore confines his search to the actual laws that govern the processes of change observable in the world.

Comte maintained that in each of the three stages there is to be observed a progression from complexity to simplicity, from multiplicity to unity. The theological stage, for example, began with fetishism, moved to polytheism and reached its perfection in monotheism. The metaphysical stage began by postulating a variety of abstract entities and reached its consummation in the one basic entity of Nature. In the positive stage the number of basic natural laws will diminish as science progresses and, though the perfection of this stage may never be attained by man, it would consist in the ability to trace all observable phenomena back to the operation of one single fact, such as a force like gravitation.

It was from Saint-Simon that Comte borrowed the use of the word 'positive' (with the accompanying term 'positivism') to refer to the third stage, for he regarded scientific knowledge as certain and reliable. By contrast he used the term 'negativism' as a derogatory label for those beliefs and pre-scientific dogmas which, resting only on the authority of tradition, are quite unreliable. The term positivism has come to be used since that time for a variety of differing philosophical positions; what they all have in common is the rejection of all traditional metaphysics and the contention that the only valid forms of knowledge are those gained by the scientific method.

Comte believed his law of three stages to be immediately perceptible to all who had a knowledge of the history of science. He contended that all sciences had their origin in the theological stage and that though some were then reaching the positive stage, they still retained traces of the earlier two stages through which they had passed. Moreover he contended that in the growth of each person to intellectual maturity, one starts as a child in the theological stage, moves as an adolescent into the metaphysical stage and only in adult maturity, if at all, does one reach the positive stage. He believed that in cultural history the move from the first to the second stage had occurred several times, especially so at the Reformation and the Enlightenment, but only in his own day was the third stage being reached. Once again we meet with the analogy between modernity and man's coming of age.

The main section of Comte's magnum opus was an attempt to show how an encyclopaedic unification of all knowledge could be achieved, on a strictly scientific basis, by arranging the sciences in a linear series proceeding from the simplest to the most complex. He concluded that there are five fundamental sciences – astronomy, physics, chemistry, biology and social physics – each of which is dependent in part on its predecessor, and all of which are to be prefaced by mathematics, which provides the human mind with the necessary tools for scientific research in the sciences proper. The earlier of these sciences had already passed through the first two stages while the more complex ones were still at the theological or metaphysical stage.

Because of this presumed necessary sequence, Comte believed that it was not until biology had reached some maturity in the positive stage that social physics would fully emerge and be seen as the science which interlocked all the others into a grand unity. Social physics, for which he coined the term sociology in 1839, was thus to be a kind of queen of the sciences. By 'sociology' he meant a comprehensive discipline which linked history, morals and politics. It was, in his view, methodologically similar to biology in that both proceed from the study of organic wholes. But whereas a biological organism is unified by an encasing skin, a skeleton or a nervous system, the social organism is unified by cultural, moral and political factors. These form the cement which binds society together.

As soon as the new discipline reached some maturity he believed it would supply the scientific basis for the reorganization of society, which, in his view, was so necessary to resolve the crisis from which European civilization appeared to be suffering. Education, for example, which up until that time had been theological and metaphysical, would be 'replaced by a positive education, in tune with the spirit of our time, and adapted to the needs of modern civilization'.[6]

Comte believed the human mind was passing through a general revolution. This had begun with Bacon, Descartes and Galileo and would soon be brought to a consummation by the completion of the positive philosophy in the study of social phenomena. He contended that this revolution would modify, more profoundly than all earlier revolutions of thought, the whole of human existence, both individual and social. It would outclass even the ancient transition from a polytheistic world to a monotheistic one.[7]

One of the great assets Comte saw in his positive philosophy was its capacity to present a completely coherent system of all knowledge such as had never existed before, even in the best minds. He recognized at the same time, however, that there could be no finality about the formulation and unification of knowledge, for one of the essential differences between his positivism and all former philosophy was the recognition of the purely relative character of all human knowledge. In view of the confident optimism which positivism has tended to exude, it is important to remember that it was Comte's belief that the best which men could achieve would be ever closer approximations to the ultimate truth. 'Once the purely relative nature of all our knowledge comes to be recognized', he said 'our theories, under the natural dominance of the social point of view, will aim solely, with regard to a reality that can never be absolutely revealed, at approximations as satisfying as the corresponding stage of the great human evolution in each epoch permits.'[8]

In spite of this caveat Comte believed man was entering a great new era, in which the growth of positivism would not only bring to the individual a mental harmony which had previously been impossible to attain, but would also create at the social level an intellectual and moral communion which would prove to be more complete and stable than that achieved by any religious tradition in the past.[9] We may say that, as Comte saw it, traditional religion was to be superseded by positivism and, since belief in God was to be replaced by confidence in human society, theology was to be superseded by sociology.

Thus Comte had his own particular way of expounding the religious transition he saw taking place in the post-Enlightenment era. The place occupied by God in the thought of post-Axial man was to be taken by human society or Humanity in the new era of positivism. Humanity had become for Comte *Le Grand Etre*. In his view Humanity constitutes one grand, complex organism, living a continuous and virtually immortal life in accordance with its own laws of development, which it is the task of sociology to unfold. It is society, and not the individual, which holds the key to the understanding of reality. The individual, once divorced from society, is an unreal abstraction. Every person exists, as such, only because he is a member of a family, then of a city or nation, and finally of Humanity, which consists of all nations on earth.

From the vantage point of his positivist stage, Comte naturally believed that all the former religious traditions were now to be superseded but this did not mean that they were false. They were appropriate and true for the previous stages through which Humanity had passed, just as a child's beliefs are in a form appropriate to his mental level but need to be replaced by maturer forms later. Comte believed, therefore, that the great religious teachers of the past should be honoured and whatever was of permanent value in their teaching should be retained or freshly expressed.

On the grounds that the era of positivism then being entered required its own form of religion, analogous to the traditional religions of previous eras, Comte proceeded to promote and expound the new Religion of Humanity, founding the Positivist Society of Paris in 1848. The guiding principle of the new religion (drawn from Saint-Simon) was 'Live for Others'. For this Comte actually coined our now common term 'altruism'. Not content with elaborating an ideology, Comte proceeded to establish a Positivist 'Church', so close to Catholicism in its externals that Carlyle called it 'Catholicism without Christianity'. Positivist philosophers were to be priests, Comte himself being the Supreme Pontiff. They were to be ordained only after a long period of study and probationary service. It would be their function to preach positivism, to celebrate the sacraments (for which an elaborate cultus had been constructed), to give counsel, to mould public opinion, to be physicians and to create works of art. Women were to be given a place of special honour. Comte replaced the Christian Year with a Positivist Calendar of 13 months, each of 28 days and each named after one of the makers of Western civilization, such as Moses, Archimedes, Aristotle, Caesar, Paul, Shakespeare, Descartes. The Positivist Era (PE) began with 1789 as the Year One.

Of course all this was far too artificial to attract widespread support, even though small scattered communities survived into the twentieth century. The British philosopher J. S. Mill was at first keenly interested in Comte's major work, corresponded with him and even helped him financially, but he took strong objection to Comte's attempt to institutionalize positivism in this religious form. Yet, shorn of its crudities, Comte's massive sociological analysis of history was just as thorough as that of Karl Marx. The diverse fate of the two systems, however, is very striking. Comte's attempt to create the new religion of the positivist age was a dismal failure: Marx, who abhorred all religion, unintentionally became the founder (as we have seen above) of the most widespread new 'religion' of modern times. 'Likewise', as Andreski drily remarks, 'the Communist habit of worshipping their stalwarts, building them monuments and mausolea, naming streets, towns, buildings and what not after them, is much more in line with Comte's project of replacing the Christian saints by positivist figures, than with Marx's insistence on the unimportance of individuals. Above all, the notion that their doctrine and programme were based on Science – as well as the name "scientific socialism" for them – in all likelihood occurred to Marx and Engels in consequence of reading Comte. So, though in a rather perverse way, a number of Comte's crucial projects have been implemented by the worshippers of the man who had nothing but contempt for Comte's Utopian schemes.'[10]

In spite of his defects and oddities Comte remains important for two reasons. Firstly, he enunciated in a clear and systematic way the fact that the advent of empirical science has led mankind into a new kind of intellectual era and that this must be reflected in his religious aspirations, beliefs and practices. Secondly, he pioneered the new human science of sociology. We now turn to one of Comte's most important disciples, Emile Durkheim (1858-1917), who once remarked that sociology had come to birth with Saint-Simon and Comte and had remained up until his time an essentially French science.

Durkheim was the son of a rabbi and studied Hebrew

in his youth with the intention of entering the rabbinate. He experienced some kind of religious crisis while under the influence of a Catholic teacher; he settled for a secular career and became a lifelong agnostic. He always spoke of Judaism and Christianity with respect but, for himself, he was committed to science and humanity. Like Comte, he found in sociology an adequate replacement to fill the role once played by theology. But unlike Comte, he had no wish to turn sociology into a cultic religion. Yet he often spoke of society in a way which implied almost metaphysical overtones. Because of what society is as the source of ideas, morality, and even the personal life of the individual, it takes the place of God in a post-theistic age. Bellah has referred to Durkheim as the 'high priest and theologian of the civil religion of the Third Republic and a prophet calling not only modern France but modern western society generally to mend its ways in the face of a great social and moral crisis'.[11]

Whereas Comte had wanted to turn positivism into a religion with sociology as the queen of the sciences, Durkheim became increasingly fascinated by religion because of the central and essential role he believed it played in society. 'It was only in 1895', he later wrote, 'that I had a clear sense of the capital role played by religion in social life . . . It was for me a revelation . . . all my earlier researches had to be revised anew in order to be put in harmony with these new views.'[12]

Durkheim came to believe that what gives cohesion to a human society is in fact religion. Without it there can be no durable society. This means, first, the acknowledgement that every society expressed the moral and spiritual forces which gave it cohesion in the form of religion. Secondly it means that to ask which of all the religions is the true one is to ask the wrong question. Every living religion is in a sense true, so long as it is adequately fulfilling its role of giving unity and cohesion to a society. 'In reality, then, there are no religions which are false', wrote Durkheim. 'All are true in their own fashion; all answer, though in different ways, to the given conditions of human existence.'[13]

For such reasons Durkheim was led to devote more than ten years of the last part of his life to the study of religion. He chose, in particular, the religion of the Australian Aborigine on the grounds (as he believed) that it represented the simplest and earliest known form of religion and yet contained all the essentials of religion, as it later evolved into more sophisticated forms. He published his study as *The Elementary Forms of the Religious Life* and it has become a classic, even though parts of it would today be seriously questioned.

Durkheim believed the essence of all religion to consist in the division of man's world into two areas which are mutually exclusive – the sacred and the profane – and that there is no religion where this division is not found.[14] What is the reason for this? How did men come to make this division? For the religious practitioner, of course, these questions do not arise; the reality of the sacred/profane dichotomy is simply a fact which has impressed itself on human consciousness and requires no explanation. From the point of view of post-Enlightenment man, who has been experiencing increasingly the absence of a sense of the sacred,[15] Durkheim looked for an empirical reason for this previously universal phenomenon. He concluded that man had felt himself confronted by a dualistic world because he experienced a duality in his own nature. When man finds himself involved in a moral and spiritual struggle – in its simplest form, a struggle between a man and his conscience – he recognizes that there is something which transcends him, stands over against him, is superior to him and commands him.

This experience, argued Durkheim, is not an illusion but stems from the fact that we are members of a society, and on it we depend not only for our survival but for our very humanity. What is experienced as standing over the inner self is the impact of society upon us. Man lives a dual life – the life of a self-determining individual and the life of a social being under the direction of the society on which he depends and which has given him his humanity. This duality is experienced as a spiritual encounter and is often one of tension. Durkheim believed the totemism of the Australian Aborigine exemplifies the rise of this duality in a primal society and explains the origin of the sacred/profane dichotomy and the subsequent rise in beliefs, in spirits, gods and other non-material forces. The 'god' of the clan he took to be the totemic principle, which is 'nothing else than the clan itself, personified and represented to the imagination under the viable form of the animal or vegetable which serves as the totem'.[16]

All religion, concluded Durkheim, originated out of the moral pressures which the group exerts upon the individual members. Religious forces are in fact 'moral powers because they are made up entirely of the impressions this moral being, the group, arouses in those other moral beings, its individual members'.[17] Durkheim conceived the social group almost as a living entity with a life of its own, over and above the sum-total of that of its members. Just as in the context of theistic religion God was believed to have initiated that religion by some process of divine revelation, so Durkheim maintained that it is the moral being of society which is the origin of the religious beliefs and practices of the individual. It causes man to construct (in his imagination) another world above the real world where his profane life is lived, and to this higher world he attributes superiority and ultimacy – it is the realm of the sacred.

At a time when religion was becoming discredited in the

eyes of some, Durkheim was reasserting its essential importance. Religion he believed to be firmly founded on reality, not a supernatural reality however but a natural one. 'Religious forces are therefore human forces, moral forces', he said.[18] 'We can say that the believer is not deceived when he believes in the existence of a moral power upon which he depends and from which he receives all that is best in him; this power exists, it is society.'[19] Durkheim thus came to look at religion in a positive light as something very meaningful and reasonable; it is the system of ideas and practices by which men objectify and mediate to themselves the moral powers of the society of which they are members. So long as religion is faithfully performing this, its primary function, it is manifesting 'an eternal truth that outside of us there exists something greater than us, with which we enter into communion'.[20] So essential is this function of religion that it can be said, asserted Durkheim, 'that the fundamental categories of thought, and consequently of science, are of religious origin'.[21] But 'If religion has given birth to all that is essential in society, it is because the idea of society is the soul of religion'.[22]

Since religion is not an illusion but the representation of society itself in symbolic form, then, said Durkheim, 'there is something eternal in religion which is destined to survive all the particular symbols in which religious thought has successively enveloped itself. There can be no society which does not feel the need of upholding and reaffirming at regular intervals the collective sentiments and the collective ideas which make its unity and its personality'.[23]

At the same time as Durkheim was affirming the permanent function of religion he fully recognized that he lived in an age of transition, in which the traditional religious forms and symbols were fast becoming obsolete and needed to be replaced by something more adequate.

'The old gods are growing old or are already dead', he said, 'and others are not yet born.'[23] Because of the essential relationship between society and religion, however, it meant that for the continuance of a viable human society religion was 'destined to transform itself rather than to disappear'.[24] Otherwise society would disintegrate through uncertainty and confusion. He looked forward to the coming day 'when our societies will know again those hours of creative effervescence in the course of which new ideas arise and new formulae are found which serve for a while as a guide to humanity'[25] but confessed that at that stage it was impossible to say by what symbols the new faith would come to expression and to what extent they would resemble the symbols of the past. He knew they could not be artificially constructed as Comte had tried to do. He was just as sure that science could not take the place of religion, as Comte's positivism implied and as scientism assumes to be the case. What science in general can do, including the human sciences in particular, is to determine some of the perimeters within which the new symbols will take shape, but it cannot provide the religious forms. 'Faith is before else an impetus to action', he said, but 'Science is fragmentary and incomplete' and 'life cannot wait'.[26]

This is not the place to sketch the subsequent development of sociology and outline the variety of schools of thought which have subsequently arisen within it. Our purpose has been served by showing from the work of these French pioneers the extent to which the birth of sociology has thrown quite a new light on the origin, substance and function of religion. Sociologists today are usually much more modest than Comte in what they claim for their particular human science. Sociology has not become universally recognized as the queen of the sciences. Even so, there has been a certain tendency on the part of some people to expect it to take over the role (formerly played by theology) of enabling man to solve life's problems. Sociologists are prepared to discuss almost any subject X under the heading of 'The Sociology of X' in much the same way as theologians used to speak (and often still do) of 'The Theology of X'. The reason for this is that, on the assumption that we live in a post-theistic age, then human society becomes the empirical source of the individual's very humanity. Instead of a supernatural God, it is society which has made a person what he is.

It remains briefly to summarize the impact of sociology on religion. However much the French founders of sociology may be criticized by both later sociologists as well as others it must be conceded that the rise of sociology has shown the necessary relationship which exists between religion and society. Never again can we afford to ignore the sociological factors present either in the condition of our humanity or in the religion which shapes our behaviour and expresses our basic beliefs. Sociological factors may not be the only ones to be taken into consideration but they are very important ones. Much more of the content of religion originated in social forces than previously men ever dreamed of.

But if sociology has given general support to the contention of Feuerbach that religions are man-made, it has nevertheless opened up a more plausible and ultimately more fruitful explanation of the human origin of religion. Feuerbach attributed too much to the creative mind of the individual. Sociology has shown that the reason for the rise of religion is much more complex. Moreover, if we follow Durkheim's emphasis, we avoid the implication that religion is basically illusory and arrive at a much more positive appreciation of the role of religion than Marx was prepared to allow. Indeed Durkheim adds strong support to the general contention of this book that while the Enlightenment seriously threatened religion in both its primal and post-Axial forms, it heralded not the end of religion but its transition to new forms. Sociology, as Durkheim saw this new way of understanding man, confirmed the essential and lasting importance of religion for the preservation of all that is essentially human.

Sociology, however, is not the only human science and cannot by itself tell us all we need to know about the human condition and about the nature of man's religion. Sociology fastens attention on the moral and spiritual forces of the natural world which impinge on the individual from the outside. We must now turn to the human science which fastens attention on the moral and spiritual forces which impinge upon the individual from within – the science of psychology.

CHAPTER 11

THE COPERNICAN REVOLUTION IN THE SCIENCE OF THE SOUL

Ever since humans began to reflect on the nature of their condition they have used such concepts as spirit, soul and mind to refer to the presumed organs of their inner life, which enabled them to think and reason, and to participate in that high level of consciousness which, perhaps more than anything else, appears to distinguish the human species from all other known living creatures. But whereas man's physical body is tangible and open to public investigation, man's inner life is private and apparently inaccessible to others and, in part, even to himself. Each of us has first-hand experience only of his own inner life and can reflect upon this by introspection. We are quickly led to make the assumption that our fellow humans have inner experiences just like our own. Indeed it is only because of the shared cultural tradition into which we are born, that our own innate potential for human self-consciousness has been nurtured. But whether we think of the spirit (the seat of vitality), the soul (the seat of personality), or the mind (the seat of the intellect), this presumed inner organ has long eluded human investigation just because of its hidden and non-physical character. The attempt to understand the inner life of man belonged necessarily therefore to the realm of traditional metaphysics.

We have seen that one of the effects of the Enlightenment

was to question, and virtually undermine, the Western metaphysical tradition. It was only to be expected that this would lead, in turn, to a revolution in the understanding of man's inner life; and so it did, resulting in the birth of the new science of psychology. The significance of this for religion can hardly be overestimated, for religion has been just as much concerned with the inner, or spiritual, life of the individual person, as it has been with the social life of man. If it is true, as van de Pol has said, that 'Modern psychology provides a totally new understanding and judgment of the sexual, emotional, ethical, moral and religious existence of man',[1] then a radical change in religion becomes inevitable.

The new science of psychology grew out of the Western metaphysical tradition and partly because a perennial philosophical problem had never been satisfactorily solved. It was the question of how the soul (or inner life of man) is to be related to the body (or physical life of man). Are body and soul two quite independent entities, are they interdependent, or are they ultimately one? The Western world had inherited two somewhat different answers from the Greek philosophers. Plato had opted for a dualistic view of man, seeing him composed of a mortal body which housed, indeed imprisoned for the time being, an immortal soul. The Christian view, and even the Jewish view, in spite of their Semitic origins, came to be greatly influenced by this. Aristotle, however, had taught a more monistic view of man (too complex to attempt to summarize here) and this entered into Western Christian thought through Aquinas and the medieval Scholastics.

The problem was raised again more sharply for the modern world when Descartes, departing from the Scholastic tradition, moved to a position closer to that of Plato. Descartes differentiated very clearly between body and mind. He believed they interacted upon each other through the medium of the brain and particularly through the pineal gland. Spinoza, as we have already seen, found the dualism of Descartes unsatisfactory and replaced it with a monistic view both of the world and of man. This, in turn, had some bearing, as we have also seen, on the two opposing ways of conceiving a monistic world that were dominant in the nineteenth century. Either, mind was claimed to be the one and only basis of reality (as the Idealists in general and Hegel in particular contended), or else, physical matter was believed to be the prime reality (as the materialists such as Hobbes, de La Mettrie, Feuerbach and Marx maintained). A third way of attempting to solve the problem of mind-body relationship was that of Leibniz (1646-1716). He held that man's bodily and spiritual activities arc independent, but exist in perfect parallel unison. He likened body and soul to two clocks which, though independent, always show exactly the same time because they are wound and regulated by the same hand.

An approach somewhat analogous to that of Leibniz was taken by Gustav Theodor Fechner (1801-87), during the very time when the German philosophical world was divided between idealism and materialism. He was both a genuine scientist and also a devout Christian who strongly believed in the sacred world. So he tried to bridge his two interests by asserting that reality is both spiritual and material at the same time; but since the spiritual is not accessible to the senses we must learn about it, as well as the laws governing its relation to the material world, through the doorway of the latter. He was by occupation a professor of physics, but after moving into the fields of medicine, philosophy and theology, he founded what he called psychophysics.

Another who assumed the independent existence of both a spiritual and a material world, but who tried to understand why they seem to match each other so perfectly was

Alexander Bain (1818-1903). He contended that every mental activity had its physical counterpart. These pioneering psychologists, being still closely tied to philosophy, were attracted to such theories of psychological parallelism, out of the need to avoid the difficulties in any absolute form of dualism. Henryk Misiak notes that 'as the ties with philosophy grew looser and those with science closer, interest in this theory and in other theories of body-mind relation gradually waned. The dichotomy of man, implicit in parallelism, was to be replaced by a developing notion of the unity of man as an organism. Psychological thought leaned toward monism and away from dualism. Moreover, the focus of psychology was changing from the mind to behaviour'.[2]

Just as the physical sicences were already throwing light on problems which earlier speculative philosophy had wrestled with but been unable to solve, so it was the empirical science of physiology which was instrumental in bringing new understanding to the mind-body problem and in serving as midwife to the birth of the new science of psychology. The one usually acknowledged as the father of psychology, Wilhelm Wundt (1832-1920), as well as another equally famous psychologist, William James (1842-1910), were both medical graduates who became professors of physiology before they turned to psychology. During the first half of the nineteenth century the developing biological sciences of physiology and neurology made various discoveries which meant that certain beliefs about man which philosophy had entertained for centuries, had to be abandoned and replaced by new ones. For example, it was shown that the energy which caused body muscles to move was not some mysterious force of a spiritual kind but was a nervous impulse which could be located and measured under laboratory conditions.

It was becoming clear that metaphysical philosophy was

not the most effective discipline for solving the problems of man's inner life and that the biological sciences were going to be able to provide much more positive results. Indeed there was a risk for some time that the new science of psychology would lose its independent identity and simply become a branch of physiology. Although Wundt was the man who rescued it from this fate, he himself actually called it 'physiological psychology' at first, in order to distinguish it from the psychology of the philosophers, which continued to be known into the twentieth century as 'Mental Philosophy'. (It is interesting to note that the actual term 'psychology' is thought to have been coined by the Protestant Reformer Philip Melanchthon (1497-1560), who meant by it simply 'the study of the soul'.)

While Wundt remained something of a dualist in his philosophical approach to the study of man, he nevertheless adopted some of Fechner's experimental methods, ruled out metaphysics completely and laid the foundations of the new science. The chief reasons why it constitutes a new way of understanding man, which has the effect of challenging the beliefs long assumed by the Christian tradition, are these. It dispenses with the traditional religious and metaphysical terms, such as soul, spirit and mind, as being of no value to the empirical investigator. It looks for the ways in which man's feelings, emotions and thoughts arise from tangible and this-worldly origins and, to the extent to which it has been successful, has provided alternative explanations to those inherited from traditional supernaturalism, explanations which modern man tends to find much more convincing.

Of course, psychology, like other empirical sciences, soon renders itself vulnerable if it claims too much. If it claims, for example, that the explanations of religious experience provided by psychology are the only valid explanations, or if it insists that the only meaningful and valid form of knowledge is that which is obtained and verified by empirical science and that truth is confined to that which can be empirically established, then it is over-reaching itself and falling prey to inconsistency for these are dogmatic and metaphysical claims which cannot be empirically verified. Sometimes the behaviourist school of psychology, pioneered by J. B. Watson (1878-1958) and continued by B. F. Skinner (1903-), tends to give this impression when it insists that psychology is simply the objective study of the behaviour of organisms and that such words as soul, minds and consciousness are illusory terms.

Before psychology had gone very far in exploring the mental activities of man, and while the implications of it for religious experience were as yet scarcely glimpsed, a further d velopment took place which was destined to be more threatening to traditional religion than all the other discoveries of psychology. This development originated with Sigmund Freud (1856-1939), whose name and some of whose basic terms have now become part of our everyday language. Freud himself referred to this development as psychoanalysis, for it did not arise out of the growing science of psychology but out of the clinical practice of psychiatry. It soon began to revolutionize psychology, however, and affected its future course. It presented such a new image of man that its far-reaching impact has been likened to the revolutions of thought associated with the names of Copernicus and Darwin. Misiak writes, 'As Copernicus destroyed the illusion of the earth's and of man's central position in the universe, and Darwin destroyed the illusion of man's uniqueness in living nature, Freud dealt a lethal blow to man's perhaps greatest illusion – that of being master of his thoughts and actions'.[3]

The year 1895 marked the birth of psychoanalysis. It basically represents the discovery of a whole area of man's psychic life of which we were previously unaware, and because we are at no time conscious of it, it is simply referred to as the 'unconscious' or the 'subconscious'. Freud was not the first to use the term. Paracelsus (1495-1541), that most original physician and philosopher of the Renaissance, postulated the existence of the subconscious. He influenced the German mystic Jakob Boehme (1575-1624), who in turn influenced Hegel, Schelling and others. Schelling influenced Karl Gustav Carus (1789-1869), a medical professor at Dresden, who in his book on the *History of the Development of the Soul* in 1846, maintained that the key to the conscious was to be found in the sphere of the unconscious. How much Freud was aware of all this we do not know. It was his great contribution to produce the clinical evidence to support the concept of the unconscious and to show some of the ways in which it operates.

Psychoanalysis is both a theory of the human psyche and a therapeutic method. We are concerned here only with the first. Previously the human psyche had been thought to consist solely of the stream of consciousness, accompanied by the memory. To speak of unconscious psychical processes had appeared to be nonsense. In the light of psychoanalysis (or what hereafter we may refer to by the looser and less dogmatic term of 'depth psychology'), it becomes necessary to abandon this overvaluation of the conscious. The unconscious now came to be recognized as the general basis of the human psyche, and within this larger whole is contained the smaller sphere of the conscious. 'The unconscious is the true psychical reality', said Freud. 'In its innermost nature it is as much unknown to us as the reality of the external world, and it is as incompletely presented by the data of consciousness as is the external world by the communications of our sense organs.'[4]

One of the models Freud used for the psyche was a

pyramidal structure of three levels, which he referred to as the conscious, the preconscious and the unconscious. The conscious level may be likened to the visible tip of an iceberg, most of which is submerged in the water. Just beneath the surface is the preconscious. It stores such material as memory data which, while not continually in our consciousness, may be readily recalled to consciousness. Beneath that again is the largest, and in some ways most important, level of all – the unconscious. This is a vast storehouse of past thoughts, impressions, experiences (some of which can be recalled to consciousness by special methods such as hypnosis), primal instincts and dynamic forces. Experiences which we find painful or shameful are relegated to the subconscious. When this is done by choice Freud called it 'suppression'; when it occurs involuntarily he called it 'repression'.

The most important aspect of the unconscious is that the material contained in it does not simply become dormant, as do living forms which are frozen into inertness in a freezing chamber. It remains active and continues to influence our conscious life, often being the hidden motivation behind our feelings, thoughts and actions. Thus the reasoning we consciously offer for these may not be nearly so clear and transparent as we think, but may often be a form of rationalization of actions which have been primarily motivated by unseen forces. The psychic content of the subconscious may be the motivating cause of slips of the tongue, mistakes and even accidents we suffer. The simplest illustration is supplied through the phenomenon of hypnosis, a state of induced sleep in which the subject surrenders consciousness and is controlled by the hypnotizer through the power of suggestion. The latter may command his subject to perform a simple action a short time after he regains normal consciousness. When he awakes the subject proceeds to do this, even though he has no idea why he feels compelled to do so. It is just as if the hypnotizer programmed the subject's unconscious during the hypnotic state.

If the unconscious is so hidden away by its very nature and is not even accessible to introspection, how is one to learn anything about it? Freud's great contribution was to show that there are some ways of penetrating into the unconscious. Dreams, for example, far from being nonsensical and meaningless, can prove to be a gateway to the unconscious. 'The interpretation of dreams', said Freud, 'is the royal road to a knowledge of the unconscious activities of the mind.'[5] In our dreams, taught Freud, the repressed experiences, the unresolved conflicts and the unfulfilled wishes of the past day are free to come to the preconscious level, but they do so in disguise, translating themselves into symbolic forms, often of the weirdest kinds. Freud taught that the dream has two contents. There is the *manifest* content, which the subject remembers on waking. There is the *latent* content, which it is the task of the analyst to uncover, for it holds the key to the purpose and meaning of the dream, and brings into the open the particular conflict, which is troubling the unconscious sphere of the psyche.

On the basis of his practical experience of penetrating into the unconscious by such methods, Freud constructed a model for the understanding of the human personality. It consists of three components – the *Id*, the *Ego* and the *Super-Ego*. The Id is the oldest and most primitive of the mental provinces and the most inaccessible part of our personality. It is thing-like rather than personal. It is in direct physical contact with the bodily instincts of sex and hunger and gives mental expression to these basic needs. It is motivated by the pleasure principle, i.e., the desire to see these instinctual drives satisfied. To this end it is irrational and quite amoral. The Id contains everything which is innate, i.e., physically inherited; it has no direct relations with the external world.

The Ego is that part of the psyche (originally wholly Id) which, according to Freud, has come under the influence of the external world and, as a result, has developed into an entity distinguishable from the Id. The Ego has been principally shaped by the individual's own experience. It is the organized part of the Id, assuming conscious control of voluntary movement and having the task of self-preservation. It stores up experiences in the memory, responds to external stimuli and keeps the instinctual claims of the Id in check. The processes in the Ego may become conscious but are mainly located in the preconscious. The Ego has to do with what we call reason and reality while the Id generates unbridled passions. The Ego is organized and strives for integration, whereas the Id is a seething chaos. Unconscious processes in the Id may be raised to the preconscious level and incorporated in the Ego, while preconscious material in the Ego may be repressed and shifted back into the Id. The pleasure that the Ego thus generates would be at a deferred and more mature level than that of the Id. Freud preferred to say that the Ego replaced the impulsive pleasure principle of the Id with the *reality principle*, in that the Ego takes consciously into consideration the conditions imposed by the external world.

In the course of personal development a third psychical component emerges, which Freud called the Super-Ego. It is derived from the influence of parents, teachers and the whole social and cultural tradition which is mediated to the individual through men. (Here we have the psychological explanation of the way in which the moral forces of a society transcend its own members, as Durkheim insisted.) The Super-Ego internalizes and perpetuates the moral imperative of the parents in particular and of society in general. It sets moral standards and ideals. The Super-Ego has long been known popularly as the 'conscience'.

The Super-Ego stands over the Ego as a kind of critic or censor and if it is developed to an abnormal degree has the power to inhibit the functioning of the Ego and make a person neurotic. The Ego has the function of mediating between the amoral drives in the Id and hypermoral dictates of the Super-Ego. Where the conflict becomes too painful, or the Ego becomes overpowered by either the Id or the Super-Ego, the person becomes neurotic or, in extreme cases, psychotic, rigidly resorting to various defence mechanisms, such as regression, fantasy, projection and displacement.

The complex human psyche, as Freud came to describe it, has extraordinary creative ability. This clearly manifests itself when the cortical control is released by the artificial effect of drugs or in sleep. It is well exemplified by the quality of the poetry which S. T. Coleridge is said to have composed while under the influence of opium. Another fascinating example is related by Freud concerning the composer Tartini (1692-1770). He is said to have had a dream in which he sold his soul to the Devil, who thereupon seized a violin and played a sonata of exquisite beauty. When the composer awoke he at once wrote down what he could recollect of it and the result was his famous 'Trillo del Diavolo'.[6]

Even though Freud's theories and concepts have been challenged and in part rejected by later psychoanalysts, some of his own disciples making a variety of modifications, the fact remains that Freud blazed a new trail in our understanding of the inner life of man and one which has far-reaching consequences for religion. 'The consequences and implications of modern psychology', writes van de Pol, 'have not yet reached the general public and have yet to cause a shock in the circles of conventional Christianity.'[7]

The chief reason for this is that just as the physical

sciences discovered natural explanations for phenomena in the external world, to explain which man had previously found it necessary to resort to supernatural causes, so Freud, by drawing attention to this hidden area of the human psyche, now offered natural explanations for experiences which had traditionally been attributed to divine causes. While this fact does not, by itself, make the former explanations invalid (for some may argue, as they have done with the rise of other natural explanations, that this is simply the way in which God operates) nevertheless it has greatly weakened the power of the former explanations to win conviction.

Let us now look at some of the ways in which depth psychology has affected what was commonly thought to be religious experience. When man had strange and disturbing dreams, when he heard voices which clearly came from no external human source, when he experienced sudden flashes of insight which he had not reached by conscious reasoning, when men felt themselves suddenly possessed by spiritual forces, when men experienced sudden conversion or ecstatic trances, etc., they took it to be certain evidence of the influence of supernatural forces upon them; there may now be a quite natural explanation in every case. Man, according to depth psychology, has a much more complex psyche than he previously thought. The forces bearing down upon his Ego need no longer be attributed to God, the Holy Spirit or the Devil. They may come from his Super-Ego (which embodies the impact of society) or from his Id (which hides his innate impulses). Thus, to take a few specific examples, the Christian's experience of temptation, Luther's encounter with the Devil, Paul's experience on the Damascus road may all admit of natural explanations.

It is easier for people influenced by the Christian tradition to look at this problem more objectively by turning to another religion, such as Islam. Muhammad is reputed to have received the Qur'an, Sura by Sura, by divine revelation through the medium of angels. In most of it God speaks in the first person. Muhammad appears to have received much of this material while in a trance-like state and, according to tradition, was utterly bewildered by it in the early stages. He and all later Muslims had very good reason to believe that divine revelation was the only possible explanation of how this material should have come into the mind of an illiterate Arab. Depth psychology has not invalidated the Muslim explanation but it has made possible an alternative explanation which, in the context of the modern world, will strike most non-Muslims at least as the more likely one. The material in the Qur'an reflects beliefs, narratives and biblical allusions, all of which could readily have come to the conscious attention of a merchant Arab of the seventh century AD, who had an enquiring mind and an intensely sincere personality. These influences entered Muhammad's mind from the cultural traditions around him. The high poetic quality of the form in which the utterances eventually came forth from him, under conditions of ecstasy, is perfectly consistent with the workings of the human psyche, as Freud has enabled us to see it. Previously, one either had to acknowledge the divine source of the Qur'an or accuse Muhammad of being an impostor. The natural explanation provided by depth psychology resolves this dilemma.

All people who remember at least some of their dreams already possess first-hand confirmation of the creative power of the psyche below the conscious level. Thus we have, in this common experience, some evidence for regarding the subconscious as a fertile seedbed for the vividly picturesque imagery (winged angels, horned devils, hellish tortures), for the myths of the other-world (such as journeys to heaven and risings from the dead) and for the complex symbolism of, say, the Book of Revelation, all of which have constituted such an important part of most traditional religion. Indeed some later psychoanalysts have become experts in the study of ancient mythology, finding it to be closely related to the continuing dream experiences of the human species. Feuerbach and Durkheim, each in their own way, produced natural theories for the origin of religious beliefs. Freud opened up still another possible source, which supplements and clarifies the earlier ones.

A further way in which depth psychology has provided natural explanations for 'religious experience' is in the moral sphere. People are often acutely aware of an intense moral struggle going on inside them. Paul could not have described it more lucidly than in his classic statement in Romans 7 – 'I do not understand my own actions. For I do not do what I want, but I do the very thing I hate'. Men have been justifiably puzzled to know whom their true self has been struggling with. Paul concluded, 'it is no longer I that do it, but sin which dwells within me'. Others have concluded they were struggling with the power of the Devil within. Paul was perhaps not far from the Freudian explanation, if we equate his term 'flesh' with Freud's Id. Similarly, when people have found a sudden release from bondage to a habit which tormented them, they have concluded they were saved by divine grace – by the invasion, that is, of divine power from without. In Freudian terms it would mean, however, simply that a deep-seated conflict had become resolved, thus restoring to the Ego the peace and freedom it sought.

There are still further moral implications. So long as the psyche could be wholly identified with the conscious self, a person could be assumed to bear complete responsibility for his actions good or bad. In the light of depth psychology the situation is no longer as simple as that. Praise and blame can no longer be apportioned in the former simplistic way. If it is true that the amoral forces of the Id or the overpowering influence of the Super-Ego play an important, but unseen, role in the decision-making process, to what extent is the Ego to be held responsible for all of his decisions and actions? If a compulsive do-gooder is being unduly motivated by an over-active Super-Ego, is he such a saint as he may appear on the surface? Moral issues are thus raised, which we need not attempt to solve here. But we should note how often in a court of law the report of a psychiatrist is nowadays called for, in order to enable the court to apportion responsibility and blame with more justice.

We have now sketched some of the ways in which depth psychology has threatened the traditional forms of religion. Freud himself came to the unequivocal conclusion that religion is an illusion. (Incidentally he accused philosophy also of clinging to an illusion,[8] but since, in his view, philosophy interested only a tiny group of individuals it had but little influence on mankind whereas religion was a tremendous force and could do much harm.) He conceded that religion had played an important role in the past, especially in building up a world-view of incomparable consistency and coherence, but this world-view he saw to be progressively dissolving under the influence of modern science and it had been left to psychoanalysis to show how empty and unsatisfying it had become.

It must be remembered that Freud was using the term religion in a somewhat narrow and (in our view) inadequate way. He defined it as 'certain dogmas, assertions about facts and conditions of external (or internal) reality, which tell one something that one has not oneself discovered and which claim that one should give them credence'.[9] He maintained that psychoanalysis could now satisfactorily explain not only the origin of these beliefs in the ancient world but also their perpetuation until the present. The religious image of a Father-God ruling over the world was simply, he said, the projection of the nursery context against the backdrop of the larger world experienced by the adult. A person 'looks back to the memory-image of the overrated father of his childhood, exalts it into a Deity, and brings it into the present and into reality. The emotional strength of this memory-image and the lasting nature of his need for protection are the two supports of his belief in God'.[10]

Freud believed the perpetuation of this basic religious belief in the modern world to be a dangerous illusion for it leads men into a false sense of security. 'It seems not to be true', he said, 'that there is a power in the universe which watches over the well-being of every individual with parental care and brings all his concerns to a happy ending . . . it is by no means the rule that virtue is rewarded and wickedness punished . . . Dark, unfeeling and unloving powers determine human destiny; the system of rewards and punishments, which according to religion, governs the world, seems to have no existence.'[11] Beliefs of this kind Freud regarded as bearing 'the stamp of the times when they originated, the ignorant childhood days of the human race'.[12] To continue to hold such beliefs, at a time when the human race is reaching adulthood, is to be compared with the neurosis of an adult who avoids facing the harsh realities of life by regressing to a childhood state of mind. He said neurosis could be described as a private religious system and religion as a universal obsessional neurosis, 'which the civilized individual must pass through on his way from childhood to maturity'.[12]

It is relatively easy to challenge and dismiss some of the more extravagant aspects of Freud's attack on religion and by applying his own psychoanalytical approach one may suspect that his own upbringing as a nominal Jew in a predominantly Catholic Vienna had not a little to do with the ferocity of his attack. Few are today convinced by his theories of the origin of primitive religion and of the Judaeo-Christian tradition, as they elaborated respectively in his books *Totem and Taboo* and *Moses and Monotheism*. But when all this has been said, there still remains a solid core to the attack of depth psychology on much traditional religion and this cannot be ignored. There would be more widespread support for Freud's claim 'that religious ideas have sprung from the same need as all the other achievements of culture: from the necessity of defending itself against the crushing supremacy of nature'.[13]

Just as in the young science of sociology, the first frontal attack on religion was followed by a more positive appreciation of the function of religion, so we find that post-Freudian psychoanalysts began to look at religion in a more favourable light. This is particularly so with the work of Carl Gustav Jung (1875-1961), who started as a disciple of Freud and made a distinct break with him in 1912. There is a popular impression that Freud was an arch-enemy of religion and Jung was a friend, but this needs to be qualified. Neither affirmed religion to be true in any supernatural sense and Jung did nothing to restore the belief in the divine origin of religion. But, partly because they set out from different conceptions of religion, they arrived at different conclusions. Freud had been primarily criticizing the Judaeo-Christian tradition he had known in Vienna. Jung looked at religion more broadly, in a way which was applicable to the non-theistic traditions as well. Freud's critique of the traditional image of God made from the standpoint of a humanistic ethic could almost be termed 'religious', in that it brought him closer to the company of the ancient Israelite prophets. Jung, on the other hand, was in danger of raising the unconscious into a religious phenomenon and making it the human replacement for the lost God.

Jung agreed with Freud that the complexity of the psyche is due to the presence of the unconscious. Both agreed that it is no longer possible to regard the human mind at birth as a *tabula rasa,* as Locke had earlier done. But whereas Freud saw it filled with biological urges, Jung went further and claimed that the unconscious is both a depository of past human propensities and also 'full of germs of future psychic situations and ideas'. As a result 'completely new thoughts and creative ideas can also present themselves from the unconscious – thoughts and ideas that have never been conscious before. They grow up from the dark depths of the mind like a lotus and form a most important part of the subliminal psyche'.[14] (We have already noted examples of this psychic creativity in the references above to Coleridge, Tartini and Muhammad.)

This does not mean that the mind of the new-born infant contains ideas, which are transmitted from past generations. Jung noted that the images seen in dreams are much more vivid and picturesque than those witnessed in waking life and these are strikingly analogous not only to those found in the dreams of people from other cultures, but also to those described in ancient mythology. This led him to postulate the existence of what he called archetypes. These are aptitudes 'which direct all fantasy activity into its appointed paths and in this way produce, in the fantasy-images of children's dreams as well as in the delusions of schizophrenia, astonishing mythological parallels such as can also be found, though in lesser degree, in the dreams of normal persons and neurotics. It is not therefore, a question of inherited *ideas* but of inherited possibilities of ideas.'[15] Nietzsche, incidentally, had once asserted that in dreams some primeval relic of humanity is at work which we can scarcely reach any longer by a direct path. To borrow a term from computer science, we could say that the embryonic psyche of an infant is already 'programmed' with what Jung called 'archetypes'.

Now it is reasonable to suppose that just as the human physical body is a museum of its long evolutionary past (e.g., the appendix and the remains of a tail) so the psyche, being housed and based in the physical organ of the brain, also (through the Id) inherits from the distant past certain dispositions or aptitudes. Some parallel confirmation of this has more recently been provided by the study of how the young child acquires language. It was once thought to depend upon the simple mechanism of repetition. It has now been shown that this by itself is not nearly adequate to acount for the speed with which language is acquired in the early stages. The young child already possesses an unexpected capacity for language learning.

The archetypes, according to Jung, represent the basic outlines of psychic activity which the human being inherits from the distant past and which channel in a broad way the directions to be followed by the embryonic psyche. 'They form the structural dominants of the psyche in general.'[16] They did 'not ever come into existence as a phenomenon of organic life, but entered into the picture with life itself'.[16]

Jung contended that all the most powerful human ideas men have ever had go back to archetypes and that this is particularly true of religious ideas.[17] He said, 'The essential content of all mythologies and all religions and all isms is archetypal'.[18] Man in fact can no more cut loose from these than he can jump out of his body or grow four arms. But at every new stage of development through which human civilization passes, he must find a new and appropriate way of relating the life of the past which still exists in him, with the life of the present.[19]

The discovery and exploration of the unconscious area of the human psyche constitutes the third Copernican revolution by which empirical science has led modern man into a new religious situation so far as his self-understanding is concerned. Further, various contentions of Strauss, Feuerbach, Darwin, Durkheim, Freud, Jung and Eliade all become interconnected at this point. Darwin opened our eyes to the lowly origins and very long history of the human species. Feuerbach recognized the role of the human imagination in the way man fashions his gods. Strauss saw the positive significance of myth. Durkheim emphasized the social origins of the human condition and of the latter's expression in religious belief and practice. Eliade maintained that society can never completely dispense with myth. Freud showed how the external social pressures are internalized in the hidden depths of the psyche. Jung contended that the archetypes or primordial images form a 'collective unconscious', which is a vast reservoir of the images and symbols (in their embryonic form) by which man relates himself to his world.

There has been a tendency in the post-Enlightenment period for some to agree that man has entered into quite a new cultural era but to see it as one marked by the shedding of all religion as the empirical sciences penetrated and dissolved one mystery after another. It is true that many of the former natural phenomena which constituted a mystery to man are no longer felt to be so. For the most part these mysteries were external to him – in nature, or up in the heavens. More recently, mystery has been reappearing, but in new locations. Not only is there the mystery of a now much vaster universe in both space and time, but there is the mystery within man himself, within his own unplumbed depths.

Prior to the Enlightenment Western man felt he could speak quite confidently about a spiritual world, about God the Creator Spirit and about his own spiritual entity, the soul. When these first came to be questioned, during and after the Enlightenment, the solution was thought by some to be simply a matter of discarding the superstitions of former ages. Men of the future would live by facts and not by myths. More recently we have come to appreciate how much man needs symbols and myths by which to live. Man is a symbol-making creature. Some of his symbols he consciously creates, as in the sciences. Some of them, as in man's religious experience, rise out of his unconscious.

But while man needs symbols just as much as he did before, there is nevertheless an important difference in the post-Enlightenment age. 'The fact is that in former times men did not reflect upon their symbols', said Jung, 'they lived them and were unconsciously animated by their meaning.'[20] Today we do reflect on our symbols. We recognize the symbolic character of such words as 'spirit', 'God', 'soul'. We even know something of the way in which the symbols come to birth within the human psyche. The fact that they have a natural origin rather than a supernatural one does not in itself mean that we can dispense with symbols and myths.

Yet neither can man return to the blissful innocence of his pre-Enlightenment condition. Like Adam and Eve of old, man's eyes have been opened and he knows himself and his world as he did not know them before. The former mysteries may have vanished but new enigmas have appeared to take their place. How can one relate oneself to the ultimate issues of human existence by means of symbols when one knows them to be symbols? Modern man has not been delivered from the ultimate mystery but has been placed on a different plane of enquiry within which to respond to it. Modern man's situation holds open many new possibilities but is also pregnant with danger. 'Modern man does not understand how much his "rationalism" (which destroyed his capacity to respond to numinous symbols and ideas) has put him at the mercy of the psychic "underworld" ', wrote Jung. 'He has freed himself from "superstition" (or so he believes) but in the process he has lost his spiritual values to a positively dangerous degree. His moral and spiritual tradition has distintegrated, and he is now paying the price for this break-up in world-wide disorientation and dissociation.'[21]

It is often remarked that whereas a person formerly went to the priest for spiritual healing, he now turns to the psychiatrist for mental health. Even the terms are similar. The ecclesiastical term 'curate' simply referred originally to one who was in charge of the 'cure of souls'. But that is just what is meant literally by the term 'psychiatry'. It is not surprising that in recent years there has been an identity crisis in the priesthood and the ordained ministry of the Churches. It is no longer as clear as it used to be just what the role of the professional clergyman really is. It is also very noticeable that in an attempt to rediscover the genuine role of Christian ministry there has been a distinct shift of emphasis in the direction towards counselling, of a kind which makes much use of the insights provided by depth psychology.

Of all the sciences, psychology as the new science of the soul has most seriously undermined the traditional interpretation of man's religious experience. But to compensate, it has also, perhaps, opened more alternative doors to enable man to re-appraise his religious nature and the fact that he is a creature whose very humanity depends upon the symbols and myths by which he lives.

There is a further difficulty, however. Not only has Western man's confidence in his traditional religious symbols and in the viability of his religious experiences been undermined by the philosophy, science and psychology which have emerged from within Western culture, but he has been forced to acknowledge in a way which has never been so acute since the first four centuries, that in other large areas of the world there have been religious traditions quite different from his own, which, on the face of it, have long proved acceptable alternatives. How is he to reconcile this with the long tradition that the Judaeo-Christian tradition alone possesses the truth? To this further cause for unsettlement we must now turn.

CHAPTER 12

FROM ABSOLUTISM TO RELATIVISM IN A PLURALISTIC WORLD

❖

It was noted in Chapter 2 that one of the special features of a post-Axial form of religion has been its capacity to assume an identity of its own, independent of the ethnic ties of its place of origin. This enabled it to spread, crossing over ethnic and cultural boundaries. Buddhism, Christianity and Islam exemplify this feature the most clearly. By the early Middle Ages only those areas geographically remote from either the Middle East or northern India had been left untouched by one of these three. Wherever they spread, they displaced or absorbed the pre-Axial forms of religions which they encountered. Each of them claimed to be the final and absolute truth for all people, irrespective of colour, class, race or sex. It was *the* truth, which was believed to supersede all the beliefs of pre-Axial religion. Because all three made absolute claims, however, they could not readily displace or absorb each other. Indeed the extent to which they penetrated successfully into one another's territory was minimal. Further, the fact that Buddhism did not displace or absorb Hinduism in India, or Confucianism and Taoism in China, shows perhaps that these also were post-Axial in character, even though less missionary. In the same way Judaism could not be absorbed by either Christianity or Islam.

The capacity to spread and convert, which we find in

these three missionary religions, served to increase the confidence which their religious practitioners had in their respective faiths. Christianity established a more or less unified world of its own in the West (Christendom), Islam established its own world (Dar al-islam)[1] from Spain to India and Buddhism penetrated the whole of the Orient. Of these three, Western Christianity went furthest in the direction of establishing a complete and almost self-contained world. For all practical purposes it was as if, to Christians, the rest of the world did not exist. Christians became completely convinced of the absolute truth of their religion. This is why they could barely tolerate the presence of Jews within Christendom. Their attitude towards such non-Christians as they knew about was one of self-confidence and condescension. This is succinctly illustrated in the will of Robert Boyle, the father of modern chemistry, who, at his death in 1691, left a trust fund to provide annual lectures 'proving the Christian religion against notorious Infidels, to wit, Atheists, Theists [*sic*], Pagans, Jews, and Mohametans'.

But to what extent was this confidence in the absolute truth of Christianity simply a cloak for the natural confidence one feels in what is familiar and known? Once any post-Axial religion, including Christianity, became thoroughly integrated with the total culture of a specific area (and this has usually meant some sort of synthesis with the pre-Axial religion it encountered), then, the longer it remained confined to the same area, the more it tended to assume the ethnic character of pre-Axial religion. That is why, in the modern missionary expansion we shall presently refer to, it has often been difficult to distinguish between Westernization and Christianization. The bearers of Western culture to the non-Western world chauvinistically assumed the superiority of their own culture to the 'foreign' cultures they encountered. Was their culture superior because it was grounded in Christianity (Christian missionaries certainly believed it to be so) or was Christianity believed to be the final truth, simply because Westerners had for so long been moulded in it? For what one has been shaped by often appears to be self-evidently true. We are now to examine still another way in which the advent of modernity has challenged traditional Christianity.

The rise of the modern world (today becoming a global village) brought an end to the long period of geographical isolation which Western Christendom had experienced and to the spiritual security it provided. Just as the first two Copernican revolutions, already referred to, vastly expanded Western man's view of cosmic space and cosmic time, so the successful voyages of the early explorers, such as Vasco da Gama, Columbus, Abel Tasman and James Cook, effectively brought within the horizon of Western man first-hand knowledge of other human cultures, some of them as sophisticated as his own. Over the last 500 years, but particularly during this century, Western man has been forced to come to terms with the fact that Christianity is only one of several post-Axial religious traditions.

The fact of the globe's religious pluralism caused Western man, at least as early as the Enlightenment, to search for a basic, simple and natural religion, which could be conceived as being a primal religion which underlies all the diverse forms of religion. Rousseau painted a rosy picture of the simple but noble savage. Hume, who (as we have seen above) may be considered the forerunner, if not the founder, of the modern disciplined study of religion, showed a growing, if limited, knowledge of the world's religions in his *Natural History of Religion*. However inadequate his observations may appear to be today, he was already raising what was to be an increasingly critical problem and that is how the absolute claims of Christianity are to be related to the diverse and rich religious experience of man outside the Judaeo-Christian stream.

Hegel was concerned with this problem from the outset and wrestled with it at much greater depth than did Hume or any of the deists. He was the first to speak of Christianity as the Absolute religion, a term which conceded some value in the other religions but which claimed, nevertheless, that in the course of cultural evolution in all its complex diversity, Christianity was to be seen as the goal and crowning achievement of all man's religious search and aspirations.

Yet Hegel was already stepping outside the limits of the orthodox Christian viewpoint. The vast majority of traditional Christians, on the other hand, were not yet aware of the coming problem. Still completely confident in the superiority and absolute truth of Christianity, they saw the opening up of the new world as a divinely-given opportunity for the implantation of the true faith in virgin soil. Christian missionary expansion had begun with the Portuguese and Spanish Catholics as early as the sixteenth century and was particularly successful in Central and South America. The nineteenth century brought the most striking period of Christian expansion, particularly for Protestantism. Latourette, therefore, devoted to it three of his seven volumes on *The History of the Expansion of Christianity*. In 1814 there were only a few hundred Protestant missionaries in overseas countries; a century later there were 22,000. So successful was the missionary expansion thought to be that at the beginning of the twentieth century the American Methodist layman John R. Mott (1865-1955) was calling for the 'The Evangelization of the World in this Generation'. To most Western churchmen Hinduism, Buddhism, Confucianism and Islam were just as pagan as the tribal religion of Melanesian cannibals, and the finality of the truth of Christianity was never held to be in any real doubt.

Only a few saw the matter differently. One of these was

Frederick Denison Maurice (1805-72), a liberal Anglican theologian.[2] When he delivered the Boyle lectures for 1847 (note their above-mentioned purpose!), he made a plea for Christians to study the non-Christian religions with a view to acknowledging their positive values. He argued that since the Bible teaches that 'God has not left himself without witness' and that he raises up unexpected servants for the performance of his will, Christians should look for the way in which non-Christian faiths already embody some elements of the Christian revelation. He suggested, for example, that the rise of Islam should perhaps be seen as an example of divine judgment on the debasement of Christianity that had occurred by Muhammad's time. Other liberal Christian leaders, like Frederick Temple in *Essays and Reviews*,[3] expounded the Hegelian approach of seeing the non-Christian religions as being partially true, rather than false, on the grounds that they were divinely-inspired human searches for that fullness of truth which had been revealed only in Christianity. J. R. Illingworth wrote in *Lux Mundi*, 'The pre-Christian religions were the age-long prayer. The Incarnation was the answer . . . In short, the history of the pre-Christian religion is like that of pre-Christian philosophy, a long preparation for the Gospel'.[4]

During the latter half of the nineteenth century a start was made with the serious and objective study of the sophisticated cultures of India and China; several University Chairs in the History of Religion and the Comparative Study of Religion were established, particularly among the colonizing nations of Europe. These moves did not receive much encouragement from churchmen, however, and were often looked upon with suspicion by the theological and biblical scholars of divinity faculties. Their concern is reflected in the witticism attributed to Cardinal Newman, 'The study of comparative religion makes one comparatively religious'. It was feared (perhaps justifiably so) that an appreciative understanding of other religious traditions, particularly post-Axial ones, could have the effect of undermining conviction in the absolute truth of the Christian faith.

Increased acquaintance with other religions did not necessarily mean that Christians would be tempted to convert (say) to Islam, Buddhism or Hinduism. (In the twentieth century, however, a small but significant number of Westerners *have* embraced a faith of Oriental origin.) The threat being posed to Christianity by a greater knowledge of non-Christian religions was rather seen to be this. When one looks at a religious tradition such as Buddhism or Islam from the outside, one can readily appreciate the historical, sociological, economic and geographical factors which helped to determine its origin, its character and its subsequent development. The Christian is then likely to turn back to his own tradition and view it in a new light. He may find in Christianity also many of the human and this-worldly factors which are to him so clearly evident in the other religions. Christianity is then seen to be one religion among others, instead of being wholly unique. What the Christian had long believed to be the final, absolute and divinely revealed truth comes to be seen only as relative, partial and of largely human origin, even if still superior in some respects to the non-Christian faiths. The growing awareness of the non-Christian religions has proved to be a threat to Christianity, therefore, not because Christians were tempted to convert to a foreign faith, but because it caused them to see Christianity increasingly as an historically-conditioned phenomenon like the others, and hence lacking in final authority. The knowledge of man's past religious diversity, which modernity brought to the Western world, consequently had the effect of supplementing those other factors which, as we have seen in earlier chapters, were already causing the erosion of confidence in traditional Christianity.

The majority of churchmen, increasingly caught up in the vision of the modern missionary enterprise, and still completely confident in the finality of Christian truth, had not yet seen in what way the non-Christian religions could constitute a threat. This fact was illustrated by the mood present in the Parliament of the World Religions held at Chicago in 1893. Representatives of the major non-Christian religions were encouraged to be present at what was ostensibly an occasion for promoting mutual goodwill and understanding, but it turned out to be a patronizing display of Christian chauvinism. When, in the closing session, Swami Vivekananda (1863-1902) made a plea that henceforth no religion should attempt to make converts from the others, his remark struck the predominantly Christian audience as so odd that it was greeted with applause from only one person.

Of those churchmen who did see how necessary it was to explore the significance of Christianity's encounter with the non-Christian faiths, perhaps the most important was the Lutheran theologian Ernst Troeltsch (1865-1923). From an early age, he later confessed,[5] he found himself caught up in a conflict between his historical education on the one hand and, on the other, with the theological education, to which he had been led out of a desire to find a viable and meaningful religious position on the main issues of life. Out of this conflict he came to the conclusion that Christianity was destined to decline into stagnant obscurantism unless it faced up to the increasing historical consciousness which was at that time undermining its claims to be the final and absolute truth.

Troeltsch set himself the task of trying to resolve this conflict in his book *The Absoluteness of Christianity and the History of Religions* (1901). He set out from what was to him the self-evident premise that since the eighteenth century the modern world had been developing a new kind of culture, uniquely different from the ancient and medieval cultures by reason of the new awareness of history, which had resulted from the expansion of 'men's horizons both backward into the past and laterally across the entire breadth of the present'.[6] As a result of this it was coming to be realized that it was the ebb and flow of historical change, rather than supernatural causes, which had been 'the matrix out of which all world views took shape'.[6] What had once, within each culture, been taken to be absolute, was now seen to be relative to the historical flow of events and circumstances. The claims of Christianity also, like those of the other great religious movements, had been caught up in this maelstrom of historical relativism.

How could Christianity defend itself against this threat of historicism (as Troeltsch called it)? It had been common to make appeal to miracles, particularly the miracle of the Incarnation, as evidence of the truth of Christianity. The trouble is that other religions claim their miracles also. The Muslim, for example, sees the revelation of the Qur'an to Muhammad as a self-authenticating miracle. There is no way in which the historian, *per se*, can 'believe the Christian miracles and deny the non-Christian'.[7] In any case, Hume had already shown that miracles, if understood as violations of the laws of nature, could not be defended by reason but must be accepted on faith. Therefore they could not be appealed to in any sense to 'prove' the faith. Further, Strauss had already effectively shown that the crucial affirmations of Christianity were expressed in the language of myth rather than in historical testimony.

So Troeltsch turned to examine, in much greater depth, the alternative defence of the finality of Christianity which had been pioneered by Hegel. This sets out, as we have seen, from the conviction that religion in essence is the self-realization of the divine Spirit in human history. There can therefore be only one true religion, but it is latent in all the historical forms of religion. In Christianity, according to Hegel, this essence of religion had reached its full, final and absolute form. Troeltsch showed that the Hegelian approach to the problem was unsatisfactory. In the first place, the historian of religion can in no way isolate and define this universal principle or essence of religion; what Hegel had taken to be this essence turned out to be merely a watered-down version of Christianity, in much the same way as the natural religion of the deists had been a reduction of Christianity. What is more, the historian cannot even find in Christianity an absolute, unchangeable and permanent essence, of which the various Christian forms are the manifestation. (This latter fact has been demonstrated many times in the twentieth century, as different groups of Christians have come into irresolvable conflict with each other in their respective claims as to what constitutes the *sine qua non* of Christianity.) There is no universally acceptable way of separating the essence of Christianity from the cultural dress in which it has become clothed, i.e., in separating the kernel from the husk. As Troeltsch said, 'the actual absoluteness of the kernel always absolutizes the husk as well, while the actual relativity of the husk always relativizes the kernel in turn'.[8]

Troeltsch was forced to concede, somewhat reluctantly perhaps, that in the light of modern historical consciousness the claim of Christianity to be the true and final form of the essence of religion was just as vulnerable as were non-Christian claims. Each of the great religions is found by the historian to be a unique movement, shaped and defined by the historical circumstances through which it lives. 'History is no place for "absolute religions" or "absolute personalities" ', he said.[9] 'The Christian religion is in every moment of its history a purely historical phenomenon, subject to all the limitations to which any individual historical phenomenon is exposed, just like the other great religions.'[10] The modern historical study of religions has shown that Christianity, just as much as all other religions, is inextricably bound up in the course of human history with many other factors, sociological, economic, geographical, ideological, etc., each of them exerting an influence in their own place and time.

Yet Troeltsch was still reluctant to surrender to historical relativism all the truth claims of Christianity. He tried to find a solution by claiming that 'Christianity is the pinnacle of all religious development thus far and the basis and presupposition for every distinct and meaningful development in man's religious life in the future. There is no probability that it will ever be surpassed or cut off from its historical foundations as far as our historical vision can reach'.[11] In the context of the apparent Christianization of the globe then taking place, this claim may have seemed self-evident to all Christians and even a few Orientals. Three-quarters of a century later it is far from self-evident. Indeed it exemplifies the very relativism which lay at the heart of the problem. Even Troeltsch conceded that, in making such a claim, one was making a transition from scientific discourse to an affirmation of religious faith.[12]

It is not surprising, therefore, that he later modified his claims still further. His preparation for his classic work, *The Social Teaching of the Christian Churches*, impressed upon him how thoroughly personal and inward is all religious experience, including Christian experience. This means that the various forms which a particular tradition may take, depend very much on the intellectual, social and national conditions within which its adherents live. Troeltsch's further study of Hinduism and Buddhism convinced him that their claims to validity were just as genuine within their respective settings as that of Christianity was in its, that they too were humane and spiritual, making the same inner appeal to their followers that Christianity did to Christians.

Troeltsch set out his modified position in a lecture prepared for delivery at Oxford.[13] Here he conceded that Christianity's 'primary claim to validity is thus the fact that only through it have we become what we are, and that only in it can we preserve the religious forces that we need . . . We cannot live without a religion, yet the only religion that we can endure is Christianity, for Christianity has grown up with us and has become a part of our very being'.[14] Here the subjective, and hence the historically relative character of religious faith is rather surprisingly acknowledged. It means, of course, that while the Christian may remain inwardly convinced of the validity of the Christian faith for himself, it 'does not preclude the possibility that other racial groups, living under entirely different cultural conditions may experience their contact with the Divine Life in quite a different way and may themselves also possess a religion which has grown up with them, and from which they cannot sever themselves so long as they remain what they are'.[15]

The importance of Troeltsch for our present purpose is not that he successfully solved the problem posed by religious pluralism but that his very failure to do so (in spite of his keenest efforts) highlights the gravity of the new situation in which Christianity found itself. Troeltsch was fully aware of this. Even in *The Absoluteness of Christianity* he had warned that the effects of modern historical thinking 'call for a rethinking of every aspect of the religious phenomenon'.[16] In 1923 he went further and said, 'All that is certain is that Christianity is at a critical moment of its further development and that very bold and far-reaching changes are necessary, transcending anything that has yet been achieved by any denomination. I have in this respect become more and more radical and super-denominational whilst at the same time I have come more and more to regard the specific kernel of religion as a unique and independent source of life and power'.[17]

Troeltsch clearly foresaw that if Christianity failed to find a satisfactory solution to the precarious predicament in which historical relativism had placed Christianity along with the non-Christian religions, it would seriously affect the whole missionary enterprise on which the Churches were at that time still enthusiastically engaged. Although the so-called higher religions were likely to supersede the tribal religions, none of them, he believed, had the capacity to displace others of the same order. Troeltsch contended that, in the new global situation in which Christianity found itself, the proper missionary approach (not only for it but for all the higher religions) was not to aim at conversion but at mutual understanding. He believed this would bring spiritual benefit to them all. Only a few were prepared to listen to him at the time, but subsequent history to date has tended to confirm the wisdom of this proposal.

Troeltsch's work appeared at what may now be seen as a critical turning point in the whole Christian enterprise of modern missionary expansion. Indeed his book was followed by a vigorous theological debate. He was regarded by many Christians as an enemy of Christianity. What in fact he had done was simply to bring out into the open, and to enunciate clearly, the way in which the new historical consciousness was already undermining the long unquestioned exclusiveness of Christian claims. From the Enlightenment onwards, of course, there had been increasing criticism of the truth claims of Christianity, but much of the criticism had come from those who no longer regarded themselves as Christians. Troeltsch, however, was speaking as a theologian of some repute, for it was not until 1915 that he moved from his chair of theology at Heidelberg to one of the history of philosophy and civilization at Berlin. It was out of his enquiries as a theologian that Troeltsch had come to the conclusion that, in the new era which had been entered, the absolute claims of Christianity could no longer be defended as valid and the Christian was required to rethink the Christian position and its relation to other religions in the light of the new historical consciousness.

The first signs of such a re-thinking made their appearance in the decision of some American churches to send a commission to the Orient under the chairmanship of Professor W. E. Hocking to study the missionary situation. Their report, *Rethinking Missions, a Laymen's Inquiry after a Hundred Years* (1932), is said to have fallen like a bombshell on the American Churches. It appeared to place Christianity on a more or less equal footing with the religions of the East. Although it still saw a place for the Christian missionary, it regarded his aim, not as the winning of souls for Christ but as that of encouraging with non-Christians a mutual sharing of religious experience. It foresaw, not the wholesale conversion of the East to Christianity, accompanied by the virtual disappearance of the non-Christian religions, but the continued existence of all of them, in a pluralistic situation where they would leaven one another, in preparation for their subsequent consummation in a world faith which drew from them all.

In his own book, *Living Religions and a World Faith,* Hocking affirmed the need for some unifying world faith in the new global situation, but believed that Christianity in its traditional form was not yet ready to serve in that capacity. He described three ways in which the new world faith might manifest itself. The first was by 'Radical Displacement'. This had been the policy of the Christian missionary movement. It meant that the Oriental had to choose between Christianity and his own traditional religion. Hocking believed the interests of divine truth were not served by such an either-or choice and the time had come for Christians to discard this policy. The second way he called 'Synthesis'. He had considerable sympathy with this approach, since it allowed for the preservation and fusion of the values of the East with those of the West. But in the end he rejected it because it smacked of compromise and over-accommodation. The third way, and the one which Hocking favoured, was what he called 'Reconception'. It meant that each religion would think through its own heritage afresh, not alone but in dialogue with the practitioners of other religions and in the light of the spiritual values the others embodied. Hocking himself was confident that, instead of diminishing the figure of Christ, this procedure would enhance it and that when the new global faith eventually emerged, it would still basically consist of the worship of the God and Father of Jesus Christ.

Needless to say there was strong Christian reaction to *Rethinking Missions* and to Hocking's call for a new global faith. It was condemned by the Dutch missiologist, Hendrik Kraemer (1880-1965), as a 'total distortion of the Christian message, which would lead to the suicide of missions and an annulment of the Christian faith'.[18] An international missionary conference was called together at Tambaram, India, in 1938 and, for this, Kraemer was invited to write the preparatory study, *The Christian Message in a Non-Christian World*. He conceded that the religion of mankind was passing through a period of transition and that this called for a fundamental re-orientation of the Church. He insisted, however, that, in the new forms of religious encounter then taking place, it was absolutely essential for Christians to continue to recognize the unique and exclusive character of the divinely-revealed Christian message and to keep it sharply differentiated at all points from whatever spiritual and moral values were, quite admittedly, to be found in the non-Christian religions. Kraemer continued to champion this cause for the next 25 years.

While many Christians found Kraemer's firmness very

encouraging, in view of whatever doubts they were beginning to entertain, the Tambaram conference by no means unanimously supported him. Already there were Asian Christians from India and China who were not only wanting to distinguish between Christianity and the Western forms of culture in which it had been long integrated, but they sought the freedom to integrate Christianity with their own indigenous cultures.[19] They argued, for example, that the Vedas or Chinese Classics, respectively, were for them a more appropriate spiritual preparation for the proclamation of Christ than were the Jewish Scriptures of the Old Testament. Kraemer was adamant that the revelation of God in Christ was absolutely unique and this meant that the witness of the prophets and Apostles contained in the Bible place the latter in an altogether different class from the Holy Scriptures of all other religions.

Kraemer, and indeed much of the Protestant world, received considerable support from Karl Barth (1886-1968), the most influential Protestant theologian of the day. Barth's solution to the problem of how to defend the finality of the Christian Gospel against the eroding effects of historical relativism was simple, but perhaps more ingenious than successful. Barth set out from the Christian assertion that, in Jesus Christ (as testified to in the Bible and in the Church), sinful man encounters divine revelation, i.e., God's self-offering and self-manifestation. The Christian is the one who responds to this in faith and obedience. He may reflect upon it (this is the task of Christian theology) but if he questions it, or attempts to defend it by appeal to any external criterion (as Troeltsch had done), he is already moving out of faith into unbelief.

Barth drew a very sharp distinction between revelation and religion; revelation demands faith but religion is an expression of unbelief, a form of idolatry, in that it arises out of man's search for God, man's attempt to achieve his own salvation. It is in the light of the revelation of God in Jesus Christ that all religions are judged to be unbelief. Christianity also, in so far as it has historically taken the form of one religion among others, stands under the same judgment. No religion is true, not even the Christian religion; but religion can become true, wherever men listen to the divine revelation in Jesus Christ. Barth's solution, therefore, to the question Troeltsch had raised was to assert in effect that it was not a proper question for a Christian to ask. To the non-Christian and to the external observer, it would appear that Barth doggedly refused to acknowledge that any real problem had been raised for the Christian, either by historical relativism, or by the presence of the great non-Christian religions within the new global horizon.[20]

Through the middle decades of the twentieth century the influence of Barth was strong and widespread. H. Richard Niebuhr once spoke of it as the 'the Barthian captivity of the history of modern Christian thought'. When the Barthian influence began to wane, from the sixties onwards, the problem originally posed by Troeltsch was still there, waiting to be faced afresh. In the meantime the Christian missionary enterprise had been undergoing quite drastic shifts of emphasis. The direct implantation of Western forms of Christianity was giving way increasingly to the rise of new, indigenous forms of Christianity in Asian countries. Western Christian missionaries had been forced out of mainland China altogether, leaving the Christian seed implanted there to develop its own most appropriate forms of life. By way of contrast, religious movements of Eastern origin have now entered the so-called Christian West and though their impact is as yet very small in numbers, they have nevertheless gained a foothold and may be seen, in relation to Christianity, as counter-missionary movements. Of even more significance, we find that, for sociological reasons rather than religious ones, quite largish Muslim, Hindu and Sikh communities are now permanently domiciled in Western countries such as Britain. The rapid expansion of Christianity, so clearly hoped for at the beginning of this century, appears now to have ground virtually to a halt and, at the home base, may even be in retreat. The respective prognoses of both Troeltsch and Hocking now seem to be somewhat closer to the way modern religious encounter is taking place than are the hopes of either Mott or Kraemer.

The mood of Christian contact with non-Christian, both in the West and in the East, has changed from one which aims at complete conversion, to one of open dialogue and sharing in an atmosphere of mutual respect.

After a religious consultation with Hindu, Buddhist, Muslim, Jewish and Roman Catholic colleagues in Manila, in 1960, even Kraemer, while not wishing to depart from his former position, nevertheless confessed that it had become clear to him 'that in our world of today, where the inward and spiritual life of men will have to find entirely new forms of expression now that the old ones are disintegrating or proving themselves inadequate, for all the major religions the paramount problems are the same'[21] and that 'one of the most fruitful forms of genuine communication between the religions would be if we were to steep ourselves in one another's problems and be ready to serve one another in word and deed'.[21]

The attitude of the Roman Catholic Church to the non-Christian religions has also changed significantly as a result of the Council Vatican II. In its 'Declaration on the Relation of the Church to non-Christian Religions' Vatican II declared, for example, 'The Catholic Church rejects nothing of what is true and holy in these religions . . . The Church, therefore, urges her sons to enter with prudence and charity into discussions and collaboration with members of other religions. Let Christians, while witnessing to their own faith and way of life, acknowledge, preserve and encourage the spiritual and moral truths found among non-Christians, also their social life and culture'.[22] None of these drastic changes in attitude could have been foreseen in the opening decades of this century.

All of this is in strong contrast with the mood which prevailed in the growing missionary movement of the nineteenth century, when Christians were so convinced of the truth of the Christian message that they regarded it as self-authenticating. They believed it would be sufficient simply to proclaim the Gospel message and to translate the divinely-given Bible into the local vernacular and these would be readily welcomed. It is true that there were some examples of mass conversion, but these were chiefly in tribal cultures. Among countries where the higher religions prevailed, progress was almost invariably very slow. Of course Christians could still supply reasons. It was due, they said, to the sinful state of man which blinded him to the truth; missionaries must simply persevere with patience and love. It was still believed that when the Christian message was listened to without prejudice, it would so meet the spiritual needs of all men that its truth would be transparent and need no further defence.

Two hundred years of missionary expansion around the globe have not wholly borne out this initial confidence. What can we learn about the post-Axial religions in general and about Christianity in particular from the present situation? We are brought back to the problem which Troeltsch failed to solve. The truth of Christianity may appear self-evident to the person who is already Christian or who has already been at least partly moulded by Western culture. But the truth of Buddhism may appear equally self-evident to the person who is a practising Buddhist or who has already been moulded by Buddhist culture. But if one looks for some external and universally acceptable criterion, such as reason, empirical evidence, or history, by which to justify the truth of one religion against the claims of others, one draws a blank. Each person has his or her own reasons for embracing or retaining a particular religious faith, reasons which those outside of that faith are unlikely to find equally convincing. The Christian Gospel is more likely to win conviction in those areas long permeated by Christianity than elsewhere; by the same token, within the cultural context conditioned by any other of the higher religions (say Buddhism) then its essential message (the four Noble Truths) is more likely than any foreign faith to appear plausible and convincing. In this pluralistic situation religious conviction has come to depend quite largely on the hidden prior cultural conditioning. The acknowledgement of this state of affairs has constituted the threat of historical relativism, since it first came to be recognized.

If inter-faith encounter were the only new factor in the modern religious scene, then we would have a relatively simple case of religious pluralism. The situation is more complex than that. The inter-faith encounter is itself a contributing factor to the more deep-seated process of religious change. What has been happening in the advent of the modern world is that, for the reasons sketched in previous chapters, a new world-view is taking shape, which does have the power to win universal conviction. This has been transported all over the globe in the last 200 years by powerful Westernizing influences. Each culture has been experiencing a growing tension between its own traditional world-view and the new global one which has come out of the West. *This* tension has often been felt more urgently than that which exists between competing religious faiths of the post-Axial type. The suggestion was made as early as the Second World Missionary Conference at Jerusalem in 1928 that, instead of competing with one another, all the higher religions should assist one another in their fight against the common foe of secularism. All this means that each of the great religious traditions is today entering a period of change and testing more critical than any which has been experienced since its time of origin. This applies as much to Christianity as to any of the others, even though it was from within the Christian West that the modern world-view has emerged.

Encounter with one another, and even more with the forces of modernism, does not mean, however, that religions are simply dying. It is true that some are. More correctly, some aspects of traditional religion are fading away. It is also true that religion is showing remarkable vitality, but it is a vitality which is being expressed in ever increasing diversity. Instead of the world being captured and unified by one homogeneous faith, as Hocking believed would be the case, religious pluralism has become the order of the day. The sciences and associated factors are tending to provide a view of the physical world which is substantially shared by all around the globe. But religion, in so far as it is that in which people manifest their ultimate concern and find their sense of fulfilment, is becoming more diversified and individualized. However strongly a person may hold his religious convictions, it is becoming increasingly unrealistic for him to expect that all men will want to share them. He must be content to see them as his personal convictions which he holds for reasons which he, at least, finds personally convincing. Whereas in the past, religions can now be seen to have been relative to the tribe, society or shared cultural tradition, they are tending in the new era to become relative to the individual. The increasing number of faiths by which men choose to live are related to the historical and social context in which they are found. Man's foreseeable future is one of religious pluralism, in which the element of relativism, however much one may try to be delivered from it, can never finally be eliminated.

CHAPTER 13

SECULARIZATION – A PROCESS OF RELIGIOUS CHANGE IN TWO STAGES

It is now time to take up again, and to discuss more explicitly, the main thesis of this book (as concisely stated near the end of Chapter 1), namely that in the long and complex history of man's religious experience there have been two major transitions or thresholds of change – the Axial Period and the Age of Enlightenment – and that, further, there is an inherent relationship between these two thresholds in that they may be regarded as two successive steps in the one process, a process of secularization.

In Chapters 5-12 we have been examining the evidence for maintaining that the Age of Enlightenment has proved to be a watershed in the history of religion, initially for Western Christendom, but subsequently for all mankind, in that what there took place has been transported round the world and is now influencing all cultures and religious traditions. At the end of the last chapter we referred to the taking shape of a new world-view which is today winning conviction on a global scale.

In this chapter we shall first of all discuss some of the dominant features of this new world-view, drawing upon and gathering together the trends which have been continually coming to the fore in the previous chapters. Then it will be shown that, of all the words which might be used to describe these features of the transition to modernity, the most satisfactory one is 'secularization', provided we restore to it its original root meaning. Thereafter the transition to modernity will be compared with the Axial Period in an attempt to demonstrate that in some important respects there is an intrinsic relationship between the two, the second being in part a further development, and in part re-direction, of the first.

In Chapter 2 it was maintained that one of the very important differences between pre-Axial and post-Axial religion was concerned with the general character of the world-view which prevailed in each. The Axial Period marked a transition from a basically monistic world-view to a dualistic one in which the sacred, divine, eternal, spiritual and invisible sphere of reality was felt to be clearly separable from the secular, human, temporal, material and visible sphere, even though it impinged upon it at a number of vital and strategic points. At the end of Chapter 4 we briefly noted, in anticipation, the most significant ways in which man's religious outlook was changing during the Age of Enlightenment. In the light of the last eight chapters we must now fill out that brief outline.

The first and chief thing to be said is that, partly as a result of the Copernican revolution in cosmology and partly as a result of related factors, the duality present in the world-views of post-Axial religion has been replaced by a view of the world which emphasizes its underlying unity. Bellah expressed it this way, 'In the world-view that has emerged from the tremendous intellectual advances of the last two centuries there is simply no room for a hierarchic dualistic religious symbol system of the classical historic type. This is not to be interpreted as a return to primitive monism: it is not that a single world has replaced a double one but that an infinitely multiplex one has replaced the simple duplex structure'.[1]

In the experience of modern man the plausibility of the

existence of an unseen spiritual world has been diminishing, leaving this tangible, empirical world as the one and only real world which mankind finds it both possible and necessary to make his response to. This world still contains much which is puzzling and unknown to man, and some of it may for ever elude him. But it is a world which can no longer be adequately understood by the former two-world dichotomy of natural and supernatural. This is reflected in the fact that modern man has experienced an increasing loss of the sense of the sacred in those very places, times and persons where the spiritual and supernatural world was once believed to impinge upon the empirical world.

In one area of human experience after another (as we have been seeing in the preceding chapters) what was once believed to be supernatural has come to be seen as belonging to the natural world, what was thought to be of divine origin has been found to be of human origin, what was treated as absolute, has come to be recognized as relative. Even though the symbol-system of the post-Axial religions may continue to possess real value and importance for many people in the new religious era mankind has entered, they are increasingly being recognized to be this-worldly in character. Further, each of the historic religions pursues a kind of historical existence in this world of change; each had a beginning, each has manifested a capacity to change and to diversify, to flourish and to decay, and each will presumably come to an end, even if it were yet to last for a million years. Post-Axial religions, just like the tribal and archaic religions they have come to displace, are seen by modern man to be largely the constructs of the human imagination, even though they are responses to what concerns men ultimately.

The recognition of the this-worldly origin and character of all pre-modern religion, coupled with the loss of the sense of the other-world, has had the effect of revaluing and upgrading the one real world with which man has to deal and to which he must make some kind of response. This was well expressed by Troeltsch when he wrote, 'If the absolute authority has fallen which, in its absoluteness, made the antithesis of the divine and human equally absolute, if in man an autonomous principle is recognized as the source of truth and moral conduct, then all conceptions of the world which were especially designed to maintain that gulf between the human and the divine, fall along with it. With it falls the doctrine of the absolute corruption of mankind through original sin, and the transference of the ends of life to the heavenly world in which there will be deliverance from this corruption. In consequence, all the factors of this present life acquire an enhanced value and a higher impressiveness, and the ends of life fall more and more within the realm of the present world with its ideal of transformation'.[2]

The enhanced value which the modern world-view has restored to this world of space and time implies two things of fundamental importance for the new forms in which religion manifests itself in the new era. The first is that ultimate reality (or whatever man responds to as his ultimate concern and which he may refer to as the 'ultimate', the 'unconditioned', the 'ground of being' and which the various post-Axial religions have referred to as God, Brahman, Nirvana, Tao and so on) must be sought *within* this world rather than *outside* of it, assuming it is to be found at all. The second is that the sense of personal fulfilment, which it is one of the functions of religion to provide, must be conceived as possible of attainment within the limits and conditions imposed by this-worldly human existence.

The first of these facts is reflected in the way in which modern man has either (through atheism) denied the reality or existence of any God, conceived to be external to, or wholly transcendent with respect to, the world of space and time, or else (through various forms of pantheism or panentheism) has attempted to modify the traditional theism to be consistent with a monistic view of reality. We have already noted this in such men as Spinoza and Hegel. It may equally be seen in such thinkers as Teilhard de Chardin, Martin Buber and Paul Tillich. The concept of God as pure and absolute spirit, dwelling in a world of absolute spirit, has become increasingly problematical. Even the notion of a *creatio ex nihilo* appears to be ruled out, for in whatever way the physical energy of which the universe is composed is to be related to the 'ground of its being' (i.e., whatever may be conceived as conditioning it and providing it with form and order) the complete absence of the basic physical stuff of the universe is not a state of affairs which is any more readily conceivable.

It is true that the traditional monotheism of the three major religions of the Western world has always attempted to balance the transcendence of God with some element of immanence, and this was particularly so in Christianity with its doctrines of the Incarnation and of the indwelling of the Holy Spirit. But whereas, in the classical forms of Christianity, the experience and understanding of the immanence of God tended to be overshadowed by the sense of the transcendence of God, all attempts of Christianity to adapt itself to the conditions imposed by the modern world-view are likely to be marked by a reversal in the priority to be attributed to these two complementary modes of the ultimate reality. By way of demonstrating this reversal, one may point to the presence of the charismatic movement within Western Christianity. At a time when the Western world has suffered an increasing loss of the sense of divine transcendence, there has been a resurgence among charismatics of the sense of divine immanence. As has been already illustrated by the transition from theism to deism and from deism to atheism, it has become increasingly difficult to affirm as transcendent what has not first of all been existentially experienced as immanent. What ultimately concerns man is not to be conceived as inhabiting another world than this but rather as permeating the whole of this physical universe.

The replacement of the dualistic world-view of post-Axial man by the monistic world-view of modern man has its counterpart in the radical change in self-understanding which modern man has come to experience. Post-Axial man saw himself as essentially a spiritual entity temporarily inhabiting a physical body, the particular relationship between soul and body depending upon which post-Axial tradition one found oneself in. In all of them, however, the final and eternal destiny of this essential self was conceived to be in another world than this, either after one lifetime (as in the Western religions) or after an indeterminable succession of rebirths within this world (as in religion of Indian origin). Man was a creature who had a foot in both worlds. In striking contrast with this view, modern man has come to see himself as a finite, indivisible, physical organism whose nature and destiny can no more be readily conceived as being clearly divided between two different forms of existence – a physical and a spiritual. Admittedly man, though a physical organism, has the potential to realize for himself a spiritual dimension to his this-worldly existence (Feuerbach along with subsequent materialists and humanists always conceded this and indeed were often anxious to affirm it); but it is a spiritual dimension which remains dependent on a person's physical existence. Moreover, even a man's spiritual potential is conditioned, in part, by the biochemistry and physiology of his physical existence as well as by the cultural tradition in which he was nurtured.

The fact that in the new era man finds himself living in

one world, vast though it is, and sees himself as a physical organism, an earthling with a finite existence, does not mean that he has no further need of religion. It is true that the pre-modern religions may no longer meet his needs, particularly in their traditional form, for they came to expression within the context of different world-views. If religion is defined as man's response to the ultimate issues of life, then modern man, no less than his forebears, is required by the very nature of human existence to make his response to the kind of world he finds himself in. That response will provide the religious forms of the new era.

Whereas pre-Axial man simply inherited the religion of the society into which he was born, and whereas post-Axial man, in so far as he came to question inherited tradition, found himself attracted to the authoritative teachers through whom he believed the truths of the other world to have been revealed, the advent of modernity has thrown each individual man back on his own resources. He must now assume responsibility which he previously thought he could transfer to others, responsibility for thinking things out for himself, for finding meaning to life and formulating goals and values. Modern man finds that he must work out his own salvation or perish. He can no longer find ultimate satisfaction and fulfilment by giving himself in blind subservience to an external authority, whether it be a teacher of divine truth, a guru, an infallible Bible or an ideology, for that would be to opt out of the full potential of the humanity he is now called upon to attain.

The fact that mankind has reached a new religious era does not mean that everybody is ready or willing to enter it. The responsibility it throws back upon the individual is daunting and rather frightening. It is only to be expected that in the social trauma of man's coming of age there will be many examples of the reactionary resurgence of one or other of the pre-modern forms of religion, for these offer security and certainty in a time of growing uncertainty and insecurity. The manifestation of various forms of religious reaction should not be allowed to blind us, however, to the new forms which religion is taking in spite of them. The traditional institutions of the post-Axial religions are crumbling, mostly because they are the social manifestation of the other-world which is now receding and of the authority believed to emanate from it. Modern man has been winning his freedom from institutionalism and from external authority and learning to find his own individual place and identity, irrespective of the accidents of race, colour, nationality, class, sex or age which happened to apply to him at any particular time.

There is another side to the responsibility man now has to learn how to bear. He must find himself, and achieve fulfilment, not only as an individual but as a corporate species. He is now, by means of his technology, in control of the future of his planet home as he has never been before. Because of the complexity of modern life in industrialization, in international economic interdependence, in rapidly expanding population and in the finiteness of the earth's non-renewable resources, man has thrown off the authority of his former institutions only to become more dependent than ever on the co-operation of his fellowmen and even on the cultural inheritance of his forefathers. Into the bargain he must now recognize his share of responsibility for the earthly conditions which the future generations, as yet unborn, will eventually inherit from him.

It is within the context and in the light of all the above factors which characterize the situation in which modern man finds himself that there rises to the surface again the age-old questions which lie at the root of man's religious nature. Is there any purpose and meaning in life, and if so what is it? What is there about the nature of this world which causes men to ask such questions and to respond in faith and hope? Or perhaps the question should now be rephrased – How is one to put purpose and meaning into the raw material of human existence so that, as a human being, one may attain some measure of fulfilment?

Always in the past man has used symbols, signs and rituals when he has attempted to respond to what he took to be ultimate reality and to reflect on the ultimate issues which confronted him. He assumed these to be the tokens, gifts and revealed truths from a higher world. The fact that modern man is much more aware of the human origin of all of these religious phenomena of the past does not mean that he must abandon them. Indeed man cannot retain his humanity without the use of symbols of one kind or another (as the use of language so clearly illustrates) nor can he reflect on the ultimate issues without resorting to them. The difference between modern man and his predecessors, however, is that he is forced to recognize that they are symbols.

Pre-modern man did not need to distinguish between the symbol and the reality to which it pointed or which it was believed to mediate. Modern man must make the distinction. This may be illustrated by the particular use of symbolism in religious narrative, which we now call myth. For post-Axial man the myth did not merely *symbolize* the reality; it *was* the reality. Religious affirmations such as 'Jesus rose from the dead', 'Gautama became the Buddha, the enlightened one', were proclaimed as *a priori* truths. They did not need to be proved or defended. They were not stepping-stones to the truth; they *were* the truths for their respective faiths.

Just as modern man has lost his former sense of the sacred and his conviction that he possessed absolutes revealed from another world, so also has he lost a religious language and terminology which is universally acceptable and transparently clear. The former myths and religious symbols have become ambiguous, unclear and opaque. Some of them have died altogether. Whether he creates new symbols to replace the old or whether he continues to use some of the old symbols, one thing is clear. In striking contrast with the pre-modern situation, modern man has become aware that all of his symbols are themselves of human origin. The human character and this-worldliness of his religious language and symbols have become apparent as never before. For better or for worse his eyes have been opened and he knows the nakedness of the human condition. He finds himself naked and alone in the vast universe. To cover his nakedness (that is, to find a meaning to life, to establish an identity for himself, and to find fulfilment in this human existence) he must respond to the reality of his situation by clothing himself in garments of his own making. It is by the religion with which he clothes himself that man becomes more than an animal. The humanity of his condition is dependent upon religion. The fact that modern man recognizes that all the paraphernalia (symbols, etc.) of religion are of human creation has placed him in a dilemma of a quite serious and critical kind. Man needs a religion in order to remain human and to experience spiritual satisfaction; but he cannot find spiritual satisfaction in what he has himself created.

There is a widespread feeling that something quite serious and radical has happened to mankind in the modern world. This feeling has led to a confusing and wide-ranging set of words in an attempt to describe or interpret just what it is which has been and still is taking place. Our times have been described as enlightened, scientific, technological, secular, post-Constantinian, non-religious, post-Christian and post-traditional. Each of these, when more fully expounded, conveys some useful insight into the nature of the modern world. Indeed one cannot expect the many-faceted character of modernity to be wholly contained or fully described in one word. There is one word, however, which has been widely used, and which is perhaps more useful than most others, to refer to what has been happening on this side of the watershed of change marked by the Enlightenment. That word is 'secularization'.

The meaning of the word needs to be clarified, however, or else it merely leads to a good deal of confusion. First it must be clearly distinguished from 'secularism'. 'Secularization' is a descriptive term. It implies no value judgment and is intended to describe a process of change which is reasonably discernible to the objective and neutral observer. 'Secularism', on the other hand, refers to an ideology, the set of values and convictions held and promoted by the secularist, such as the belief that education should be divorced from and kept free from ecclesiastical control.

Unfortunately 'secularization' has been too often defined by specific reference to religion and 'secular' has been treated as if it were the antonym of 'religious'. For example, Bryan Wilson writes, 'By secularization we mean the process whereby *religious* thinking, practice and institutions lose their social significance'.[3] Peter Berger, another sociologist, says 'By secularization we mean the process by which sectors of society and culture are removed from the domination of religious institutions and symbols'.[4] Alisdair MacIntyre, a philosopher, refers to secularization as 'the transition from beliefs and activities and institutions presupposing beliefs of a traditionally Christian kind to beliefs and activities and institutions of an atheistic kind'.[5]

This practice of defining 'secular' and 'secularization' in terms of 'religion' is unsatisfactory for several reasons. First, it not only assumes that it is relatively easy to define religion (when in Chapter 1 we noted how difficult this task is) but, into the bargain, it implies a particular definition of religion which we earlier discarded as being too narrow to be universally applicable. Secondly, where 'secular' is defined in terms of religion, we are given little insight into what it really is but learn only what it is not. Thirdly, the relationship between 'religious' and 'secular' is built into the definition so that there is little point in discussing the effect of secularization on religion since, by definition, secularization must entail the erosion and eventual abolition of all religion and such terms as 'secular Christianity' are rendered self-contradictory.

Now it is true that when 'secular' first came into English usage it was used in opposition to 'religious' but the latter term meant something very different in the late medieval context from what it generally means today. For example, because the parish priest lived and worked in the world he was referred to as 'secular' in contrast with the 'religious' who lived according to the rules of his order and often in monastic seclusion from the world. Obviously this does not mean that the parish priest was non-religious in the modern sense of the term religious. Indeed the first use of the term 'secularization' was in reference to the process by which a 'religious' was granted permission to leave the monastic order and pursue his (often none the less Christian) vocation in the context of the ordinary world.

This earlier use of the term 'secular' actually provides us with the key to its basic meaning, and one which will lead us to the most satisfactory definition of 'secularization'. 'Secular' is derived from the Latin *saeculum*, which originally referred to a span of time, such as a 'generation' or an 'era'. This meaning has been long preserved in the liturgical phrase *ad saecula saeculorum*, meaning 'to one age after another' or 'for ever and ever'. As was also the case with the equivalent terms *aeon* and *'olam* (in classicel Greek and Hebrew, respectively), this originally temporal term acquired a spatial connotation. 'This present age' came to mean 'this present world' and the 'age to come' came to mean 'the world to come'.

If we reclaim this earlier meaning of 'secular', then its nearest synonym is 'this-worldly' and its antonym is 'other-worldly'. We are now in a position to define secularization without making any explicit reference to 'religion'. Secularization may be legitimately and profitably defined as that process of change which consists of an increase of this-worldliness, i.e., the process in which man focuses his attention increasingly on this world and decreasingly on an imagined or postulated other-world. Further, since religion was earlier defined without specific mention of a particular world-view, such as a dualistic one, we are left free to discuss the effects of secularization on religion.

There is nothing very novel about this definition and indeed it had this emphasis when the secularist movement arose in the nineteenth century. The leading British secularist, G. J. Holyoake, tells us in *The Origin and Nature of Secularism* (1896), that the word 'secularist' was first used to signify a way of thinking. In actual fact 'secularism' first appeared in an issue of *The Reasoner* on 25 June 1851 and it was explained to its readers as having to do with the issues 'which can be tested in this life'. *The Reasoner* described itself as a journal which concerned itself with *this world*. It was about 1864 that the word 'secularization' first came into modern usage to describe a discernible process of social and intellectual change.

Owen Chadwick has admirably described this intellectual change in his Gifford Lectures *The Secularization of the European Mind in the Nineteenth Century*, and here he pertinently quotes some words of Rénan written in 1868. 'Whether one is pleased or not, the supernatural is disappearing from the world: only people not of this age have faith in it. Does this mean that religion must crash simultaneously? Indeed not. Religion is necessary. The day when it disappears the very heart of humanity will dry up. Religion is as eternal as poetry, as love. It will survive the demolition of all illusions . . . Under some form or other, faith will express the transcendent value of life.'[6] This makes clear why secularization should not be regarded as necessarily anti-religious. The process of secularization leaves the future of religion as an open question. W. B. Hodgson made a similar point in a lecture on *The Secular, the Religious and the Theological* (1850), where he said, 'Secular means belonging to the Saeculum or Age, or period of life on this earth, as distinguished from eternity or life to come. It should never have come to mean the opposite of *religious*. The fact that something may be described as secular does not preclude it from also being religious. Thus rightly considered the secular is religious in its tendency and issue; the religious is secular in its application and practical development'.[7] Harvey Cox strikes the right note, therefore, when he writes, 'Secularization is man turning his attention away from worlds beyond and toward this world and this time'.[8]

It will hardly be disputed that the process we have been describing in this book as taking place in Europe from the fourteenth century onwards is just what Cox succinctly described in his definition of secularization. In the 15th edition of the *Encyclopaedia Britannica* it is described[9] as 'a movement in society directed away from other-worldliness to this-worldliness. In the medieval period there was a strong tendency for religious persons to despise human affairs and to meditate on God and the after-life. As a reaction to this medieval tendency, secularization, at the time of the Renaissance, exhibited itself in the development of humanism, when man began to show more interest in human cultural development and the possibilities of his fulfilment in this world. The movement towards secularization has been in progress during the entire course of modern history'.[10]

But though the advent of the modern world has certainly been marked by an increase of this-worldly interest there is more to be said. In so far as religions of the post-Axial type have been other-worldly in their ultimate goals the move to modernity admittedly does appear at first sight to be anti-religious in character. But this rests on the assumption that religion must be other-worldly, and that the only genuine form of religion is that which conforms to the post-Axial model. Now it must be conceded without question that pre-Axial man was religious even though his religion was rather this-worldly, by comparison with that of post-Axial man. We must be open to the possibility therefore that on this side of the second major threshold of change new forms of religion may be in the process of coming to birth, which are neither other-worldly, nor dependent upon the natural/supernatural dichotomy. For although the Axial Period involved a shift from a one-world view to a two-world view and modern secularization has involved a shift from a predominantly dualistic world-view to a one-world view, it is clear that modern man is not simply reverting to the religious situation which obtained before the Axial Period, even though there are some broad features in common between the world-views of primal man and modern man.

Instead of regarding the Age of Enlightenment as something which simply cancelled out the distinctive characteristics of religion introduced by the Axial Period, these two thresholds of radical religious change are more appropriately seen as successive steps in the one process, the second having ultimately been made possible by the first. Let us now examine ways in which the two thresholds of change may be related, looking first at what they have in common.

First of all, in both watersheds there was a radical questioning of the inherited traditions. In the Axial Period it was the privileged few who asked the questions and formulated the new answers. Among them were the prophetic founders and authoritative teachers of the post-Axial religions. Through these men religious change gradually permeated through the masses and spread over cultural boundaries. The authority of past tradition was effectively questioned, undermined and superseded by appeal to a higher authority, an authority believed to come from an other-worldly source, and to be mediated through the founders. One set of final answers and absolute moral demands was replaced by a new set, which was believed to have originated in a higher world.

The second threshold of change brought a fresh period of questioning. This time it was on a broader front and has continued to spread, gathering in all who are willing to participate in the exercise. It requires both courage and confidence to question accepted absolutes. This time (as we have seen above in the transition from heteronomy to autonomy) the higher authority which gave modern man the courage and confidence to question traditional absolutes was found within man himself, rather than in a higher world.

The modern phase of questioning continues. The time for expecting a final set of answers, and a code of unchangeable absolute moral demands, has been superseded. Each individual is now being thrown back more and more upon his own initiative and personal judgment. Instead of accepting the ultimate truth on the basis of an external and higher authority, he is now being challenged to carry through the quest for himself (not, of course, without the help and guidance of others, by means of mutual and continuing dialogue). Modern man must learn to formulate for himself the answers he finds most deeply satisfying and the moral imperatives he finds most inwardly compelling.

Secondly, both transition periods have had the effect of accelerating change. In the Axial Period man was emancipated from a relatively static and permanent cultural tradition, one which had slowly evolved as a result of the complex interplay of cultural forces over which man could exert quite minimal conscious control. In post-Axial religion there was greater possibility of change and development in that man, while still required to be subservient to an external authority, was nevertheless required to make a more positive contribution. Since the external authority was seated in another world, it had to be interpreted in each new set of this-worldly conditions. This is why post-Axial religions manifested change and development, i.e., they had a life and a history in a way in which pre-Axial religions did not.

In crossing over the threshold to modernity man underwent a further stage of emancipation, being freed from bondage to all external authority and becoming autonomous in the best sense of that word. In the modern era man, in spite of all remaining limitations, is freer than he has ever been to become the person of his own choice. He is being gradually emancipated from whatever has been depersonalizing and stereotyping in the past, such as cultural conditioning, class stratification, race, colour, sex and age. Each individual is being freed and encouraged to develop his own human potential in the way which does most justice to the physical, intellectual and spiritual dimensions of the human condition. Of course there are still severe limits, set by the physical, finite and mortal character of the human condition, but they are being reduced to their minimum.

This freedom which so characterizes modern man is simply the progressive development of what chiefly originated in the questioning which took place at the Axial Period. We had earlier noted that it was a feature of the post-Axial religions, in contrast with what had preceded, that they required from their prospective practitioners a positive decision or choice. Religion was no longer something one was born into. To become a Buddhist, Christian or Muslim, one had to make a deliberate choice (even if, in the course of religious conversion, one might feel a higher power was exerting an influence). The advent of modernity has not only intensified the need to choose, and increased the range of choices, but also has led man to become aware, as never before, that he must make the choice, by his own unaided efforts, and then bear the responsibility for what ensues from it.

The more freedom the human individual acquires, and the more he is required to become a decision-making creature, the more he contributes to change. Once again we earlier noted that the prophetic origin of the post-Axial religions meant that the component of change came to be built into the tradition. Not only was it that component which led, in the fullness of time, to the second major step in the secularizing process, but it became magnified during the second transition period. Since the end of the eighteenth century change has become the order of the day and it is still accelerating. Whereas ultimate reality (religiously referred to as God) was once conceived to be changeless, the same yesterday, today and for ever, it is now conceived as having the attribute of change, even to the point sometimes of being identified with the process of change itself (as in Process Theology).

So far, in comparing the two major thresholds of change, we have been looking at the ways in which the transition to modernity extended or intensified something already initiated at the Axial Period. There are other ways in which the modern religious era may rather be seen to have synthesized apparently opposing components from both the pre-Axial and post-Axial forms of religion. For example, for modern man there is only one real world, just as for pre-Axial man there was only one world. For pre-Axial man, however, there were no such things as inanimate objects; the whole world was alive and pregnant with the kind of consciousness which he experienced in himself. Post-Axial man not only clearly distinguished between animate and inanimate objects but became so impressed by the fact of consciousness and by his capacity for spirituality that he found it necessary to divide reality into two worlds, a material and a spiritual. For modern man these two realities have once again been rejoined in an indivisible unity. There are no wholly inanimate objects and no non-physical, self-subsistent spirits, but rather one universe of basic energy which possesses the potential to be organized in an amazing variety of complex forms and modes. What modern man has in common with pre-Axial man is the fact that he sees himself as an indivisible part of an intricate, developing, ecological, planetary system and that his own destiny and the future of his species depend on the way he relates his life to it. What modern man has in common with post-Axial man is the belief that man, unlike other creatures at present known to us, has the potential for the highest spiritual destiny attainable on this planet.

There is a second way in which the concerns of pre-Axial and post-Axial man have become synthesized for modern man. Pre-Axial religion had evolved out of the necessity of seeking provision of the basic needs of food, shelter, protection and regeneration. It was primarily concerned with what may be called the physical aspects of the human condition. Post-Axial religion, on the other hand, was primarily concerned with the welfare and ultimate salvation of the human spirit and was sometimes almost exclusively so. Post-Axial religion tended to ignore, or treat as quite secondary, the physical side of life. Modern man, seeing himself as an indivisible psychosomatic organism, is concerned with the welfare and destiny of the whole man, both physical and spiritual. Health or wholeness is equally applicable to the body, the mind and the spirit. In the same way the dissolution of the other-world means that modern man, like pre-Axial man, is concerned with the preservation of this world on which his life and destiny rest. This concern is manifested in such things as the conservationist movement, the need to husband non-renewable resources, population control, and the accommodation of human practices to the processes of nature. But like post-Axial man, modern man distinguishes between what is lasting and what is ephemeral. He still seeks for the quality of eternity, but he seeks it within the context of his own world. So he sees the continuing value of the *other* world of the post-Axial symbol system to be in the fact that it interpreted and spelt out for him the meaningfulness of life in *this* world.

Thirdly, the religion of modern man has this in common with that of pre-Axial man – it is, at least for the foreseeable future, unnameable. Some therefore are inclined to say that modern man has no religion or is becoming religionless. Others, such as sociologist Thomas Luckmann, have referred to the religion of modern man as the 'invisibie religion'[11] and Robert Bellah has drawn attention to 'civil religion',[12] using a term first coined by Rousseau.

The reason why the religion of modern man cannot be named is that, first of all, modern man is still only at the very beginning of becoming adjusted to the new era of this-worldliness. The vast majority of men still think of themselves as adherents of one or other of the post-Axial religions. Yet in practically all men there is some element of the new secularity and it is growing in spite of all that men try to do to hold it at bay.

The religion of modern man is unnameable for two further reasons. It is a distinctive feature of the modern religious situation that the channel for ultimate authority has been internalized, each person becoming both the formulator and the critic of his own particular religious stance. This leads to diversity and on the grand scale. Even the nameable religious traditions from the post-Axial period are dividing and diversifying still further, since the advent of modernity. Just because religion is becoming much more of a personal and almost a private affair, it does not need to be named. Indeed there is a certain resistance to names in the modern religious era. Men do not want to be known by labels, such as Christian, humanist, agnostic, to which they are expected to conform. They want to be known for themselves; they want to be free to be themselves, free to change and grow to greater maturity; labels, while they serve to give identity, also exercise a hampering, depersonalizing effect.

On the other hand, the religion of modern man, unnameable though it is, has this in common with the post-Axial religions; it supersedes all previous religions, both pre-Axial and post-Axial. It not only crosses ethnic and cultural boundaries; it crosses the boundaries of the post-Axial religions. The modern man of Christian background, for example, may find he has more in common with the modern man of Muslim, Jewish, Hindu or Buddhist background than he has with the person who is rigidly and blindly committed to traditional Christianity. Ecumenism is a product of the modern religious era. In the long run it cannot stop short at an exclusively Christian ecumenism or a Buddhist ecumenism; it cannot even stop short at an ecumenism of the higher religions of the post-Axial order (as has sometimes been suggested). The word ecumenical is derived, it should be remembered, from the Greek *Oikumene* (the whole of the inhabited world). Ecumenism by its very nature, therefore, must grow ever wider until it embraces all men, accepts them in all the diversity which flows from their countless individualities, and appeals to them on the basis of what they all share in their common humanity.

In its simplest (but also necessarily very simplistic) form, the relationship between the two major thresholds of religious change may be put thus. Pre-Axial man was in bondage to the world which had brought him forth and in which he evolved to consciousness. In his religion he expressed, and tried to come to terms with, the forces he found confronting him and which he conceived as spiritual powers of a divine order immanent within the world. The Axial Period enabled man, in a variety of ways, to project these forces into a world of their own. He still believed he was subject to them and that his eternal destiny lay with them. But, at the same time, he achieved a relative freedom which he had not known before. Immanence had given way to transcendence. These powers were now 'off his back', as it were; they were no longer 'breathing down his neck'. He was free, at least in part, to regard the world as *his* world. Previously he could not till the soil, cut down a tree or catch a fish, without performing the appropriate ritual which would have the effect of propitiating, or forestalling the wrath of, the higher powers which oppressed him. The projection of the primitive sacred/profane dichotomy into the dualistic world-view made possible the desacralization of much of the tangible world. The visible world became less sacred to the extent to which the unseen other-world became more so. It was the first major step in the process of secularization.

In the second threshold of change secularization took desacralization a step further. The collapse of conviction about the other-world resulted in a desacralization of those particular places, objects, seasons and persons which were believed to be the meeting points between the two worlds. Man thus entered into even greater freedom. He freed himself from priestly authority and ecclesiastical control. He became free to examine critically the 'revealed' codes of behaviour and the 'divinely appointed' social structures. Whereas, at the Axial Period, a once oppressive sense of divine immanence had been replaced by an other-worldly form of transcendence, the dissolution of that other-worldly transcendence left man with a greater sense of freedom than he had ever felt before.

The freedom achieved by modern man is not, of course, unlimited. It is not to be identified with licence, even though in testing out his newly-won freedom man has sometimes fallen into the trap of thinking that it is. He is not free to believe wholly what he wishes or do wholly what he likes. He is free to make some changes in his world but he is not free to create his world *de novo*. His world already exists. He must come to terms with the world as it really is, and not as he, in a flight of fancy, would prefer it to be. Religious faith is man's response to ultimate reality and not to a figment of his own imagination. It is ultimate reality which still transcends man, which encounters him in all his freedom and which calls forth the religious response from him. This is true for all men, whether they are emancipated moderns or adherents of one of the more traditional faiths. 'It is impossible for man to lose transcendence without ceasing to be human', said Karl Jaspers.[18] But whereas for post-Axial man transcendence was believed to be seated in another world and whereas for pre-Axial man it was immanence rather than transcendence which held him in bondage, for modern man immanence and transcendence may be said to have become fused into one.

In the one real world in which modern man finds himself existing and of which he is a part, then in order to retain his humanity and, if possible, to experience his human potential even more fully, he *must* make his response to ultimate issues; and that is what it means to be religious. The ultimate issues which confront him emerge from *within* this world and sometimes even from within himself, because of the greatly increased responsibilities placed upon him in the exercise of his greatly increased freedom.

We have been speaking of this increased freedom enjoyed by modern man in terms of autonomy. It was said earlier that during the Age of Enlightenment Western man rebelled against his heteronomous state and became autonomous. This must now be qualified. If man could have become completely autonomous, either as an individual or as a species, then man would indeed have ceased to be religious, for he would no longer have any ultimate concern. It is the false belief that modern man *has* become completely autonomous, *is* wholly free, acknowledges *no* form of transcendence, which has led some to assert that the new era is basically a non-religious one. But while it is true that completely autonomous man would cease to be religious, he would also lose the dimension of depth to his life; his life would become shallow and meaningless; in fact he would be losing some of the most significant features of his humanity.

Absolute autonomy, therefore, is not the final and complete answer to the inadequacies of the heteronomous condition from which man has been delivered by the transition to modernity. Early in the post-Enlightenment period a new term, 'theonomy', came to be coined to resolve this dilemma between the polar opposites of heteronomy and autonomy. Fruitful use has been made of this term, for example, by Paul Tillich[14] and Hans Küng.[15] The inadequacy of heteronomy *per se* is that it holds man back from the development of his full human potential by smothering initiative and creativity. The inadequacy of autonomy *per se* is that it robs man of the motivation for self-fulfilment by causing him to think he is a creature who is a law unto himself, an end in himself and hence without a goal or meaning. There is a relative value in both heteronomy and autonomy in that each points to a weakness in the other. This relative value is preserved if each is seen to be grounded in theonomy and neither is treated as an absolute in itself. Theonomy 'means autonomous reason united with its own depth. In a theonomous situation reason actualizes itself in obedience to its structural laws and in the power of its own inexhaustible ground', said Tillich.[16] 'Theonomy is the condition of the possibility of the moral autonomy of man in secular society', said Küng.[17]

The secularization of the human condition which has resulted from the two major periods of religious change does not, therefore, leave man in a religionless state. But it does call for new religious forms, that is, new ways in which secularized man will come to understand the reality which ultimately concerns him and new ways in which he will express his existential response to that reality.

CHAPTER 14

WHY DID SECULARIZATION COME OUT OF THE WEST?

❖

Having traced the steps by which we have arrived at the modern religious situation, and having described this long cultural development in terms of two basic thresholds of change in a total process of secularization, we are now faced with the question of why the second transition originated in only one place, Western Europe, whereas the first transition or Axial Period, took place in three or four different geographical areas more or less simultaneously and without any known influence upon each other. Why did modernity come to birth in the West and not in the Islamic world or in India or in China?

We must concede the possibility that it may be nothing but an accident of history. Admittedly there is much in this world which appears to be simply the result of chance. During this century physicists have been coming to the unexpected conclusion that certain atomic processes occur in an entirely haphazard way, thus implying that there is a component of chance to be found in the most basic stuff of the physical universe. If that is the case in the very simplest forms of inorganic matter, how much more likely is pure chance to be present in the much more complex scene of human history, resulting as it does, from the unplanned interplay of innumerable human wills. In any case, it is a well-known fact that some of the most important scientific and technological advances have resulted from chance discoveries.

To regard *all* human events and social changes to be the result of pure chance, however, is no more consistent with the observable data than the contention that everything is completely determined. The ancient Democritus was much nearer the truth when he said, 'Everything existing in the universe is the fruit of chance and necessity'. From primitive times down to the contemporary age of science, the human mind has been much impressed by the order, constancy and purpose which it believed to be observable in the world, even in the midst of movement and change. Indian religion, in its doctrine of *karma*, even raised the law of cause and effect in human behaviour to the status of an eternal cosmic principle. This did not lead the Indian mind, however, to concern itself with any purposeful design in history. In the monotheistic religions of the West, by contrast, it was the general course of history which was believed to be in no sense the result of chance, but rather the manifestation of the purposeful will of God. When the modern historian looks for the factors which contributed to an event or movement, he does not need to be committed to either of the above views. Like the scientist, he can concede a considerable degree of scope to pure chance and yet at the same time find that there are frequently very plausible reasons which help to explain events, trends and cultural change.

What we can look for, therefore, and hope to find, is not the clear proof of why the modern world could not have come to birth anywhere else but in Western Europe, but rather those factors which may have served as catalysts of change and which were more prominent there than anywhere else. Even if it were to become clear that there is a probable causal connection between the Judaeo-Christian tradition and secularization, it does not mean that modernity was the inevitable and only possible conclusion of that particular path of faith. Nor does it imply that the modern secular world is just what the authoritative bearers of that tradition were expecting or ultimately looking for. Max Weber has convincingly shown in his study of *The Protestant Ethic and the Spirit of Capitalism* that the long-term results of an ideology are often quite other, and perhaps even the reverse of, those which have been intended.[1] It is certainly true that the majority of contemporary Christians do not see modern secularization in any real sense as the logical and necessary consequence of the Judaeo-Christian tradition; rather they treat it as an enemy to be overcome or at least held at bay.

We may leave aside for the moment the question of whether modern secularization is to be welcomed or deplored and simply ask to what extent the Judaeo-Christian tradition already possessed within it the seeds of the modern religious era, and possessed them, perhaps not exclusively, but to a greater degree than the other post-Axial religions. Ever since Hegel welcomed the post-Enlightenment age as the time for the realization of Absolute Spirit, for which, in his view, traditional Christianity had provided the necessary prior stage, there have been historians, scientists, philosophers, sociologists and theologians who have contended, though in a wide variety of ways, that there is an inherent connection between modernity and the Christian foundations of the Western world.

Nobel Prize-winner Jacques Monod, for example, in claiming objectivity to be the *sine qua non* for the rise of empirical science, suggests that 'if this unprecedented event in the history of culture occurred in the Christian West rather than in some other civilization, it was perhaps partly thanks to the fundamental distinction drawn by the Church between the domains of the sacred and the profane. Not only did this distinction allow science to pursue its own way (provided it did not trespass on the realm of the sacred); it prepared the mind for the much more radical distinction posed by the principle of objectivity'.[2] We have already pointed out in the last chapter how, at the Axial Period, the projection of the primitive sacred/profane dichotomy into a dualistic world-view had the effect of largely desacralizing the tangible world, in which man, thereafter, enjoyed a relative freedom and authority.

Philosopher and scientist C. F. von Weizsäcker (1912-) claimed in his Gifford Lectures that the rise of modern science and of the secularization to which it has contributed, cannot properly be understood or accounted for except against the background of the biblical doctrine of creation and this in spite of the counterclaim which is often made, namely that the ancient Greeks are the real progenitors of modern science. 'The concept of exact mathematical laws of nature, which was only dimly present in Greek thought, gained far greater convincing power by means of the Christian conception of creation. Thus I think it is a gift of Christianity to the modern mind.'[3] He concluded that 'the modern world owes its uncanny success to a great extent to its Christian background', being 'the result of the secularization of Christianity'.[4]

Similarly philosopher A. N. Whitehead, in a lengthy discussion on the origin of modern science in his *Science and the Modern World*, became convinced there is 'but one source for its origin. It must have come from the medieval insistence on the rationality of God, conceived as with the personal energy of Jehovah and with the rationality of a Greek philosopher . . . In Asia, the conceptions of God were of a being too arbitrary or too impersonal for such ideas to have much effect on instinctive habits of mind . . . My explanation is that the faith in the possibility of science, generated antecedently to the development of modern scientific theory, is an unconscious derivation from medieval theology'.[5]

Sociologist Peter Berger not only contended that 'Protestantism served as a historically decisive prelude to secularization' but agreed with a number of contemporary biblical scholars 'that the roots of secularization are to be found in the earliest available sources for the religion of Israel', in other words that 'the "disenchantment of the world" begins in the Old Testament'.[6]

Harvey Cox, following the lead of another theologian Friedrich Gogarten, expounded the view that secularization is the legitimate consequence of the impact of the Old Testament on world history. In his widely read book, *The Secular City*, he argued that in the religion of ancient Israel, as preserved in the Old Testament, there are to be found three basic components of modern secularization. The Hebrew doctrine of creation was the beginning of the disenchantment of the world of nature. The Hebrew insurrection in Egypt, leading to the Exodus under Moses, was the beginning of the desacralization of politics. The prohibition of graven images was the beginning of what he called the 'deconsecration of values'. (We shall elaborate this below.)

Perhaps each of those we have quoted has over-simplified the connection between the Judaeo-Christian tradition and the coming of the modern world but sufficient has been cited to make it worth our while to explore the issue further. It will have been noted, however, that while modern secularization came to birth in the Christian West, the roots of it seem to be not so much in the classical forms of Christianity as in the much older Jewish heritage out of which Christianity itself sprang. By retaining the Hebrew Bible as the major part of the Christian canon of Holy Scripture, Christianity never became divorced from its Jewish origins, even though a large amount of that Israelite heritage lay dormant for a long time, at least until the Reformation.

If there is any truth in the thesis we are about to explore, namely that there is a causal connection between the Old Testament and the coming of the modern world, then this would mean that the ancient Israelite ancestors of the Jewish people have played a remarkable and unique role in the whole development of human culture in the last three thousand years. The term 'chosen people', by which the Jews have long been known, may have to be looked at afresh, even by the neutral observer. When one views the history and influence of the Jewish people against the background of the many and diverse cultures the world has known in e last three millennia, the Jews do strike one as a most 'peculiar people', to use an Old Testament phrase.[7]

The first amazing fact is that the people of ancient Israel, through its Jewish descendants, has retained its identity over a time span of about 3000 years (even longer if one accepts the historicity of the earlier and somewhat shadowy patriarchs), and this in spite of the fact that it has always been relatively small in numbers and that, for the last 2500 years, it was forced to live in the widely scattered state known as the Diaspora. This remarkable phenomenon further means that in the history of the Jewish people, more than in any other cultural tradition, we are able to trace a clear thread of continuity through religious forms of the pre-Axial, post-Axial and post-Enlightenment types. Tribal Yahwism was the pre-Axial form. Through Moses and the prophets this was transformed into the post-Axial religion of Judaism. In the post-Enlightenment period the Jews were among the first to feel the impact of the modern form of secularization and subsequently Zionism became a particularly clear and interesting example of a secularized form of a post-Axial religion.

The second significant fact to recognize is the widespread extent of Jewish influence outside of Judaism proper and much of it quite unintentional. Through one Jew, Jesus of Nazareth, Judaism inadvertently gave birth to Christianity, the most widespread of all the post-Axial religions. And another Jew, Saul of Tarsus, became the first and most important missionary and theological interpreter of Christianity to the Gentile world. While Muhammad was an Arab and not a Jew, it is apparent to non-Muslims, if not to Muslims, that Judaism was a very significant influence in his life, as the reading of the Qur'an will quickly demonstrate. It was from Judaism that both Christianity and Islam inherited the monotheistic basis of their respective faiths. It was from the Jewish institution of the synagogue that both Christianity and Islam inherited the very distinctive phenomenon of congregational worship, something taken for granted in the West but unknown in the East. It was because Judaism had already evolved an authoritative canon of Holy Scripture that Christianity and Islam also became 'peoples of the book'.[8] Thus through the much larger Christian and Muslim communities, Judaism has been indirectly influencing the whole Western half of the world for more than a thousand years.

There is more yet. A new and more secularized form of religion regards as its founding father another man of Jewish extraction, Karl Marx. Since Marxism bears within its structure some of the distinctive marks of Judaism (as has already been made clear in Chapter 8), it means that Judaism has, again quite unintentionally, influenced a further large section of mankind, including this time, through its impact on modern China, by far the largest portion of the Eastern world.

The fact that the extensive spread of Jewish influence has been indirect and unintentional should not cause us to dismiss it (as the findings of Max Weber already referred to bear witness). It is true that neither Jesus of Nazareth nor Karl Marx were typical or orthodox Jews, and Muhammad was not a Jew at all; yet the paths of faith associated with these men undoubtedly owed much to

Judaism. The fact that Jewish influence spread so far, in spite of the orthodox interpreters of Judaism rather than because of them, suggests that something extremely powerful was latent within the principles of Judaism, which not even Jews themselves fully realized. We shall be looking at these principles presently.

In the meantime it is worth noting that throughout religious history the heretics have often proved more interesting than the wholly orthodox and have usually had the more creative minds. If it is true that the greatest sons of Judaism have come not from the centre of Jewish orthodoxy but from the periphery of Jewish life, it is only what one should expect from a growing, creative religious tradition. It has been the function of the Torah-true Jew simply to perpetuate the tradition, so that from time to time, when the time was ripe, a non-conformist Jew, living on the boundary where Judaism meets the Gentile world, could be the instrument of creative new thought. There cannot be a boundary unless a centre is continuously preserved; yet it is the boundary, rather than the centre, which has provided the growing edge.

Actually when one looks through a list of the great pioneering spirits of the Western cultural tradition the number who turn out to be of Jewish extraction is out of all proportion to the relatively small size of the Jewish community. Let us look at some examples. Philo of Alexandria (c. 25 BC-c. AD 40) attempted to commend the Jewish heritage to the Gentile intellectual world of his day by building a bridge between Holy Scripture and philosophy. In doing so he not only fashioned the allegorical tool of biblical interpretation which Christians were soon to borrow from him and use for more than 1500 years, but he achieved such a synthesis of Hellenistic philosophy and Jewish faith that he laid the foundations for the Christian pursuit of theology, a fact which contributed to the total neglect of him by the later rabbinical Judaism.

The man often reckoned as the greatest Jewish philosopher of all time, Maimonides or Moses ben Maimon (1135-1204), was held in considerable suspicion by his fellow-Jews and the publication of his *Guide for the Perplexed* provoked a storm of Jewish protest. The fact that Aquinas borrowed from him three of his proofs of the existence of God illustrates the extent of his influence outside of Judaism. Even though later Jewish tradition came to value him, and to accept as authoritative his *Thirteen Articles of Faith,* he also stood on the growing edge of faith and his creative work was a foretaste of what would be required of religious thinkers in the transition to modernity.

We have already had occasion to name several of Jewish extraction among the makers of the modern world of thought – Spinoza, Marx, Durkheim and Freud. Others which could be added to the list are physicist Albert Einstein (1879-1955) and philosopher Martin Buber (1878-1965), both of whom have become much more widely honoured outside of Judaism than within it. None of these were synagogue-going Jews. Einstein wrote in 1929, 'I believe in Spinoza's God, who reveals himself in the orderly harmony of what exists, not in a God who concerns himself with the fates and actions of human beings'.

What is it about the Jewish path of faith which has caused it, indirectly, to have exercised such an extensive influence? Is it because, more than its post-Axial rivals, it has had the capacity to be more in touch with the reality of man's situation, more down to earth, so to speak? Let us look at some of the dominant emphases of the Jewish tradition (as preserved in the Old Testament) which could be regarded as pointers to the modern world and hence be accepted as reasons why modernity emerged out of the Judaeo-Christian West. Five points will be selected, though others could readily be added.[9]

The first thing to note is that the Old Testament retained much more of the monistic world-view of its pre-Axial origins than did the other post-Axial religions. The concepts of heaven and Sheol (the underworld of the dead), which were conceived as compartments of the one world in pre-Axial times, went through a process which virtually eliminated their former significance. The sun, moon and heavenly bodies all lost their former divinity and became created objects; they were desacralized. Even though heaven continued to be thought of as the dwelling-place of God (see below), it was not an eternal world. It was said to have been created with the earth and it would pass away with the earth. Thus the heavens and the earth belonged to the one created system. As time went on 'heaven' simply became a synonym for God, just as Sheol became a euphemism for death. In the Old Testament there is no eternal world; there is no other world than this and this is the world which God created and which remains his sole concern.

The consequence of this is that in the Old Testament the ultimate destiny of man was never conceived as being anywhere else than on earth, even though during the later age of apocalyptic thought, it was hoped that a new and transformed earth would cataclysmically replace the present one. The Platonic doctrine of the immortality of the soul (with its corollary of a projected soul world) is quite foreign to the Old Testament. Thus, whereas the Christian and the Muslim came to set their hopes on an other-worldly heaven, the Buddhist trod the path which led to Nirvana and the Hindu practised renunciation in order to be reabsorbed into Brahman, the Old Testament saw man as a finite, mortal creature, made from the dust of the earth and destined exclusively for this earthly existence.

The second point is linked with the first. Towards this

one and only real world – tangible, physical and earthy though it is – the Old Testament encouraged a very positive and appreciative attitude. In its myth of creation it asserted that not only had God made everything which exists in this world but that 'God saw everything that he had made and behold it was very good'.[10] Israelite Psalmist and poet recounted the wonders of the natural world with awe and gratitude.[11] The sages and prophets of Israel were not blind to the tragic and evil experiences to be frequently encountered within human existence but these did not cause them to judge this to be a fallen and depraved world and to seek an escape from it into some perfect world elsewhere. Rather were they led to hope for the future renewal of *this* world, even to the point of doing something practical to make that hope a reality. The earth, with all its problems and frustrations, was not only man's only home but was believed to have great potential; it could become the dwelling-place of God.

The general burden of the Old Testament is not that the earth is irretrievably corrupt but that it is to become so perfect as to manifest the rule (or kingdom) of God. It taught men to look forward to the time, not when man would go to heaven, but when God would come down to earth. Heaven was not an other-worldly reality but the ideal which was to be made a reality on the earth at that time when 'the earth shall be full of the knowledge of the Lord'.[12] It is a typically Jewish thought which is expressed in the Lord's Prayer, 'Thy Kingdom come. Thy will be done on earth (in reality) as it is in heaven (the ideal)'. Also very Jewish is the vision (even though found in the Christian Apocalypse) of the holy city coming down to earth out of heaven and the proclamation, 'Now at last God has his dwelling among men! He will dwell among them and they shall be his people and God himself will be with them'.[13]

This leads us to the third point, namely, that the Old

Testament expresses just as positive a view of the human condition as it does of the earth. The myth of the Garden of Eden is a penetrating description of what the Israelites knew the human condition to be, both psychologically and existentially; but neither in the Old Testament nor in later Judaism did it give rise to a doctrine of original sin and of the total depravity of man (as it did in Christianity). The Old Testament quite properly acknowledged man's potential for wrong-doing, i.e., for falling short of the mark, but in contrast with Christianity it also stressed the capacity which remains in man for gaining the upper hand over the temptations which beset him and for making a complete turn around (in Hebrew *teshuvah*) by his own unaided efforts, thus enabling him to step back on the path which leads to fullness of life. The Old Testament (and later Jewish thought) is quite unashamedly Pelagian in this respect. This is even clearly implied in the Parable of the Prodigal Son told by Jesus.[14]

The Old Testament reflects a much higher estimate of the potential ability in man and of his place in the order of creation than had usually been the case in pre-Axial religion (where man was often regarded as the plaything of the gods) and even than that found in the other post-Axial religions. Even though man was acknowledged to be a physical organism (made from the dust of the earth), yet he is said to have been made in the image of God,[15] to be in himself very little less than God and to be adorned with glory and honour.[16] Man participates with God in the creative and ordering process. For example, he is said to have been invited to name the other creatures, that is, to give them an identity. Here is an early hint of something we widely acknowledge today – the way we understand the world, the order we discern in it, even the scientific laws we enunciate, are all largely the construction of the human mind, which we have imposed upon the world.

Being only a little less than God means that man is in a situation which brings both stress and responsibility. On the one hand (as the ancient myth explained), being like God is the result of having one's eyes opened and of knowing good and evil and it involves the loss of the paradisean state of existence in which all other creatures live. On the other hand, it means that man has been placed in a position of authority and power. God's creation has become man's world; man has been given dominion over all other creatures and must take over responsibility for such things as promoting the agriculture by which life is sustained.

It is also important to note that in the Old Testament it is the human species as a whole to which the God-like character, functions and authority are being transmitted and not simply to individual men in their capacity as king, lord, aristocrat or priest. Whereas pre-Axial man often treated slaves, foreigners and lower classes as sub-human animals and whereas the post-Axial religions often saw the divisions in human society (castes, aristocracies, priesthoods, ruling families) as part of the eternal and divine order, the Old Testament fastened attention increasingly on the humanity which all men and women have in common rather than on the roles or stations in life which particular individuals may happen to have. When one compares the Old Testament law-codes with those which were contemporary with Israel in the ancient world, the humanitarianism of the Hebrew Bible stands out sharply. In giving legal expression to this humanitarian concern the Old Testament itself refers back to the Exodus event – 'You shall remember that you were a slave in the land of Egypt'.[17] The deliverance from Egyptian slavery was seen as an earnest of the freedom into which all mankind had the right to enter. The Israelite prophets displayed an unprecedented passion for social justice and a special compassion for the underprivileged (the widow, the orphan and the alien). The many ways in which, in the modern world, the equality of all men is being acknowledged (abolition of slavery, rejection of priestcraft and autocracy, the rise of democracy and socialism, the plea for human rights) may all be seen as the natural fruit of seeds found in the Old Testament.

Fourthly, we must look at the new and very distinctive way in which the concept of God came to be understood in ancient Israel. The fact that it became the foundation of all Western monotheism bears testimony to its importance. But it also tends to blind us to its uniqueness since we tend to take for granted what we have long been used to. Instead of trying to evaluate the significance of Israel's view of God against the background of the modern (and partly justifiable) atheistic protest, we must look at it within the context of the ancient world.[18] Then we notice a quite remarkable thing about the Old Testament. Absent is the multiplicity of gods and goddesses, such as we find in the Mesopotamian Epic of Gilgamesh or in the Hindu Vedas and Mahabharata. The very simplicity of the central affirmation of the Old Testament stands out – 'The LORD our God is one'. Absent also are the theogonies which were a feature of pre-Axial religion. In the Old Testament the concept of God has been almost completely stripped of the customary mythology (i.e., it has been largely demythologized).

This means that God, the creator and foundation of all reality, is unlike anything man had previously worshipped. God is impossible to describe or portray. No man can ever see God. God cannot be grasped (even by the human mind). God cannot be manipulated or mastered. In so far as naming was often thought of as identifying and hence gaining some degree of control, the God of Israel could not even be adequately named. Characteristically, therefore, when Moses asked for the name of him who addressed him from the burning bush he was told, 'I AM who I AM'.[19]

In contrast with the indescribable Nirvana (of Buddhist thought), the attributeless Brahman (of Hindu thought), the eternal Tao which cannot be named (of Chinese thought), the God of Israel could be *heard*. He was, in fact, a voice – the voice of ultimate authority on all things relating to man and his place in the world. This fact introduced into the concept of God an element which has remained practically unique in all of religious history. The God of ancient Israel primarily has to do with the course of human history and, in so far as he can be defined at all, it is in terms of history. To the Israelite, God is the One who brought the people of Israel out of Egypt, delivered them from slavery and led them into a new land. The events in which, for good or ill, they were successively involved in that land, continued to be the chief manifestation of the reality of God to them, the significance of these events being interpreted through the prophets, or spokesmen, of God.

When we compare the Old Testament with the Holy Scriptures of post-Axial religions outside the Judaeo-Christian stream, we find it unique in the attention it gives to human history. Indeed it contains first-class historiography which is centuries older than that of the Greek historians. The reason for this is that the history of the human race upon the earth, rather than some divine events in a projected other-world and rather even than the cyclic processes of nature, constituted the real concern of the God of Israel. To translate this into modern and non-theistic terminology we may say that the Old Testament teaches that the issues which are man's ultimate concern are to be found on earth and in what happens to men in the course of their historical existence. The central place given to history in the Old Testament meant that while the physical world was largely desacralized and conceived as being entrusted to man, man's attention was not at the same time being directed to some other-worldly sphere in order to find his ultimate concern. His ultimate concern was to be discerned within the course of human history. Israel's God was primarily the Lord of history.

The fifth point follows from the unique character of the Old Testament concept of God, and is expressed in the second commandment, 'You shall not make any graven image and shall not worship or bow down before any likeness of anything in heaven or earth'.[20] This means that the only God who can be legitimately worshipped is unlike anything to be found in the whole universe. It means that the gods of the nations are idols. It means that much of what is usually taken to be religious is in fact false, and like all falsehood, is not to be tolerated. An iconoclastic zeal became a very distinctive characteristic of Judaism and was inherited by Christianity and Islam. It is the reason for the Puritan reformations which have tended to be a feature of these three religions and it has also unfortunately led, when opportunity offered, to religious intolerance and persecution.

Although the iconoclastic zeal was originally expressed as a prohibition of graven images, the spirit of it can readily be extended to all other religious phenomena whereby men treat an object, a practice or a belief, as if it contained the ultimacy which is proper only to God, who himself can never be fully comprehended. The Israelite prophets themselves, for example, turned their attention to the traditional practice of sacrifice, and called for the abolition of this survival of pre-Israelite religion. The Israelite priests were scandalized by what they heard the prophets say. Even most modern biblical scholars have found it hard to accept that the prophets meant just what they said and have usually softened the tone of their oracles by interpreting them as a call for the *reform* of the sacrificial cultus rather than its *abolition*.[21] In the end the sacrificial cultus *was* abandoned in the Jewish tradition, not by choice but by force of historical circumstances.

In the transition to modernity many religious beliefs and practices have been questioned and subsequently abandoned. Instead of regarding this as apostasy it may have to be seen, in some if not in all cases, as the outworking of the ancient and quite proper rejection of idolatry. Much modern atheism, for example, is a protest against false religious beliefs and against superstitious practices, out of a concern for truth. In so far as traditional beliefs about God have been rejected by the appeal to truth or to what Tillich called the 'God beyond God', then the transition to the 'post-theistic' age is not so much the abandonment as the fulfilment of this quite extraordinary component in the ancient tradition of Israel.

Similarly we have noted that one of the features of the modern mind is the acknowledgement that there are no known absolutes. There are no religious dogmas which one can accept as the final and absolute truth. There are no moral codes which are to be obeyed as beyond question. Such a situation, discomforting though it may be, is completely consistent with the long-term working out of the second commandment. This is why Cox spoke of the Sinai Covenant as involving the 'deconsecration of values'. It was the forerunner of today's situation in which all the former absolutes have been relativized. This does not mean that values are no longer important. It means that man can no longer opt out of his responsibility for being continually involved in the process of evaluating. As Cox says, this 'relativization of all human values, one of the integral dimensions of secularization, stems in part from the biblical opposition to idolatry'.[22]

The above five points briefly illustrate how the seeds of modernity are to be found in the Old Testament and may go some way to explaining why secularization came out of the West. At the time of its birth Christianity inherited these secularizing trends from Judaism. For example, Christianity emerged out of the Jewish institution of the synagogue and not out of that of the Temple; and the synagogue may be regarded as a secularized substitute for the Temple. Yet Christianity did not long continue in the direction of those secularizing trends. On the contrary, as Berger says, 'Catholic Christianity, both Latin and Greek, may be seen as an arresting and retrogressive step in the unfolding of the drama of secularization' and it was not until the Reformation that we see 'a powerful re-emergence of precisely those secularizing forces which had been "contained" by Catholicism, not only replicating the Old Testament in this, but going decisively beyond it'.[23]

Perhaps the chief reason for this is that though Christianity retained the Old Testament in its Bible (even if only after an initial struggle), it very quickly became divorced from its Jewish origins and took root in a Gentile world whose religions were of the pre-Axial order. Christianity baptized into its developing forms a considerable amount of non-Jewish components from such sources as Persian dualism, Hellenism, Greek, Roman and Teutonic religion. Islam was, in part, a protest against the resurgent mythology, idolatry and priestcraft seen to be present in the growing Christian tradition and, in making his protest, Muhammad was drawing, even if unconsciously, upon some of the very elements of the Old Testament we have just been sketching. The affirmation of the unity of God, the fierce rejection of polytheism, idolatry and of all visible representations of God, the non-priestly character of worship and the simplicity of prayer all reflect Jewish influence.

While Christianity was still in its infancy, however, it gave rise to a very distinctive doctrine which, though strongly rejected by both Jew and Muslim, is capable of being interpreted as a continuation of the secularizing forces present within ancient Israel. That is the well-known and central doctrine of the Incarnation. The difficulty is that this doctrine is open to widely diverse interpretation. But the fact that in the early post-Enlightenment period considerable appeal was made to it by Hegel, Strauss and Feuerbach (as we have already seen) is evidence of the possibility of regarding it as a step in the process of secularization.

The popular understanding of this doctrine is that God came down to earth and assumed human form in the person of Jesus of Nazareth. Such a simple identification of God with an historical person is unacceptable to both Jew and Muslim, in whose view no human being can contain the unseeable, incomprehensible God – this being a consequence of the prohibition of graven images. Even mature Christian thought has always tried to protect itself against such a simplistic view, and the complex doctrine of the Trinity evolved as a result.

What the early Christians wished to affirm by the Incarnation was that in their view Jesus of Nazareth was a meeting point between man and God. He spoke with all the authority of God. He embodied in human form all the divine qualities – the grace and truth of God. The important implication of this for our present purposes is this – not only was the human condition to be conceived as being only a little less than God, but it could in fact, in the right circumstances, embody the divine nature. When looked at in this way the doctrine of the Incarnation may be regarded as a further step in secularization; for it states that the transcendent reality referred to as God is not only to be found within the physical world rather than outside of it, but, in particular, can become manifest in the human condition.

Such a thought was too daring even for most Christians,

and as time went on Christianity developed an interpretation of the Incarnation which was almost the opposite of this. This was because it became virtually impossible to root out the ancient Gnostic view (heresy though it was said to be) which conceived Jesus as an eternal, divine and supernatural figure who, though he was believed to have once walked the earth *in the form* of a man, had never really been *completely* human. And while Christianity moved ever further in the direction of a dualistic world-view it could hardly be otherwise. Jesus came to be seen, no longer as a human being, but as a supernatural being from another world, who for a brief period of time paid a visit to our world. To the extent that this has been so in Christian thought and devotion, the original thrust of the language of Incarnation, including what we may here call its secularizing implications, became obscured and lost sight of.

The situation has radically changed. In the transition to modernity there has been an increasingly positive appreciation of the human condition. There has been a recovery of the genuine and complete humanity of Jesus. There has been a realization of the symbolic character of religious language and a recognition of the role of myth. There have emerged new ways of thinking about God (i.e. ultimate reality). All this has made it possible for the doctrine of the Incarnation to be approached in a way rather different from the traditional and crypto-Gnostic one, and one which restores and extends its original innovative character.

To achieve this, however, it is essential to move wholly into the new religious situation and not stop half way. For example, one cannot appreciate the significance of the Incarnation if one tries to combine a post-Enlightenment view of the humanity of Jesus with a pre-Enlightenment view of God. This is perhaps the weakness of the Unitarian position, as it is also of the humanist who is strongly attracted to Jesus as an authoritative teacher. It is also essential to distinguish clearly between the historical Jesus (about whom we have insufficient historical records ever to be able to gain an absolutely reliable picture) and the Christ of faith (to which the New Testament and Church tradition testify). The Christ of faith is the embodiment and projection of Christian experience, however much that was originally dependent upon the impact of the historical Jesus. The figure of Christ, the focal point of the doctrine of Incarnation, belongs not to the realm of historical data but to that of religious symbolism.

The Christian world has already become adjusted to the symbolic character of the creation myth and the story of Adam. It is commonplace today to say that Adam is not an historical figure but a symbolic embodiment of the human condition. In Adam (which is Hebrew for 'man') we are to see Everyman. Yet the myth, even when demythologized, remains deeply meaningful. Now it is the New Testament itself which first suggested the correlation between Adam and Christ, for there we read, 'For as in Adam all die, so also in Christ shall all be made alive . . . The first man Adam became a living being; the last Adam became a life-giving spirit . . . The first man was from the earth, a man of dust; the second man is from heaven'.[24]

When Paul wrote those words he was thinking within the framework of two worlds – an earthly and a spiritual. If we translate this symbolic language into the context of today's monistic world-view then it means something like this. Adam is the symbol for the whole human race in its present natural state; Christ is the symbol for what the whole human race can become. Christ symbolizes the human race in whom God has come to dwell, or, to use a phrase from Tillich, Christ is the symbol of the New Being[25] which, because of the human predicament (as symbolized in Adam), has been universally sought by man in all his religions. Even Paul did not hesitate to use the term 'Christ' both symbolically and collectively when he referred to Christians as those who are 'in Christ' and to the Church as the 'body of Christ'.

In translating the doctrine of the Incarnation into the context of the modern world-view it must also be remembered that whatever is thought of as being incarnate in the Christ figure is not God in the former supernatural and other-worldly sense. As Tillich rightly warns, the doctrine of the Incarnation is not to be confused with the 'mythology in which divine beings are transmuted into natural objects or human beings'.[26] He specifically warns against 'a literalism which takes pre-existence and post-existence as stages in a transcendent story of a divine being which descends from and ascends to a heavenly place'.[27]

A much more appropriate way of interpreting the Incarnation in the modern world is offered by John Macquarrie in his striking paraphrase of the Prologue of St John's Gospel, the very passage which inspired the term 'incarnation' in the first place, and Macquarrie presents this in the course of his attempt to reconstruct theism in the modern world.

> Fundamental to everything is meaning. Meaning is closely connected with what men call 'God', and indeed, meaning and God are the same. To say that God was in the beginning is to say that meaning was in the beginning. All things were made meaningful, and there was nothing made that was meaningless. Life is the drive toward meaning, and life has emerged into the light of humanity, the bearer of meaning. And meaning shines out through the threat of absurdity, for absurdity has not destroyed it.
>
> Every man has a share of the true meaning of things. This follows from the fact that this meaning has been embodying itself in the world from the beginning and has given the world its shape. Yet the world has not recognized the

> meaning, and even man, the bearer of meaning, has rejected it. But those who have received it and believed in it have been enabled to become the children of God. And this has happened not in the natural course of evolution or through human striving, but through an act of God. For the meaning has been incarnated in a human existent, in whom was grace and truth; and we have seen in him the final meaning or glory toward which everything moves – the glory of man and the glory of God.[28]

Much more could be cited from both the New Testament and subsequent Christian thought to support a this-worldly interpretation of the doctrine of the Incarnation, but the present purpose does not call for anything more. This brief sketch is offered to illustrate the contention that just as the Old Testament seems to have contained the seeds of the secularizing process, so also does that central Christian doctrine which has affirmed consistently the complete divinity and complete humanity of Jesus Christ.

Thus, if we are searching for reasons to explain why the modern secularized world has come out of the Judaeo-Christian West, and not from one of the other great cultural traditions, then we may have to look to significant elements which are present both in the Old Testament inherited from Judaism and in the theme most central to Christianity itself. It would have to be clearly acknowledged, of course, that if there is any such causal connection then these elements have exercised their influences almost surreptitiously and certainly in spite of, rather than because of, the authoritative interpreters of the tradition in which they are found.

Berger has drawn attention to this paradoxical situation by saying that 'Christianity has been its own gravedigger'.[29] Such a remark assumes, however, that the pre-modern form of Christianity is the only true and possible expression of it. This may be true, in which case it may have to be said that Christianity had within it the seeds of its own dissolution. But if, on the other hand, we look at the Judaeo-Christian tradition as a whole, and within the total context of all past religious experience on this globe, then we may come to view it more positively as the key to the contemporary religious situation. The long-term impact of the Judaeo-Christian tradition could even be summed up in the term secularization in that it has been a spiritual movement in which religion has become increasingly this-worldly, in which the divine has become more and more grounded in the human – a process, indeed, in which God comes down to earth.

CHAPTER 15

A PROPHET OF THE NEW AGE

❖

Even today, late in the twentieth century, there are many who emphatically deny that it is legitimate to speak of man as having entered a new religious era and they insist that the religious situation of man is in no essential way different from what it has traditionally been conceived to be. During the nineteenth century it was only a small minority of the Western world who came to believe that a new religious era had dawned. Even many of those did not realize how radical the change was, which was then taking place. There is one nineteenth-century person, however, who is worth singling out as the thinker who perhaps penetrated most deeply into the nature of the new era in man's religious experience.

Friedrich Wilhelm Nietzsche (1844-1900) may be described as the prophet *par excellence* of the new age. Martin Buber has referred to him as 'the first path-finder of the new culture', 'the awakener and creator of new life-values and a new world-feeling'.[1] R. J. Hollingdale, a translator of some of Nietzsche's works into English, said 'The twentieth century came to birth in the mind of Friedrich Nietzsche during the 1880s; and it is his particular and undying distinction that when he saw the blood-red dawn of our day he did not turn from it in distress and leave the future to fend for itself, but wearied himself to find a means whereby this new and more terrible day could be endured, welcomed and enjoyed'.[2]

Nietzsche had been reared in an atmosphere of extreme Lutheran piety, a fact which needs to be remembered when reading his fierce condemnation of Christianity. He came of a long line of Lutheran pastors but the premature death of his father left him thereafter in a household entirely composed of female relatives. His childhood experiences were undoubtedly influential in engineering what became his four pet hates – pharisaical piety, nationalism, bourgeois provincialism and domineering women.

After a school career made notable for his brilliance in classics, Nietzsche went to the University of Bonn to study theology. He soon turned back to classics. His professor, Friedrich Ritschl, regarded him as the most brilliant student he had had in his 40 years of teaching, recommending him for the Chair of Classical Philology at Basel before he had even graduated. Nietzsche was awarded his doctorate without examination and went to Basel, where he held the Chair, his only academic appointment, until he resigned ten years later, partly because of growing ill-health and partly because of increasing disillusionment with academic life. He spent the next decade in southern Europe, nursing his failing health and writing. This was his most creative period; his intellect is said to have become razor-sharp. But in 1889 he became hopelessly insane (probably as the result of syphilis) and remained so until his death. It was only after he had lost his sanity that his books came to be widely read and it has been mainly during this century that his real significance has been recognized.

Even during his student days at Leipzig, Nietzsche was beginning to lose his interest in classical philology. He was becoming fascinated with the condition of modern man, with what he called the true and urgent problems of life. He began to probe beneath the surface of Western culture with remarkable insight. His greatness was to perceive the radical character of the cultural and religious change then taking place. He saw that he lived between two ages, one already dying and the other waiting to be born. He knew that Western Christendom had come to an end. That observation is commonplace today; a century ago many found the thought offensive.

Nietzsche ceased to be a believing Christian during his schooldays. In an essay entitled 'On the Childhood of the Peoples' which he wrote at the age of eighteen he said, 'That God became man shows only that man is not to seek his bliss in eternity, but to found his heaven on earth; the delusion of a supra-terrestrial world has placed the spirit of man in a false relation to the terrestrial: it was the product of the People's childhood'.[3] Here he shows how he had already grasped the significance of the transition to modernity, described in the last chapter as secularization.

It was probably in deference to his mother's wishes and to family tradition that he began to study for the Lutheran ministry. When his mother expressed her regret at his subsequent abandonment of the study of theology, he wrote her a long letter in which he pointed out that, though the traditional belief in God might bring peace of mind and spiritual satisfaction, it did not necessarily mean that it was true; it was more important to search for truth even though the uncovering of it could be unwelcome and discomforting. 'Here the ways of men divide', he said, 'if you wish to strive for peace of soul and happiness, then believe: if you wish to be a disciple of truth, then inquire.'[4]

An important factor in Nietzsche's own search for truth was the influence of Arthur Schopenhauer (1788-1860), after he accidently came across the latter's book *The World as Will and Idea,* and became captivated by it. Schopenhauer is said to have been the first avowed atheist in Germany. He was influenced by Kant and Fichte but became strongly anti-Hegelian. He was attracted to Buddhism rather than to Christianity and also drew some inspiration from the Upanishads. Whereas Hegel prepared the way for an attitude of evolutionary optimism, subsequently to be found in both Christian liberalism and in Marxism, Schopenhauer opened the door for existentialist pessimism. For Schopenhauer the ultimate metaphysical reality is neither Mind nor Matter but Will. Will manifests itself throughout the world, operating blindly and without purpose. In the sphere of human affairs Will manifests itself in the operation of the human will, leading to self-assertion, social conflict, etc. It is the cause of all suffering and has the potential for evil rather than for good. Just as the Buddha diagnosed the suffering character of the human condition to be directly due to desire or thirst, so Schopenhauer believed all suffering to result from Will. Thus the more we exercise the will, the more we suffer. As the Buddha prescribed a path which led to salvation (or Nirvana) by the final elimination of desire, so Schopenhauer maintained that a person is delivered from suffering and unhappiness only when he is no longer involved in operations of the will. Even though death brings such a state, suicide is no answer for it involves an act of the will. Schopenhauer held that the refusal to commit suicide in order to face the worst that life might offer is the one redeeming feature of the human condition, which places man above the animals. For Schopenhauer, life has no eternal meaning and is all a tragic mistake; the only form of happiness possible is to be obtained by renunciating life and entering into painless nothingness.

When Nietzsche abandoned the Christian faith of his youth and, as he said, set sail upon a sea of doubt, the first firm ground on which he landed was Schopenhauer's pessimistic philosophy. It provided for him what he found necessary, at first, to counterbalance the extreme optimism of the post-Hegelians. He felt they were looking at life through rosy-coloured spectacles and did not see the world as it really is. They did not properly appreciate what has been called the 'tragic sense of life'.[5] Nietzsche understood himself 'as the first *tragic philosopher*'.[6] It was important that Nietzsche, through the agency of Schopenhauer, should have experienced, at least for a while, the attraction of that more negative attitude to life which is found in Buddhism and sometimes in Hinduism, for it meant that when he came to express his own maturer thoughts, there was a sense in which he superseded the post-Axial traditions of both East and West.

By the time Nietzsche was entering his most creative decade he was making his break with Schopenhauer, and indeed had never denied the value of life in the way the latter had done.[7] In his first book, *The Birth of Tragedy*, Nietzsche contended that in the spirit of Greek tragedy there was a more positive answer than that of Schopenhauer to the horrors and meaninglessness of human existence; it was possible, in spite of everything to the contrary, to face life and to affirm it as something worthwhile and even beautiful.

Thereafter Nietzsche produced about a book a year. At first these consisted of a series of essays (e.g. *Untimely Meditations*), and then for a while he expressed himself in the form of aphorisms, short pithy observations, some as short as a sentence and others forming a brief essay of several pages. Nietzsche presented no coherent philosophical system. Such was the radical character of the cultural change taking place and such was the enigmatic nature of human existence (as he saw it) that systems of thought were out of the question. His thoughts were often extremely provocative, sometimes at variance with one another, and sometimes so outrageous as to appear (at least at face value) as absurd. They were intended to jolt one out of complacency and stereotyped ways of thinking. He did not expect his readers to agree with everything he said; rather he was encouraging them to think for themselves. His books cannot be read quickly; they must be wrestled with, pondered on and responded to. They reflect the ambiguities of life, the fact that creative and destructive elements are both present in the life process.

This further means that all those interested in Nietzsche should read his works for themselves, rather than through an interpreter, so that they may personally experience his provocative jabs as well as his penetrating insights. He is open to interpretation in a variety of ways and it is questionable whether any one of these is the only true or definitive one. What follows in this chapter is simply an attempt to draw attention to some of the ways in which he strikingly expressed the predicament of modern man and showed a deep, even if incomplete, understanding of the nature of the new religious era.

More clearly than any of the nineteenth-century thinkers we discussed earlier, Nietzsche saw that the transition to modernity was not simply a matter of replacing an outmoded religion or philosophy with a new and more adequate one. The time for uncovering eternal truths and seeing how they fitted into a neat and coherent whole was past. (Of course, in one sense it had never really existed, but men had long assumed that it did.) This is partly why his own philosophy, if one can call it such, defies systematization and lacks logical consistency. He recognized that even ultimate reality itself is in a state of change and flux. He rebuked philosophers for 'starting out from man as he is now and thinking they can reach their goal through an analysis of him'.[8] They were assuming that the human condition is something which remains constant in the midst of flux, when in fact it is in the process of becoming. 'But everything has become', he said, 'there are no *eternal facts,* just as there are no absolute truths.'[8]

Nietzsche sketched the post-theistic character of the new religious age most tellingly in his now well-known little Parable of the Madman.[9] He described a madman running through the market-place with a lantern during the brightness of the morning and crying out that he was looking for God. The bystanders poked fun at him and asked him if God had lost his way or gone on a distant voyage. Thereupon he declared that mankind were all responsible for the murder of God. Because God was dead and would remain dead, it was as if the earth had become unchained from the sun and was already moving out into the cold, dark and empty space of the vast universe. That was why he had lit his lantern even though it was still light. This strange announcement silenced the onlookers and caused them to stare at him in astonishment. Then the madman was silent and threw his lantern to the ground, where it broke into pieces and went out. Then he said, 'I have come too early; my time is not yet. This tremendous event is still on its way. It has not yet reached the ears of men'.

People like Hegel, Strauss, Feuerbach and so on had recognized that mankind had entered into a post-theistic age but, in Nietzsche's view, they had not properly appreciated the stark and frightening significance of such a shattering cosmic event. Hegel, it may be remembered, was the first to have spoken of the death of God. These men optimistically assumed, however, that all the lasting values inherited from the past would still remain for man in spite of the loss of traditional theism. They had not reckoned with the fact that the death of God also meant an end to absoluteness of all values, and all truths. Nietzsche contemptuously spoke of Strauss as a 'cultural Philistine' on the grounds that he had openly renounced Christianity but continued to think and act as if nothing else had changed; Strauss had participated, along with others, in the killing of God but had not realized the full significance of this event.

According to Nietzsche, people like Strauss and George Eliot had made the mistake of thinking that Christian moral values would still remain even after the Christian God had been got rid of. 'Christianity is a system, a consistently thought out and *complete* view of things', he said. 'If one breaks out of it a fundamental idea, the belief in God, one thereby breaks the whole thing to pieces: one has nothing of any consequence left in one's hands.'[10]

Nietzsche, of Protestant extraction though he was, traced the causes of the modern dissolution of Christendom back to the Protestant Reformers, contending that the work of Luther, instead of leading to the intended rebuilding of the Church, had inadvertently set in motion the destruction of Christianity. 'But what is strangest is this', he said. 'Those who exerted themselves the most to preserve and conserve Christianity have become precisely its most efficient destroyers – the Germans.'[11] Luther, he asserted, had 'smashed an ideal that he could not attain, while he seemed to abhor and to be fighting only the degeneration of this ideal'.[12]

On the other hand, Nietzsche was strongly critical of Luther for even attempting to restore Christianity in a purified form. Nietzsche regarded Buddhism as vastly superior to Christianity and a hundred times more realistic but in his view they both belonged to the decadent past. He rejoiced in the fact that Christendom was being shaken to its deepest foundations, that the belief in God had been undermined and that the Christian-ascetic ideal was fighting its last fight.[13] He did not, therefore, like Strauss, Feuerbach and the Hegelian theologians, attempt to reconstruct a new and more adequate form of Christianity. His denunciation of Christianity was more violent than any other nineteenth-century critic and reached its peak in the *The Anti-Christ*, where he said, for example, 'I condemn Christianity, I bring against the Christian Church the most terrible charge any prosecutor has ever uttered. To me it is the extremest thinkable form of corruption . . . The Christian Church has left nothing untouched by its depravity, it has made of every value a disvalue, of every truth a lie . . . I call Christianity the *one* great curse . . . the *one* immortal blemish of mankind'.[14]

Yet it was something of a love-hate relationship which he had with Christianity. It was the love of truth which he had imbibed from Christianity which enabled him to be so critical of it. He said, 'even we students of today, who are atheists and anti-metaphysicians, light our torches at the flame of a millennial faith; the Christian faith, that God is truth and truth divine'.[15] Indeed it was this very concern for truth, hidden at the heart of Christianity, which was now, in his view, bringing about the dissolution of the historical forms of Christianity. He wrote, 'This Christianity as dogma perished by its own ethics, and in the same way Christianity as ethics must perish; we are standing on the threshold of this event. After drawing a whole series of conclusions, Christian truthfulness must now draw its strongest conclusion, the one by which it shall do away with itself . . . It is by this dawning self-consciousness of the will to truth that ethics must now perish. This is the great spectacle of a hundred acts that will occupy Europe for the next two centuries, the most terrible and problematical but also the most hopeful of spectacles'.[16]

The suggestion we have here that, if Christianity were voluntarily to bring about its own dissolution, it would be its finest hour, is unexpectedly consistent with the paradox which is central to Christianity, namely that one must die in order to live. It is not surprising then that Nietzsche, in spite of his polemic against Christianity, was attracted to some aspects of the Christ figure. 'In reality', he said, 'there has been only one Christian, and he died on the Cross. The "Evangel" *died* on the Cross. What was called

"Evangel" from this moment onwards was already the opposite of what *he* had lived.'[17] What subsequently became Christianity was in Nietzsche's view a dysangel or bad tidings and it consisted in thinking that Christianity is primarily a matter of what one believes, such as the belief that redemption comes through the supernatural power of Christ. Genuine Christianity (and according to Nietzsche there *is* such a thing) consists in the practice of living a life like that of him who died on the Cross. Nietzsche claimed that 'This "bringer of glad tidings" died as he lived, as he *taught* – *not* to "redeem mankind" but to demonstrate how one ought to live. What he bequeathed to mankind is his *practice* . . . his bearing before the judges . . . his bearing on the *Cross*'.[18]

Just as Hegel and Feuerbach had made much of the Christian doctrine of the Incarnation, so Nietzsche may be said to have turned back to the scandal of the Cross, which had long been grossly distorted. Whereas Christ had taught that whoever set out to save his soul would lose it and called man to take up their own cross and follow him, Christianity had completely twisted this to mean the offer of an assured place in some eternal world through the benefits of the Cross of Christ. Nietzsche (somewhat unfairly) laid most of the blame for this distortion on St Paul. He said it was Paul who was responsible for turning the original evangel into a dysangel until 'nothing was left bearing even the remotest resemblance to reality. Paul simply shifted the centre of gravity of that entire existence *beyond* this existence – in the *lie* of the "resurrected" Jesus . . . If one shifts the centre of gravity of life *out* of life into the "Beyond" – into *nothingness* – one has deprived life as such of its centre of gravity. The great lie of personal immortality destroys all rationality, all naturalness of instinct – all that is salutary, all that is life-furthering'.[19]

Here, as elsewhere, Nietzsche acknowledged the complete

secularity of the modern religious situation and saw the continuance of the traditional Christian other-worldliness as a threat to man's realization of his true humanity. Nietzsche scathingly rejected the dualistic world-view which Christianity had long regarded as the absolute truth of reality and which had led Christians to look for other-worldly goals and to hopes of personal immortality. He said, 'The "kingdom of Heaven" is a condition of the heart – not something that comes "upon the earth" or "after death". The entire concept of natural death is *lacking* in the Gospel; death is not a bridge, not a transition, it is lacking because it belongs to quite another world, a merely apparent world useful only for the purpose of symbolism . . . The "kingdom of God" is not something one waits for; it has no yesterday or tomorrow, it does not come "in a thousand years" – it is an experience within a heart: it is everywhere, it is nowhere'.[20]

Nietzsche believed that the traditional Christian concern with the supposed spiritual realities of the other-world, far from leading to human fulfilment, had the effect of falsifying all the real human problems of politics, of social organization and of education and of causing men to despise the basic concerns of life itself.[21] The concepts of 'God', 'soul', 'virtue', 'sin', 'beyond', 'truth', 'eternal life' are not to be considered true realities but are mere imaginings. 'The concept of "God" invented as a counterconcept of life – everything harmful, poisonous, slanderous, the whole hostility unto death against life synthesized in this concept in a gruesome unity! The concept of the "beyond", the "true world" invented in order to devaluate the only world there is – in order to retain no goal, no reason, no task for our earthly reality! The concept of the "soul", the "spirit", finally even "*immortal* soul", invented in order to despise the body, to make it sick, "holy"; to oppose with a ghastly levity everything that deserves to be taken seriously in life, the questions of nourishment, abode, spiritual diet, treatment of the sick, cleanliness, and weather.'[22]

The modern growth of this-worldly concerns (or secularization) meant, for Nietzsche, that mankind was entering on an entirely new era, one pregnant with both hope and disaster on the grand scale. He spoke of his fellow-Europeans as the 'first-born of the twentieth century'.[23] Of course there had been cultural transitions before. The transition from the ancient classical world to Christendom had involved the replacement of one set of values by another; acts previously thought to be good (such as sacrifice to the Roman gods) came to be labelled bad, and what was bad became good. In the transition to modernity another transition in values is taking place. Nietzsche believed this to be more radical than all previous transitions in that it was not simply a replacement of one set of values (long accepted as absolute) by another set of values (now believed to be the *truly* absolute); it was the transition to the state of affairs where it must be recognized that there are no absolute moral values but that man himself is seen to be the creator of values. This transition he called 'the revaluation of all values'. It is one of the themes of his book *Beyond Good and Evil*, in the course of which he says, 'There are no moral phenomena at all, only a moral interpretation of phenomena'.[24] This led Nietzsche (who in many ways is to be regarded as a man of intense moral concern) to refer to himself as 'the first immoralist'.[25]

There are two stages (as Nietzsche saw it) in the transition taking place in the moral dimension of human nature and these he expressed in a parable of the metamorphoses of the human spirit from the camel to the lion and then from the lion to the child.[26] In the traditional morality the human spirit has become weighed down with the burden of the absolutes he is bound to obey and he is like an overloaded camel crossing a waterless desert. There a metamorphosis takes place; the camel becomes a lion. This means that the time comes when the human spirit must throw off its burdens, exert its freedom and feel its strength. Where the great dragon previously said, 'Thou shalt', the spirit of the lion says, 'I will'. But though, for the new morality, it is necessary to become free, the human spirit cannot, as the lion, create new values; for this the lion must become a child. Out of a child-like innocence and making a new beginning, the human spirit 'now wills its own will, the spirit sundered from the world now wins *its own* world', and thus internalizes the process of creating values.

Nietzsche's doctrine of the revaluation of all values is all of a piece with the dissolution of the other-world, the recognition of the death of God and the awareness of the absence of any eternal moral absolutes. The new age called upon men to revalue and reverse the former 'eternal values', for in the past these had fostered what Nietzsche called the 'slave morality'. He contended that at the basis of every religion and morality of the past was the imperative 'Do this and you will be happy'. It induced a slave morality because it caused men to be dependent on the approval of God and/or of his fellows and thus it stunted moral growth, smothered initiative, crushed the freedom of the human spirit and encouraged in man the continuance of weakness, servile dependence, lack of self-confidence and spiritual suffering. Slave morality operates on the basis of what all men have in common and takes no cognizance of values peculiar to each individual. How often do we find, for example, that the man of genius, of creative spirit, must break out of the accepted morality of his time in order to be creative.

What Nietzsche hoped to see develop by the revaluation of all values was what he called 'the master morality'. This has nothing whatever to do (as has sometimes been mistakenly supposed) with a morality of mastering it over others. It is the morality of the noble type of man who 'feels *himself* to be the determiner of values, he does not need to be approved of . . . he *creates values* . . . The noble human being honours in himself the man of power, also the man who has power over himself, who understands how to speak and how to keep silent, who enjoys practising severity and harshness upon himself and feels reverence for all that is severe and harsh'.[27] Instead of becoming the slave of values, falsely believed to be absolute (but in actual fact created by others) he has become the master of the moral component of his own human condition. The exponent of master morality is the morally mature man, the man who is morally well-balanced, who, because of what he is, *must* perform certain actions and instinctively shrinks from other actions. Instead of finding happiness by conforming to certain virtues imposed from without, 'his virtue is the consequence of his happiness'.[28]

It is a grave travesty of Nietzsche's revaluation of values to interpret it as meaning the end of morality or to think that he was advocating a life of unbridled licence for man. Far from making it morally easy for man, the attainment of the master morality would make much greater demands upon men than the traditional moralities had done and it was by no means certain in Nietzsche's mind that the human race would be equal to these demands. But in so far as men met the requirements of the new age, there would emerge a new type of man, of whom there had been only very occasional examples in the past. Nietzsche called this new type the *Ubermensch*. This has been translated as 'superman' though perhaps 'overman' is preferable. (The English term 'Superman' is a misleading translation for it already has too many associations which are in sharp conflict with what Nietzsche had in mind. Although the Nazis claimed Nietzsche as their own prophet, and were encouraged to do so by Nietzsche's own sister, it is a gross misrepresentation of all that Nietzsche stood for to have his name even associated with Nazism and the popular image of the Nazi stormtrooper was almost the polar opposite of Nietzsche's *Ubermensch*.)

The concept of the Overman is chiefly expounded in *Thus Spake Zarathustra*. There he is said to be, not the man who lords it over others by virtue of his superior strength, but rather the man who has first of all channelled his own will to power towards the mastery of himself. The key to the understanding of the Overman is to be found in self-discipline. The *Over*man is the one who has *over*come MAN, i.e., himself. He is the one who has overcome the animal nature in man, who has ordered the chaos of man's warring passions, who has sublimated his destructive impulses, who has become the 'man of tolerance, not from weakness, but from strength, a spirit who has *become free*'.[29] In achieving the mastery of his humanity, the Overman is led to joy and serenity. 'The most spiritual human beings, as the *strongest*, find their happiness where others would find their destruction: in the labyrinth, in severity towards themselves and others, in attempting; their joy lies in self-constraint: with them asceticism becomes nature, need, instinct. They consider the hard task a privilege, to play with vices which overwhelm others a *recreation* . . . They are the most venerable kind of human being: this does not exclude their being the most cheerful, the most amiable.'[30]

Nietzsche did not share the optimistic view of human nature displayed by Feuerbach, Marx, Comte and later humanists, and often associated with the then popular ideas of automatic progress and continuing evolution. He knew that man has within him the potential for unbelievable inhuman savagery; he believed that the human phenomenon could end in complete disaster. 'Man is a rope over an abyss, fastened between animal and Overman', said Zarathustra.[31] In his parable in *Thus Spake Zarathustra* Nietzsche likened mankind to a tightrope walker, treading a path fraught with danger but, provided he did not fall, it would lead him from his animal origins to the attainment of his Overman potential.

According to Nietzsche, there are those who do not want to see the human attainment of the Overman. These despise the life of here and now and are weary of the earth. They poison men's minds with hopes of life in another world, for which there is no need to exert oneself unduly. Nietzsche speaks of these as the Ultimate Men and presents his readers with the choice between the Overman and the Ultimate Man. Through Zarathustra he says, 'Behold, I teach you the Superman, the Superman is the meaning of the earth. Let your will say: The Superman *shall be* the meaning of the earth! I entreat you, my brothers, *remain true to the earth,* and do not believe those who speak to you of superterrestrial hopes! . . . I love those who do not first seek beyond the stars for reasons to go down and to be sacrifices: but who sacrifice themselves to the earth, that the earth may one day belong to the Superman'.[32]

Whereas the slave morality proclaimed by Christianity leads men to the denial of life (according to Nietzsche), and encourages them to escape from the world and to find ultimate fulfilment in another world, the Overman is an affirmer – a Yea-sayer – who says Yes to life, in spite of the absence of any ultimate meaning to history or to human existence. Any significance man comes to recognize in life must be found in the present, for only the present truly exists and both the past and the future are simply imaginary. It is here that Nietzsche's existentialist stance becomes clear. It led him to make a break with the linear view of time and of history, which has so strongly characterized Judaism, Christianity and Marxism and which encourages men to look back to ultimate beginnings and to pin their hopes on a final consummation.

In contrast with the linear view of history Nietzsche minimized ends and purposes and maximized the present state of being. This may be simply understood by likening life to an unending sea journey.[33] Since there is no possibility of ever reaching land, the question of what the ultimate destination will be loses all significance, but the question of whether one is at present sea-sick or not is a matter of very great moment. The present (and hence every) moment is therefore of infinite significance; it takes on the quality of eternity. Nietzsche's replacement for the linear view of history he referred to as 'eternal recurrence'. Since there is no 'beyond' and no future but only a present which recurs infinitely, the present moment mediates, and participates in, eternity.

Since we have been long conditioned by a linear view of history it is not easy for us to grasp Nietzsche's teaching on the eternal recurrence, or even be sure that we have properly understood his intention. It is because he denies any absolute beginning or absolute end but affirms only a present moment which recurs an infinite number of times that he is able to say through Zarathustra, 'all things recur eternally and we ourselves with them . . . we have already existed an infinite number of times before and all things with us . . . I shall return eternally to this identical and self-same life, in the greatest things and in the smallest, to teach once more the eternal recurrence of all things, to speak once more the teaching of the great noontide of earth and man, to tell man of the superman once more'.[34] Instead of implying that the present moment is of no great significance because it will be endlessly repeated, Nietzsche's intention seems rather to be the affirmation of the once for all character of each individual's life and actions.

Nietzsche's doctrine of the eternal recurrence was his substitute for the now outmoded doctrine of personal immortality. It provided the motivation for morality. What one does and how one lives does really matter. There is an eternal quality about every moment. The thought of having to repeat eternally an action which does not spiritually satisfy leads one to make every decision with care. One's motto must be, 'So live that you must wish to live again'.

In similar fashion Nietzsche's doctrine of the Overman was his substitute for the now outmoded belief in God. 'Once you said "God" when you gazed upon distant seas: but now I have taught you to say "Superman". God is a supposition; but I want your supposing to reach no further than your creating will. Could you *create* a god? – So be silent about all gods! But you could surely create the Superman . . . you could transform yourselves into forefathers and ancestors of the Superman: and let this be your finest creating! . . . And you yourselves should create what you have hitherto called the World: the World should be formed in your image, by your reason, your will and your love! And truly, it will be to your happiness, you enlightened men.'[35]

It is in the notion of the Overman that the element of transcendence still finds a place in Nietzsche's thought. The Overman transcends man in his present condition but since the Overman is potentially present in the human condition, that which transcends man is also immanent. In Nietzsche's thought we find an interesting example of the balance between transcendence and immanence, referred to at the end of the last chapter. In view of Nietzsche's rejection of ends and purposes, not even the concept of the Overman should be regarded as a goal, to be reached within a linear sense of time. That is why Nietzsche also said that 'What is great in man is that he is a bridge and not a goal; what can be loved in man is that he is a *going-across* and a *going-under*'.[36]

Nietzsche shared neither the bland optimism of Hegel nor the complete pessimism of Schopenhauer. Although he saw the 'death of God' as much more disastrous for modern man than most atheists of his day did, and though he foresaw the crumbling of the whole fabric of the traditional cultures and the undermining of their value systems, there was still within Nietzsche a strong element of hope. He looked with hope to the revaluation of all values and the coming of the Overman. If mankind could so order its morality that it would favour the emergence of the Overman then the death of God would be surmounted. But in this hope Nietzsche saw absolutely no room for any easy optimism. Nietzsche was not himself a nihilist (though he has sometimes been taken for one) but he foresaw a long period of nihilism, of ferment and of great chaos.

In referring to Nietzsche as a prophet of the new age it must be clearly understood that he is not a prophet after the order of Zorathustra, the Buddha, Jesus and Muhammad. He does not unfold to us an authoritative teaching to be believed and obeyed. If he had, he would not be a prophet of the new age but simply one more prophet of the post-Axial age, of which there are many still arising in the present religious confusion. The importance of Nietzsche is not that we should applaud him and hang on his every word. Indeed the development of anything like a Nietzschean cult (there have been tendencies in this direction) would constitute a travesty of all that Nietzsche stood for. Nietzsche himself warned against it, 'there is nothing in me of a founder of a religion . . . I have a terrible fear that one day I will be pronounced *holy*'.[37]

Nietzsche's works may irritate, confuse and repel the reader as well as attract and inspire him, but in so far as they jolt him into thinking for himself then Nietzsche may be accepted as a prophet appropriate for our age and, like all true prophets, one who came before his time. Nietzsche himself said 'Only the day after tomorrow belongs to me. Some are born posthumously'.[38] The words of Nietzsche serve as a mirror, challenging us to see ourselves and our condition as we really are in this new era in which man is coming of age. We can no longer appeal to a God up there, or to former authorities – not even to Nietzsche himself. We are what we are; and what we choose to make of ourselves and of our world is over to us. We are walking a tightrope. Mankind can bring about its own ruin and even destroy this planet. All this is clearer to men today than it was when Nietzsche wrote. But there is also within us the potential for a new kind of man – the Overman. Much of what men formerly projected into the concept of God is possible of realization on earth and from within the human condition. There is a new sense in which it is possible to say – God comes down to earth.

NOTES

(For fuller publication details, where these are not supplied, consult Bibliography)

Chapter 1 Understanding Religion in Today's Changing World

1 *The Meaning of History*, pp. 1-2.
2 *The Protestant Era*, University of Chicago, 1957, p. 150.
3 *Beyond Tradition and Modernity*, p. 3.
4 *Historia Religionum*, E. J. Brill, Leiden, 1971, Vol. II, p. 355.
5 *Christianity and the Encounter of the World Religions*, Columbia University Press, New York, 1964, p. 4.
6 See *This Changing World*, ed. by J. R. M. Brumwell, pp. 261-2.

Chapter 2 The First Major Threshold of Religious Change

1 King Numa is now regarded as a legendary figure.
2 Quoted by Karl Jaspers, *The Origin and Goal of History*, p. 8.
3 ibid., p. 8.
4 ibid., p. 1.
5 R. N. Bellah, *Beyond Belief*, pp. 20-50.
6 Max Weber, *The Sociology of Religion*, p. 1.
7 Emile Durkheim, *Selected Writings*, ed. by A. Giddens, Cambridge University Press, 1972, p. 239.
8 Jaspers, op. cit., p. 4.
9 ibid., p. 2.
10 ibid., p. 2.
11 ibid., p. 4.
12 Weber, op. cit., p. 141.
13 Durkheim, op. cit., p. 240.
14 *A Study of History*, Vol. XII, *Reconsiderations*, p. 83.
15 Jaspers, op. cit., p. 8.

Chapter 3 Some Significant Steps Leading to the Modern World

1 *The Degrees of Knowledge,* Charles Scribner, New York, 1938, p. 1.
2 *A History of Philosophy,* Vol. III, 1953, p. 20.
3 The doctrine of the Swiss theologian Thomas Erastus (1524-83) that the State has the right to exercise jurisdiction over the Church in all matters both civil and ecclesiastical.
4 op. cit., Vol. III, p. 19.
5 'Christianity and the New Age', *Essays in Order,* ed. by Christopher Dawson, Macmillan Co., New York, 1931, p. 165.
6 N. Berdyaev, *The Meaning of History,* p. 129.
7 *The Crisis of Faith,* p. 46.
8 *Renaissance and Revolution,* Pantheon Books, New York, 1965, p. 39.
9 Quoted by Jacob Burckhardt, *The Civilization of the Renaissance in Italy,* George Allen & Unwin, 1951, p. 185.
10 Quoted by A. Toynbee, *An Historian's Approach to Religion,* p. 188.
11 Quoted from his *Enchiridion militis Christiani,* 1503, by Gordon Rupp in 'Erasmus Desiderius', *Encyclopaedia Britannica,* 15th edition, Chicago, 1974, Vol. VI, p. 952.
12 *The Philosophy of the Enlightenment,* p. 137.

Chapter 4 The Second Major Threshold of Religious Change

1 *Modern Christian Thought,* p. 2.
2 William Whiston, a mathematician, was removed from his Cambridge professorship in 1710 because of his Arianism.
3 Often referred to as Pyrrhonism after the Greek philosopher Pyrrho (c. 360-270 BC), the father of the Greek sceptics.
4 Descartes, *Discourse on Method,* Penguin, 1960, p. 48.
5 ibid., p. 50.
6 ibid., p. 61.
7 ibid., p. 61.
8 The first Index was issued by the Inquisition under Pope Paul IV in 1557, and is itself a witness to the emerging modern thought, since the Church believed it necessary to hold it at bay.

9 Deuteronomy 6:4. Called the Shema, after its first word in Hebrew, Deuteronomy 6:4-9 is considered the chief Jewish confession of faith.
10 E. Cassirer, *The Philosophy of the Enlightenment*, p. 167.
11 See Ninian Smart (ed.), *Historical Selections in the Philosophy of Religion*, p. 97.
12 ibid., p. 135.
13 ibid., p. 136.
14 ibid., p. 140.
15 Locke, *An Essay Concerning Human Understanding*, Dover Publications, New York, 1959, Vol. II, pp. 306-7.
16 A group of philosophical divines who flourished at Cambridge between 1633 and 1688. Influenced by Neo-Platonism and Descartes, they stood for tolerance and believed reason should be the final judge in all religious matters.
17 A term derogatively applied to Anglican divines who attached little importance to matters of dogma and liturgy.
18 John Toland, *Christianity Not Mysterious*, London, 1702, p. 6.
19 This thought has been much more fully developed by Teilhard de Chardin.
20 These were read by Voltaire when he was in England.
21 Quoted by Cassirer, op. cit., p. 166.
22 ibid., p. 170.
23 ibid., p. 163.
24 ibid., p. 135.

Chapter 5 From Religion to Philosophy

1 See *Hume on Religion*, p. 268.
2 *A Treatise of Human Nature*, ed. by Selby-Giggs, Clarendon Press, 1955, pp. 252-3.
3 *Hume on Religion*, p. 98.
4 Published only posthumously because of the offence it was expected to cause.
5 *Hume on Religion*, p. 195.
6 ibid., p. 196.
7 ibid., p. 196.
8 ibid., p. 204.

9 J. G. Hamann (1730-88) was so impressed by Hume's *Dialogues* that he translated it into German and, in response to it, developed a 'theology of faith' which strongly influenced Kierkegaard, the 'father of existentialism'.
10 *View of the Evidence of Christianity* (1794) and *Natural Theology* (1802).
11 See Willy Ley (ed.), *Kant's Cosmogony*, Greenwood Pub. Corp., New York, 1968.
12 See *Kant's Prolegomena*, ed. by Paul Carus, Open Court Pub. Co., Chicago, 1968, p. 7.
13 *Immanuel Kant's Critique of Pure Reason*, trans. by Norman Kemp Smith, Macmillan, 1929, p. 29.
14 *Kant's Critique of Practical Reason*, trans. by Thomas Kingshill Abbott, Longmans, 6th ed. 1967, p. 260.
15 ibid., p. 226.
16 See *Kant's Prolegomena*, p. 266.
17 See Patrick L. Gardiner (ed.), *19th-Century Philosophy*, p. 25.
18 Acts 17:28.
19 See Tillich, *Perspectives on Nineteenth and Twentieth Century Protestant Theology*, pp. 141-52.
20 Hegel, *Texts and Commentary*, p. 20.
21 See *Early Theological Writings*, p. 163.
22 *Lectures on the Philosophy of Religion*, Vol. I, p. 2.
23 ibid., p. 15.
24 St John's Gospel, 1:1, 4:24.
25 *Philosophy of Religion*, Vol. I, p. 33.
26 ibid., pp. 217-18.
27 ibid., Vol. II, p. 328.
28 ibid., Vol. I, p. 95.
29 ibid., p. 92.
30 *Hegel Selections*, ed. by J. Loewenberg, p. 360
31 *Philosophy of Religion*, Vol. I, pp. 79-80.
32 Quoted by J. Moltmann, *The Experiment Hope*, Fortress Press, Philadelphia, 1975, p. 35.
33 *Philosophy of Religion*, Vol. II, p. 202.
34 *The Philosophy of History*, trans. by J. Sibree, New York, 1944, pp. 321-2.
35 *Philosophy of Religion*, Vol. III, p. 86.
36 ibid., p. 89.
37 ibid., p. 91.

38 See his famous Parable of the Madman in *The Gay Science,* and briefly described in Chapter 15 below.
39 Hegel first used it in an essay 'Faith and Knowledge' (1802). In 1796 Jean Paul, a German Romantic, had written a novel *Siebenkäs,* in which the dead Christ speaks from the top of the structure of the universe and announces that God is no more.
40 op. cit., p. 154.
41 See *Philosophy of Religion,* Vol. III, p. 91, where the second phrase appears in an explanatory footnote.
42 *Early Theological Writings,* p. 292.
43 *Philosophy of Religion,* Vol. III, pp. 91-2.
44 *The Philosophy of History,* p. 328.
45 *Philosophy of Religion,* Vol. II, p. 327.
46 ibid., p. 330.
47 ibid., Vol. III, p. 77.
48 ibid., p. 107.
49 ibid., Vol. II, p. 345.
50 ibid., Vol. I, p. 219.
51 St John's Gospel, 16 : 13.
52 *Philosophy of Religion,* Vol. I, p. 219.
53 ibid., p. 218.
54 ibid., pp. 220-1.
55 op. cit., p. 115.
56 *Systematic Theology,* James Nisbet & Co., Vol 2, 1957, p. 26.
57 ibid., p. 27.

Chapter 6 From Religious Tradition to either History or Myth

1 It was later attributed to P. Annet (ob. 1768).
2 They were published in English for the first time in 1971.
3 *The Life of Jesus Critically Examined,* p. xvi.
4 ibid., p. lii.
5 For a fuller account of the material in the last two paragraphs, see Richard S. Cromwell, *David Friedrich Strauss and His Place in Modern Thought.*
6 Strauss, op. cit., p. 80.
7 This term refers to the narrative material in which the ongoing Jewish tradition elaborated the biblical stories by the free use of the imagination but for a deeply religious purpose.

8 Strauss, op. cit., p. 735.
9 ibid., p. 742.
10 ibid., p. 743.
11 ibid., p. 744.
12 ibid., p. 757.
13 ibid., p. 756.
14 ibid., p. 776.
15 ibid., p. 777.
16 ibid., p. 780.
17 ibid., p. 778.
18 ibid., p. 789.
19 ibid., p. 784.
20 ibid., p. lii.
21 ibid., p. 784.
22 *The Quest of the Historical Jesus*, A. & C. Black, 2nd edition, 1911, p. 79.
23 ibid., p. 72.
24 Schweitzer interprets Strauss thus, ibid., p. 73.
25 Quoted by Schweitzer, ibid., p. 73.
26 *A Life of Jesus for the German People*, London, 1865, Vol. I, p. 440.
27 *The Old Faith and the New*, London, 1874, pp. 8-9.
28 ibid., p. 18.
29 ibid., p. 163.
30 *The Interpretation of the New Testament 1861-1961*, Oxford University Press, 1966, p. 12.
31 *Myths, Dreams and Mysteries*, Collins, 1968, p. 38.

Chapter 7 From Theology to Anthropology

1 An Introductory Essay to *The Essence of Christianity* by Ludwig Feuerbach, Harper & Row, New York, 1957, p. x.
2 Translator's Introduction to *Principles of the Philosophy of the Future*, Bobbs-Merrill, Indianapolis, 1966, pp. xxvii-xxviii.
3 *Lectures on the Essence of Religion*, Harper & Row, New York, 1967, p. 15. He also once expressed man's earthliness in a witty epigram, *Der Mensch ist was er isst* (Man is what he eats).
4 *Principles of the Philosophy of the Future*, p. 24.

5 ibid., p. 23.
6 ibid., p. 34.
7 Quoted by Owen Chadwick, *The Secularization of the European Mind in the Nineteenth Century*, p. 169.
8 See *Principles of the Philosophy of the Future*, p. 47.
9 ibid., p. 47.
10 ibid., p. 48.
11 ibid., p. 5.
12 *Lectures on the Essence of Religion*, p. 153.
13 *Principles of the Philosophy of the Future*, p. 71.
14 *Between Man and Man*, Kegan Paul, 1947, p. 148.
15 *Principles of the Philosophy of the Future*, p. 72.
16 ibid., pp. 58-9.
17 *The Essence of Christianity*, p. 1.
18 ibid., p. 64.
19 ibid., p. 32.
20 *Lectures on the Essence of Religion*, p. 36.
21 ibid., p. 23.
22 *The Essence of Christianity*, p. xxxviii.
23 *Lectures on the Essence of Religion*, p. 233.
24 *The Essence of Christianity*, p. 226.
25 *Lectures on the Essence of Religion*, p. 121.
26 *The Essence of Christianity*, pp. 105-6.
27 ibid., p. 38.
28 *Lectures on the Essence of Religion*, p. 180.
29 *The Essence of Christianity*, pp. 105-6.
30 *Lectures on the Essence of Religion*, p. 23.
31 *The Essence of Christianity*, p. 47.
32 ibid., p. 97.
33 ibid., p. 123.
34 *Lectures on the Essence of Religion*, p. 246.
35 *The Essence of Christianity*, p. 50.
36 ibid., p. 53.
37 *Lectures on the Essence of Religion*, p. 36.
38 *The Essence of Christianity*, p. 172.
39 ibid., p. 181.
40 ibid., p. 185.
41 ibid., p. 73.
42 ibid., p. 184.
43 *Lectures on the Essence of Religion*, pp. 216-17.
44 ibid., p. 276.

Chapter 8 To a Religion Without God?

1 *Marx & Engels On Religion*, p. xii.
2 *Early Writings*, p. 218.
3 *Collected Works*, Vol. I, pp. 3, 8.
4 ibid., p. 18.
5 ibid., p. 19.
6 ibid., p. 142.
7 *On Religion*, p. 224.
8 Quoted by Tucker, *Philosophy and Myth in Karl Marx*, p. 81.
9 ibid., p. 97.
10 *On Religion*, p. 41.
11 ibid., p. 70.
12 Quoted by Tucker, op. cit., p. 110.
13 *Early Writings*, p. 239.
14 ibid., pp. 323-4.
15 ibid., p. 332.
16 ibid., p. 329.
17 ibid., p. 330.
18 ibid., pp. 330-1.
19 ibid., p. 331.
20 ibid., p. 332.
21 *The Communist Manifesto*, p. 79.
22 *On Religion*, pp. 69-72.
23 ibid., p. 72.
24 op. cit., pp. 114-16.
25 *Early Writings*, p. 256.
26 *Essential Writing of Karl Marx*, p. 207.
27 Gospel of St Mark, 1:5 (my translation).
28 *Early Writings*, p. 257.
29 *The Communist Manifesto*, pp. 120-1.
30 Quoted by Tucker, op. cit., p. 225.
31 *Myths, Dreams and Mysteries*, Collins, 1968, pp. 25-6.
32 *Early Writings*, p. 223 (italics mine).
33 *On Religion*, p. 42.
34 Milan Machovec, *A Marxist Looks at Jesus*, p. 21.
35 From 'All things bright and beautiful', written by Mrs Cecil Alexander, whose husband later became Archbishop of Armagh and Primate of all Ireland. It is an interesting

commentary that this verse has been omitted from some twentieth-century versions.

36 See Machovec, op. cit., pp. 24-7.

Chapter 9 The Impact of Science on Religion

1 *Age of Enlightenment*, p. 18.
2 This dating regularly appeared in English Bibles until the beginning of the twentieth century.
3 Regius Professor of Greek and later Master of Balliol College, Oxford.
4 Widely renowned Anglican theologian, and later Bishop of Oxford, whose trilogy of basic works was later issued as *The Reconstruction of Belief*.
5 *Lux Mundi*, XIIth edition, 1891, p. 262.
6 *The Papal Encyclicals*, ed. by Anne Fremantle, New American Library, 1963, p. 298.
7 *Lux Mundi*, 1891, p. 132.
8 *A Writer's Recollections*, W. Collins, 1918, p. 230.
9 *Lux Mundi*, 1891, pp. 73-4.

Chapter 10 A New Queen of the Sciences?

1 Quoted by Topazio, *D'Holbach's Moral Philosophy*, p. 129.
2 ibid., p. 124.
3 Quoted by I. G. Barbour, *Issues in Science and Religion*, p. 62.
4 Quoted by Topazio, op. cit., pp. 133-4.
5 ibid., p. 154.
6 *The Essential Comte*, ed. by Stanislav Andreski, p. 35.
7 ibid., p. 210.
8 ibid., p. 211.
9 ibid., p. 226.
10 Andreski, op. cit., pp. 15-16.
11 *On Morality and Society*, Selected Writings of Emile Durkheim, ed. by Robert N. Bellah, p. x.
12 Quoted by Bellah, ibid., p. xlv.
13 *The Elementary Forms of the Religious Life*, p. 3.
14 ibid., p. 41. Mircea Eliade analyses the nature of religion similarly, particularly in *The Sacred and the Profane*.

Harper & Row, New York, 1961.
15 See Eliade, op. cit., pp. 201-13.
16 *The Elementary Forms of the Religious Life*, p. 206.
17 ibid., p. 223.
18 ibid., p. 419.
19 ibid., p. 225.
20 ibid., p. 226.
21 ibid., p. 418.
22 ibid., p. 419.
23 ibid., p. 427.
24 ibid., p. 430.
25 ibid., pp. 427-8.
26 ibid., p. 431.

Chapter 11 The Copernican Revolution in the Science of the Soul

1 *The End of Conventional Christianity*, p. 94.
2 *History of Psychology*, p. 15.
3 ibid., p. 378.
4 *The Interpretation of Dreams*, p. 776.
5 ibid., p. 651.
6 ibid., p. 774.
7 op. cit., p. 90.
8 *New Introductory Lectures on Psychoanalysis*, p. 205.
9 *The Future of an Illusion*, p. 43.
10 *New Introductory Lectures on Psychoanalysis*, p. 209.
11 ibid., pp. 213-14.
12 ibid., p. 215.
13 *The Future of an Illusion*, pp. 36-7.
14 *Man and His Symbols*, p. 25.
15 *C. G. Jung: Psychological Reflections*, ed. by Yolande Jacobi, p. 38.
16 ibid., p. 40.
17 ibid., p. 39.
18 ibid., p. 42.
19 ibid., p. 46.
20 C. G. Jung, *Man and His Symbols*, p. 69.
21 ibid., p. 84.

Chapter 12 From Absolutism to Relativism in a Pluralistic World

1 Lit. an 'abode of Islam', i.e. a country where life is shaped by the ordinances of Islam.
2 His liberal views provoked a crisis at King's College, London, and he was forced to resign from his Chair of Theology.
3 See Chapter 9.
4 *Lux Mundi*, p. 50.
5 *Christian Thought*, pp. 4-6.
6 *The Absoluteness of Christianity and the History of Religions*, p. 46.
7 ibid., p. 48.
8 ibid., pp. 71-2.
9 ibid., p. 78.
10 ibid., p. 85.
11 ibid., p. 131.
12 See ibid., p. 120.
13 Unfortunately Troeltsch died before it could be delivered but it was subsequently published in *Christian Thought*.
14 *Christian Thought*, p. 25.
15 ibid., p. 26.
16 op. cit., p. 163.
17 *Christian Thought*, p. 31.
18 So said Kraemer, *Religion and the Christian Faith*, p. 224.
19 For example, see: Godfrey E. Phillips, *The Old Testament in the World Church*, Lutterworth, 1942; Robin Boyd, *An Introduction to Indian Christian Theology*, The Christian Literature Society, Madras, 1969.
20 See full discussion in Karl Barth, *Church Dogmatics*, Vol. I, Part 2, T. & T. Clark, Edinburgh, 1956, pp. 280-361.
21 *Why Christianity of All Religions?* p. 123.
22 *The Documents of Vatican II*, ed. by A. P. Flannery, Pillar Books, New York, 1975, p. 739.

Chapter 13 Secularization – A Process of Religious Change in Two Stages

1 *Beyond Belief*, p. 40.
2 *Protestantism and Progress*, (E.T.) Crown Theological Library, 1912, pp. 22-3.

3 *Religion in Secular Society*, p. xiv.
4 *The Social Reality of Religion*, p. 107.
5 *Secularization and Moral Change*, Oxford University Press, 1967, p. 7.
6 op. cit., p. 214.
7 *The Secular, the Religious and the Theological*, R. Burge, Manchester, 1850, p. 6.
8 *The Secular City*, p. 2.
9 Unfortunately this is placed under the heading of 'secularism' instead of 'secularization'.
10 *Encyclopaedia Britannica*, 15th edition, 1974, Vol. IX, p. 19. In this quote 'secularism' has been replaced by 'secularization'.
11 See his *The Invisible Religion*, Macmillan, New York, 1967.
12 See his *Beyond Belief*, pp. 168-86.
13 *The Origin and Goal of History*, p. 219.
14 *Systematic Theology*, Vol. I, Nisbet & Co., 1953, pp. 92-6.
15 *On Being a Christian*, Collins, 1977, pp. 536-8.
16 op. cit., p. 94.
17 op. cit., p. 536.

Chapter 14 Why did Secularization Come out of the West?

1 See Max Weber, *The Protestant Ethic and the Spirit of Capitalism*, Allen & Unwin, London, 1930.
2 *Chance and Necessity*, Collins, 1972, p. 162.
3 *The Relevance of Science*, pp. 120-1.
4 ibid., p. 178.
5 *Science and the Modern World*, pp. 13-14.
6 *The Social Reality of Religion*, p. 113.
7 Deuteronomy 14:2, King James Version.
8 For an elaboration of these points so far as Christianity is concerned, see F. C. Grant, *Ancient Judaism and the New Testament*, Oliver & Boyd, 1960.
9 A similar but fuller discussion is found in Part II of the author's *God in the New World*. See also Peter Berger, *The Social Reality of Religion*, pp. 113-25.
10 Genesis 1:31.
11 e.g. Psalms 145, 148, Job 38-41.
12 See Isaiah 11:6-9.

13 Revelation 21:1-3.
14 Luke 15:11-32. Note: 'He came to himself and said...'
15 Genesis 1:27.
16 Psalm 8:5.
17 Deuteronomy 5:15.
18 See G. E. Wright, *The Old Testament against its Environment*, SCM, 1950.
19 Exodus 3:14.
20 Exodus 20:4, Deuteronomy 5:8.
21 See Amos 5:21-4, Hosea 6:6, Isaiah 1:10-17, Micah 6:1-8, Jeremiah 6:20, 7:21-3.
22 *The Secular City*, p. 32.
23 *The Social Reality of Religion*, p. 124.
24 I Corinthians 15:22, 45, 48.
25 Paul Tillich, *Systematic Theology*, Vol. II, pp. 100ff.
26 ibid., p. 109.
27 ibid., p. 184.
28 Quoted with the kind permission of the SCM Press from John Macquarrie, *Thinking About God*, SCM, 1975, p. 77.
29 *The Social Reality of Religion*, p. 127.

Chapter 15 A Prophet of the New Age

1 Quoted by Maurice S. Friedman, *Martin Buber, the Life of Dialogue*, Harper & Row, New York, 1960, p. 34.
2 See Introduction to his translation of *Thus Spake Zarathustra*, p. 18.
3 Quoted by Hollingdale in *Nietzsche, the Man and His Philosophy*, p. 30.
4 ibid., p. 39.
5 The title of a book by the Spanish philosopher Miguel Unamuno.
6 *Basic Writings of Nietzsche*, p. 729.
7 ibid., p. 24.
8 *A Nietzsche Reader*, p. 29.
9 See *The Gay Science*, pp. 181f. Although the madman is, in a sense, himself, it is purely coincidental that he later became insane.
10 *Twilight of the Idols*, pp. 69f.
11 *The Gay Science*, p. 310.

12 ibid., p. 312.
13 *A Nietzsche Reader*, pp. 183f.
14 *Twilight of the Idols and The Anti-Christ*, pp. 186f.
15 *The Birth of Tragedy and The Genealogy of Morals*, p. 288.
16 ibid., pp. 296-8.
17 *Twilight of the Idols and The Anti-Christ*, p. 151.
18 ibid., pp. 147f.
19 ibid., pp. 155f.
20 ibid., p. 147.
21 *Basic Writings of Nietzsche*, p. 712.
22 ibid., p. 790.
23 *Beyond Good and Evil*, p. 128.
24 ibid., p. 78.
25 *Basic Writings of Nietzsche*, p. 736.
26 *Thus Spake Zarathustra*, pp. 54-6.
27 *Beyond Good and Evil*, pp. 176f.
28 *A Nietzsche Reader*, p. 165.
29 Quoted by Kaufmann, *Nietzsche: Philosopher, Psychologist, Antichrist*, p. 274.
30 *Twilight of the Idols and The Anti-Christ*, p. 178.
31 *Thus Spake Zarathustra*, p. 43. (wording slightly altered).
32 ibid., pp. 42, 44.
33 This simile is suggested by Hollingdale in his introduction to *Thus Spake Zarathustra*, p. 25.
34 *Thus Spake Zarathustra*, pp. 237f.
35 ibid., pp. 109f.
36 ibid., p. 44. (Wording slightly altered to bring out the German word-play.)
37 *Basic Writings of Nietzsche*, p. 782.
38 *Twilight of the Idols and The Anti-Christ*, p. 114.

BIBLIOGRAPHY

(Except where otherwise stated, the following are the English editions and published in London)

(1) *General*

BARRY, F. R., *Secular and Supernatural*, SCM, 1969.

BELLAH, ROBERT N., *Beyond Belief*, Harper & Row, New York, 1970.

BERDYAEV, N., *The Meaning of History*, Geoffrey Bles., 1936.

BERDYAEV, N., *The Beginning and the End*, Geoffrey Bles., 1952, Greenwood CT, 1952.

BERGER, PETER L., *The Social Reality of Religion*, Faber and Faber, 1969.

BRONOWSKI, J. AND B. MAZLISH, *The Western Intellectual Tradition*, Penguin, 1960, Harper & Row, New York, 1960.

BRUMWELL, J. R. M. (ed.), *This Changing World*, Scientific Book Club, 1945.

BUTTERFIELD, HERBERT, *The Origins of Modern Science*, George Bell, 1957.

CALLAHAN, DANIEL (ed.), *The Secular City Debate*, Macmillan Co., New York, 1966.

CASSIRER, ERNST, *The Philosophy of the Enlightenment*, Beacon Press, Boston, 1955.

CHADWICK, OWEN, *The Secularization of the European Mind in the Nineteenth Century*, Cambridge University Press, 1975.

COPLESTON, FREDERICK, S.J., *A History of Philosophy*, Vols. I-VIII, Burns and Oates, 1946-66, Doubleday, New York.

COX, HARVEY, *The Secular City*, SCM, 1965, Macmillan, New York, 1965.

CRAGG, G. R., *The Church and the Age of Reason*, Penguin, 1960.

CRAGG, G. R., *From Puritanism to the Age of Reason*, Cambridge University Press, 1966.

CRITES, STEPHEN, *In the Twilight of Christendom*, American Academy of Religion, Scholar Press, 1972.

CUTLER, DONALD R. (ed.), *The World Year Book of Religion, The Religious Situation* Vol. I, Evans Brothers, 1969.

DILLENBERGER, JOHN, *Protestant Thought and Natural Science*, Collins, 1961, Greenwood CT, 1977.

EDWARDS, DAVID L., *Religion and Change*, Hodder & Stoughton, 1969.

FARRER, ADAM STOREY, *A Critical History of Free Thought in reference to the Christian Religion*, John Murray, 1862.

FRANKFORT, H. AND H. A. *et al.*, *The Intellectual Adventure of Ancient Man*, University of Chicago Press, Chicago, 1946.

GARDINER, PATRICK L. (ed.), *19th Century Philosophy*, Free Press, New York, 1969.

GAY, PETER, *The Enlightenment: An Interpretation*, 2 vols. Wildwood House, 1973, Norton, New York, 1977.

GAY, PETER, *Age of Enlightenment*, Time-Life International, 1966.

GEERING, L. G., *God in the New World*, Hodder & Stoughton, 1968.

GEERING, L. G., *The Religion of the Individual in the Modern World*, Price Milburn, Wellington, 1975.

GLASNER, PETER E., *The Sociology of Secularization*, Routledge & Kegan Paul, 1977.

GOGARTEN, FRIEDRICH, *The Reality of Faith*, Westminster Press, Philadelphia, 1959.

HAMPSON, NORMAN, *The Enlightenment*, Penguin, 1968.

HILL, MICHAEL, *A Sociology of Religion*, Heinemann Educational Books, 1976, Basic Books, New York, 1973.

HIRSCHBERGER, JOHANNES, & MOISER, JEREMY, *A Short History of Western Philosophy*, Lutterworth, 1976, Westview, Boulder Co., 1977.

HOPPER, STANLEY R., *The Crisis of Faith*, Hodder & Stoughton, 1947.

JASPERS, KARL, *The Origin and Goal of History*, Routledge & Kegan Paul, 1953, Greenwood CT, 1976.

JASPERS, KARL, *Man in the Modern Age*, George Routledge & Sons, 1933, AMS Press, New York, 1976.

JOHNSON, ROGER *A. et al.*, *Critical Issues in Modern Religion*, Prentice-Hall, New Jersey, 1973.

KAHLER, ERICH, *The Meaning of History*, Chapman and Hall, 1965.

KNIGHT, MARGARET (ed.), *Humanist Anthology*, Pemberton, 1961.

KRISTELLER, PAUL OSKAR, *Renaissance Thought*, Harper Torchbooks, New York, 1961.

LIVINGSTON, JAMES C., *Modern Christian Thought from the Enlightenment to Vatican II*, Macmillan, New York, 1971.

LOEN, ARNOLD E., *Secularization*, SCM, 1967.

LOWITH, KARL, *From Hegel to Nietzsche*, Constable, 1965.

LUND, ERIC *et al.*, *A History of European Ideas*, Reed Education, 1972.

LYNCH, WILLIAM F., *Christ and Prometheus*, A New Image of the Secular, University of Notre Dame, Indiana, 1970.

MAGILL, FRANK N. (ed.), *Masterpieces of World Philosophy in Digest Form*, 4 vols., George Allen & Unwin, 1963, Harper & Row, New York, 1952.

MARTIN, D., *The Religious and the Secular*, Routledge & Kegan Paul, 1969.

MARTIN, D., *A General Theory of Secularization*, Basil Blackwell, Oxford, 1978, Schocken, New York, 1969.

MARTY, MARTIN E., *The Modern Schism*, SCM, 1969.

MARTY, MARTIN E., *Varieties of Unbelief*, Holt, Rinehart and Winston, New York, 1964, Harper & Row, New York.

MASTERSON, PATRICK, *Atheism and Alienation*, Gill and Macmillan, 1971, Notre Dame University Press, South Bend, Indiana, 1971.

MISKOTTE, KORNELIS H., *When the Gods are Silent*, Collins, 1967.

NEILL, STEPHEN, *The Interpretation of the New Testament*, Oxford Paperbacks, 1966.

O'HIGGINS, JAMES, S.J., *Anthony Collins The Man and His Work*, Martinus Nijhoff, the Hague, 1970.

PATAI, RAPHAEL, *Myth and Modern Man*, Prentice-Hall, New Jersey, 1972.

PRUYSER, PAUL W., *Between Belief and Unbelief*, Sheldon, 1974, Harper & Row, New York, 1974.

RANDALL, JOHN HERMAN, JR., *The Making of the Modern Mind*, Rev. ed., Houghton Mifflin Co., New York, 1940.

REARDON, B. M. G., *Religious Thought in the Nineteenth Century*, Cambridge University Press, 1966.

RUSSELL, BERTRAND, *History of Western Philosophy*, George Allen & Unwin, 1961, Simon & Schuster, New York, 1945.

SCHWARZ, HANS, *The Search for God*, SPCK, 1975, Augsburg, Minneapolis, 1975.

SCHWEITZER, A., *The Quest of the Historical Jesus*, A. & C. Black, 2nd edition, 1911, Macmillan, New York, 1968.
SHINER, LARRY, *The Secularization of History*, Abingdon, Nashville, 1966.
SMART, NINIAN (ed.), *Historical Selections in the Philosophy of Religion*, SCM, 1962.
SMITH, W. CANTWELL, *The Meaning and End of Religion*, Mentor, 1964.
SOROKIN, P. A., *The Crisis of our Age*, E. P. Dutton, New York, 1941.
STROMBERG, ROLAND N., *Religious Liberalism in Eighteenth-Century England*, Oxford University Press, 1954.
SYMONDSON, ANTHONY (ed.), *The Victorian Crisis of Faith*, SPCK, 1970.
THOMAS, GEORGE F., *Religious Philosophies of the West*, Charles Scribner's, New York, 1965.
THROWER, JAMES, *A Short History of Western Atheism*, Pemberton, 1971.
TILLICH, PAUL, *Perspectives on Nietzsche and Twentieth Century Protestant Theology*, SCM, 1967.
TOYNBEE, ARNOLD, *An Historian's Approach to Religion*, Oxford University Press, 1956.
TOYNBEE, ARNOLD, *A Study of History*, Vol. XII, *Reconsiderations*, Oxford University Press, 1961.
VAN DE POL, W. H., *The End of Conventional Christianity*, Newman, New York, 1968.
VIDLER, ALEC R., *The Church in an Age of Revolution*, Penguin, 1961.
VON WEIZSACKER, C.F., *The Relevance of Science*, Collins, 1964.
WEBER, MAX, *The Sociology of Religion*, Social Science Paperbacks, 1966, Beacon, Boston, 1964.
WERBLOWSKI, R. J. Z., *Beyond Tradition and Modernity*, Athlone, 1976.
WHITEHEAD, A. N., *Science and the Modern World*, Cambridge University Press, 1926.
WHITEHEAD, A. N., *Religion in the Making*, Cambridge University Press, 1927.
WILSON, BRYAN, *Religion in Secular Society*, C. A. Watts & Co., 1966.
YINGER, J. MILTON, *The Scientific Study of Religion*, Macmillan, New York, 1970.

(2) *For Specific Chapters*

CHAPTER 5

CAIRD, EDWARD, *Hegel*, Blackwood, Edinburgh, 1907, AMS Press, New York, 1883.

HEGEL, G. W. F., *Early Theological Writings*, trans. by T. M. Knox, University of Chicago Press, 1948.

HEGEL, G. W. F., *Lectures on the Philosophy of Religion*, 3 vols., Kegan Paul, Trench, Trubner, 1895.

HEGEL, G. W. F., *Lectures on the Philosophy of World History*, Cambridge University Press, 1975.

KAUFMANN, W. (trans. and ed.), *Hegel, Texts and Commentary*, Doubleday, New York, 1966.

LOEWENBERG, J. (ed.), *Hegel Selections*, Charles Scribner's Sons, 1929.

MURE, G. R. G., *The Philosophy of Hegel*, Oxford University Press, 1965.

ORYNSKI, WANDA (ed.), *Hegel, Highlights: an annotated selection*, Philosophical Library, New York, 1960.

WOLLHEIM, R. (texts selected by), *Hume on Religion*, Collins, 1963.

CHAPTER 6

CROMWELL, RICHARD S., *David Friedrich Strauss and His Place in Modern Thought*, R. E. Burdick, New Jersey, 1974.

HARRIS, HORTON, *David Friedrich Strauss and His Theology*, Cambridge University Press, 1973.

STRAUSS, D. F., *The Life of Jesus Critically Examined*, ed. by Peter C. Hodgson. SCM, 1973, Fortress, Philadelphia, 1972.

STRAUSS, D. F., *The Old Faith and the New*, E. T. London, 1874.

TALBERT, CHARLES H. (ed.), *Reimarus: Fragments*, SCM, 1971, Fortress, Philadelphia, 1970.

CHAPTER 7

FEUERBACH, LUDWIG, *The Essence of Christianity*, trans. by George Eliot, Harper Torchbooks, New York, 1957.

FEUERBACH, LUDWIG, *Principles of the Philosophy of the Future*, trans. by M. H. Vogel, Bobbs-Merrill, New York, 1966.

FEUERBACH, LUDWIG, *Lectures on the Essence of Religion*, trans. by Ralph Manheim, Harper & Row, New York, 1967.

KAMENKA, EUGENE, *The Philosophy of Ludwig Feuerbach*, Harper & Row, New York, 1967.

CHAPTER 8

DELFGAAUW, BERNARD, *The Young Marx*, Sheed & Ward, 1967.

GARAUDY, ROGER, *Karl Marx, the Evolution of His Thought*, Greenwood, Connecticut, 1976.

GARAUDY, ROGER, *Marxism in the Twentieth Century*, Collins, 1970.

GOLLWITZER, HELMUT, *The Christian Faith and the Marxist Criticism of Religion*, Saint Andrew Press, Edinburgh, 1970.

MACHOVEC, MILAN, *A Marxist Looks at Jesus*, Darton, Longman & Todd, 1976, Fortress, Philadelphia, 1976.

KARL MARX AND FRIEDRICH ENGELS, *Collected Works*, Vols. 1-6, Lawrence and Wishart, 1975, International Publishers Co., New York, 1975, 1976.

KARL MARX, *Early Writings*, Penguin, 1975, Random House, New York, 1975.

KARL MARX AND FRIEDRICH ENGELS, *The Communist Manifesto*, Penguin, 1967, *Monthly Review*, New York, 1964.

Essential Writing of Karl Marx, Selected by David Caute, MacGibbon & Kee, 1967, Magnolia, Mass., 1967.

Marx & Engels on Religion, Schocken, New York, 1964.

TUCKER, ROBERT, *Philosophy and Myth in Karl Marx*, Cambridge University Press, 2nd edition, 1972.

RUBEL, M. AND M. MANALE, *Marx without Myth*, Blackwell, 1975, Harper & Row, New York, 1976.

CHAPTER 9

BARBOUR, IAN G., *Issues in Science and Religion*, SCM, 1966, Harper & Row, New York.

Science and Religion: New Perspectives on the Dialogue, Harper & Row, New York, 1968.

DILLENBERGER, JOHN, *Protestant Thought and Natural Science*, Collins, 1961, Greenwood CT, 1977.

DRUMMOND, HENRY, *The Ascent of Man*, Hodder & Stoughton, 1894.

GORE, CHARLES (ed.), *Lux Mundi*, John Murray, 1891.

HAECKEL, ERNST, *The Riddle of the Universe*, Watts & Co., 1901.

LACK, DAVID, *Evolutionary Theory and Christian Belief*, Methuen, 1957.

MOORE, AUBREY, *Science and Faith*, Kegan Paul & Co., 1889.

MORTON, JOHN, *Man, Science and God*, Collins, 1972.

PARKER, J. (ed.), *Essays and Reviews*, Longman, Green, Longman and Roberts, 6th edition, 1861.

PFLEIDERER, O., *Evolution and Theology and other essays*, ed. by O. Cone, A. & C. Black, 1900.

RICHARDSON, ALAN, *The Bible in the Age of Science*, SCM, 1961.

SCHILLING, HAROLD K., *The New Consciousness in Science and Religion*, SCM, 1973, Pilgrim Press, Philadelphia, 1973.

TEMPLE, F., *The Relations between Religion and Science*, Macmillan & Co., 1884.

CHAPTER 10

ANDRESKI, STANISLAV, *The Essential Comte*, Croom Helm, 1974, Barnes & Noble, New York, 1974.

BERGER, PETER L., *Invitation to Sociology*, Penguin, 1968, Overlook Press, New York, 1973.

COMTE, AUGUSTE, *The Positive Philosophy*, trans. by H. Martineau, 2 vols, Kegan Paul, 1893, Bobbs-Merrill, New York, 1970.

DURKHEIM, EMILE, *On Morality and Society* (Selected writings, edited by Robert N. Bellah, University of Chicago Press, Chicago 1973).

DURKHEIM, EMILE, *The Elementary Forms of the Religious Life*, George Allen & Unwin, 1976, Humanities, Atlantic Heights, New Jersey, 1976.

GIDDENS, ANTHONY (ed.), *Emile Durkheim: Selected Writings*, Cambridge University Press, 1972.

TOPAZIO, VIRGIL W., *D'Holbach's Moral Philosophy*, Institut et Musée Voltaire, Geneva, 1956.

CHAPTER 11

FREUD, SIGMUND, *Introductory Lectures on Psycho-analysis*, George Allen & Unwin, 1949 (first published 1922).

FREUD, SIGMUND, *New Introductory Lectures on Psycho-analysis*, Hogarth Press, 1933, Norton, New York, 1965.

FREUD, SIGMUND, *The Future of an Illusion*, Hogarth Press, 1928, Norton, New York, 1975.

FREUD, SIGMUND, *Totem and Taboo*, Pelican, 1938 (first published 1919), Norton, New York, 1952.

FREUD, SIGMUND, *Moses and Monotheism*, Hogarth Press, 1939, Random House, New York, 1955.

FREUD, SIGMUND, *The Interpretation of Dreams*, trans. by James Strachey, Penguin, 1976 (first published in the translation by Hogarth, 1953), Aron Books, New York, 1967.

FROMM, ERICH, *Psychoanalysis and Religion*, Gollancz, 1951, Yale University Press, New Haven, 1950.

JACOBI, YOLANDE (ed.), *C. G. Jung: Psychological Reflections*, Princeton/Bollingen, 1973 (first published in this edition 1961).

JUNG, CARL G., *Psychology and Religion*, Yale University Press, New Haven, 1938.

JUNG, CARL G., *Man and His Symbols*, Dell, New York, 1968.

LEE, R.S., *Freud and Christianity*, Penguin, 1967 (first published 1948).

MISIAK, HENRYK AND V. S. SEXTON, *History of Psychology*, Grune & Stratton, New York, 1966.

CHAPTER 12

——, *The Authority of the Faith* (Tambaram Series), Oxford University Press, 1939.

BOUQUET, A. C., *The Christian Faith and Non-Christian Religions*, James Nisbet, 1958.

BOYD, ROBIN, *An Introduction to Indian Christian Theology*, The Christian Literature Society, Madras, 1969.

CLAYTON, JOHN P. (ed.), *Ernst Troeltsch and the Future of Theology*, Cambridge University Press, 1976.

HOCKING, W. E., *Rethinking Missions, a Laymen's Inquiry after a Hundred Years*, Commission of Appraisal, 1932.

HOCKING, W. E., *Living Religions and a World Faith*, George Allen & Unwin, 1940, AMS Press, New York, 1940.

KRAEMER, HENDRIK, *The Christian Message in a Non-Christian World*, Edinburgh House Press, 1938, Kregel, Grand Rapids, Michigan, 1961.

KRAEMER, HENDRIK, *Religion and the Christian Faith*, Lutterworth, 1956.

KRAEMER, HENDRIK, *World Cultures and World Religions*, Lutterworth, 1960.

KRAEMER, HENDRIK, *Why Christianity of All Religions?* Lutterworth, 1962.

NEILL, STEPHEN, *Christian Faith and Other Faiths*, Oxford University Press, 1970.

NEILL, STEPHEN, *A History of Christian Missions*, Penguin, 1964.

SHARPE, ERIC J., *Faith Meets Faith*, SCM, 1977.

TROELTSCH, ERNST, *The Absoluteness of Christianity*, SCM, 1972, John Knox, Atlanta, 1971.

TROELTSCH, ERNST, *Christian Thought, Its History and Application*, University of London, 1923.

VAN LEEUVEN, AREND TH., *Christianity in World History*, Edinburgh House Press, 1964.

WHITSON, ROBLEY E., *The Coming Convergence of World Religions*, Newman Press, New York, 1971.

CHAPTER 15

HOLLINGDALE, R. J., *Nietzsche, the Man and His Philosophy*, Routledge & Kegan Paul, 1965.

HOLLINGDALE, R. J. (ed. and trans.), *A Nietzsche Reader*, Penguin, 1977.

JASPERS, KARL, *Nietzsche and Christianity*, Henry Regnery Co., New York, 1961.

KAUFMANN, WALTER (trans. and ed.), *Basic Writings of Nietzsche*, The Modern Library, New York, 1966.

KAUFMANN, WALTER, *Nietzsche: Philosopher, Psychologist, Anti-Christ*, World Publishing Co., Cleveland, 1956: 3rd and enlarged edit., Princeton University Press, Princeton, 1968.

NIETZSCHE, FRIEDRICH, *The Birth of Tragedy and The Genealogy of Morals*, trans. by Francis Golffing, Doubleday & Co., New York, 1956.

NIETZSCHE, FRIEDRICH, *Beyond Good and Evil*, trans. with an introduction and commentary by R. J. Hollingdale, Penguin, 1973.

NIETZSCHE, FRIEDRICH, *The Gay Science*, trans. with commentary by Walter Kaufmann, Vintage Books, New York, 1974.

NIETZSCHE, FRIEDRICH, *Thus Spake Zarathustra,* trans. with an introduction by R. J. Hollingdale, Penguin, 1961.

NIETZSCHE, FRIEDRICH, *Twilight of the Idols and The Anti-Christ,* trans. with an introduction and commentary by R. J. Hollingdale, Penguin, 1968.

GENERAL INDEX

Abraham, 31
Adam, 89, 104, 182, 191, 296
Albertus, 50
alienation, 104–7, 142, 152–6
altruism, 199
anatta, 93
Andreski, S., 200
Aquinas, 50f, 92, 109, 209, 284
archetypes, 225–7
Aristotle, 40, 50f, 53, 68, 151, 171, 199, 209
Astruc, J., 67
atheism, 70, 76, 84, 99f, 109, 137f, 140f, 174, 188, 192, 256, 289, 292, 302
Augustine, 50, 55f, 59
Australian Aborigine, 202f
autonomy, 85–8, 274f
Averroës, 50
Axial Period, 32f, 38–42, 87, 251f, 265–73, 279

Bacon, F., 69f
Bacon, R., 51
Bain, A., 211
Barth, K., 132, 245f
Bauer, G. L., 117
Baur, F. C., 114
Bayle, P., 75f, 83, 190
Beccaria, C., 190
Bellah, R., 34, 252, 270
Berdyaev, N., 14, 54
Berger, P., 261, 280, 293, 298
Boehme, J., 100, 115, 214
Bonhoeffer, D., 84
Boyle, R., 232, 235
Brahman, 41f, 254, 285, 290
Bridgewater, Earl of, 175
Bruno, G., 64f, 72, 100, 184
Buber, M., 75, 131f, 136, 255, 284, 300
Buddha, 32f, 41f, 167, 259, 303, 318
Buddhism, 16f, 23, 30, 46–8, 93, 231f, 234, 236, 249, 302, 304
Buffon, 178
Bultmann, R., 130

Calvin, J., 61f
Cambridge Platonists, 80
Carus, K. G., 214
Casa, Carlo Della, 17
Cassirer, E., 60, 90f
catastrophism, 176
Chadwick, O., 263
Chambers, R., 178
Charron, P., 83
Chuang Tzu, 33
class struggle, 156f
Coleridge, S. T., 218, 225
Collins, A., 81–3
Common Notions, 77
Communist Manifesto, 156, 160
Comte, A., 193–201, 205, 314
Condorcet, Marquis de, 194
Confucianism, 16f, 46–8, 231, 234
Confucius, 30, 32f, 41f, 48, 167
Copernicus, 170, 172, 213
Copleston, F., 52f, 54
Cox, H., 264, 280, 292
Croce, B., 110

da Vinci, L., 58, 170
Darwin, C., 127, 147, 176, 178–82, 213, 227
Death of God, 105f, 306
deconsecration of values, 280, 292
definition of religion, 17–19
deism, 76–84, 92, 94, 109, 174f, 184, 188, 191, 256
Democritus, 277
desacralization, 280
Descartes, 69, 71–4, 79, 82, 199, 209f, 322n
D'Holbach, Baron, 189–93
Diderot, D., 84f, 178, 190
dreams, 216, 220, 225
Durkheim, E., 37, 43, 200–7, 221, 227, 284

Eckhart, 57, 103
ecumenism, 271
Ego, 216–19, 222
Eichhorn, J. G., 117
Einstein, A., 284
Eliade, M., 131, 161f, 227
Eliot, George, 124, 307
Encyclical, 182
Engels, F., 149, 151, 160
Erasmus, 60, 82
Erastus, T., 321n
Evangel, 308f
existentialism, 110, 315

Fechner, G. W., 210, 212
Feuerbach, L., 75, 110, 127f, 131–48, 149, 151–4, 155, 162f, 165, 194, 210, 221, 227, 256, 294, 306f
Fichte, J. C., 99f, 103, 302
fideism, 69, 78
Franklin, B., 190
free-thinker, 82
Freud, S., 132, 213–25, 227, 284

Galileo, 72, 170–2
Gay, P., 83, 172
Gogarten, F., 280
Gore, C., 181
Gregory XVI, 124
Grotius, H., 67, 69

Haeckel, E., 127, 179, 183f
Haggadah, 117
Hamann, J. G., 322n
Hazard, P., 66
Hegel, G.W.F., 32, 75, 100–11, 115f, 122, 125, 128, 132–5, 142, 149, 151–3, 162f, 165, 174, 180, 210, 214, 234f, 238f, 255, 278, 294, 303, 306, 318
Heidegger, M., 132
Heine, H., 98
Herbert of Cherbury, 76f
Hess, M., 153f, 157
heteronomy, 85f, 274f
historicism, 238
Hobbes, T., 67, 70, 82, 190, 210
Hocking, W. E., 243f, 247
Hodgson, W. B., 264
Hollingdale, R. J., 300
Holyoake, G. J., 263
Hopper, S. R., 54f
humanism, 55–60, 165, 256
Hume, D., 92–6, 174, 190, 233
hypnosis, 215f

Id, 216–19, 221f
Illingworth, J. R., 192, 235
immortality, 145, 285, 310
Incarnation, 104–7, 122, 142–4, 238, 294–8, 309

Index, 73, 321
Islam, 16, 23, 30, 41, 44, 46–8, 231f, 234, 236

James, W., 211
Jaspers, K., 32, 39, 40, 41, 47f, 273
Jerusalem Conference, 249
Jesus Christ, 44, 79, 82, 101, 105f, 110, 113f, 116–26, 128, 130f, 143, 158–60, 167, 173, 259, 281, 294–7, 308f, 318
Jowett, B., 181
Judaism, 46, 48, 85, 201
Jung, C. G., 224–9

Kant, I., 86, 95–101, 139f, 174, 302
Karma, 277
Kepler, J., 173
Kierkegaard, S., 100, 110, 132, 322n
Kraemer, H., 244f, 247
Küng, H., 274f

Lao Tzu, 33, 41
Laplace, 174
Lasaulx, 32
Latitudinarians, 80
Latourette, K. S., 234
Leibniz, G. W., 210
Lessing, G. E., 76, 85, 114
Livingston, J. C., 66, 105
Locke, J., 77–83, 190, 225
Luckmann, T., 270
Luther, M., 52, 59–61, 105, 137, 140, 219, 307
Lyell, C., 176

MacIntyre, A., 261
MacMurray, J., 20
Madman, Parable of the, 306
Mahavira, 33, 41
Maimonides, 284
Malthus, T., 178
Maritain, J., 52
Marsilius, 53
Marx, K., 110, 132, 134, 146, 149–67, 190, 200, 206, 210, 282, 284, 314
master morality, 312–14
materialism, 134f, 165, 188f, 210, 256
Maurice, F. D., 235
Melancthon, P., 61, 212
Mettrie, J. O. de La, 189, 210
Mill, J. S., 199
Mirandola, 56
Misiak, H., 211, 213
Monod, J., 278
Montaigne, 68f, 71, 83
Moore, A., 184
Moses, 31, 44, 70, 118, 167, 199, 280, 289
Mott, J. R., 234, 247
Muhammad, 167, 220, 225, 235, 238, 282, 293, 318
myth, 37, 40, 46, 104–6, 112f, 116–20, 125, 131, 158–62, 221, 225–8, 259f, 287f, 295f

Nazi, 313f
Neill, S., 130
Neo-Platonism, 40, 57, 134, 322n
Newman, J. H., 235
Newton, I., 96, 172–4, 178
Nicholas of Cusa, 57f, 64, 99
Niehbuhr, H. R., 246
Niehbuhr, R., 149
Nietzsche, F., 10, 101, 105, 132, 300–19
Nirvana, 42, 254, 285, 290

nominalism, 51, 138f

Ockham, 51–3
Old Testament, 284–93
Ontological Argument, 139
Overman, 313–19

Paley, W., 95
panentheism, 100, 255
pantheism, 74, 76, 81, 99f, 109, 174, 255
Paracelsus, 214
Parliament of World Religions, 237
Paul, J., 324n
Paul IV, Pope, 321n
Paul, St, 100, 219, 221, 282, 296, 309
Pelagius, 56, 287
Petrarch, 54
Philo, 283
Pius XII, 182
Plato, 40, 135, 209, 285
positivism, 194f, 197–9, 201, 205
Positivist Calendar, 199
Privy Council, 180
proletariat 156, 158–62
psychoanalysis, 213–18, 221
psychology, 209–29
psychophysics, 210
Purgatory, 63, 151
Pyrrhonism, 321n

reality principle, 217
Reformation, 60–4
Reimarus, 85, 113f, 126
Renaissance, 54–60
Resurrection, 83, 106, 113f, 116, 119–26, 130, 143, 174
revaluation of all values, 311–13
Ritschl, F., 301
Rousseau, J. J., 99, 150, 233, 270
Royal Society, 175

Saint-Simon, 193, 195, 200
scepticism, 68f, 92–6
Schelling, F. W. J., 99–101, 115, 214
Schleiermacher, 75, 99, 125, 132
Schopenhauer, A., 101, 127, 302–4, 318
Schweitzer, A., 124f, 130
scientism, 185, 205
Scotus, John, 57
secularization, meaning of, 261–4
Shema, 73, 321n
Sheol, 285
Simon, R., 83
Skinner, B. F., 213
slave morality, 312, 315
Smith, A., 190
Smith, W., 15
sociology, 189, 196f, 205–7
Spinoza, 67, 73–6, 84, 99–103, 115, 133f, 184, 210, 255, 284
Spirit, 102–10, 134, 152, 238, 278
Stein, L. von, 158
Stoicism, 40
Strauss, D., 110, 113–31, 132, 149, 151, 162f, 184, 227, 238, 294, 306f
Strauss, V. von, 32
Suffering servant, 159
Super-Ego, 216–19, 222
symbols, 228, 259f

Tambaram Conference, 244
Taoism, 30, 47f, 231
Tartini, 218, 225
Teilhard de Chardin, P., 75, 182, 255, 322n

Temple, F., 235
theonomy, 274f
Tillich, P., 14, 17, 75, 101, 109, 111, 255, 274f, 292, 296
Tillotson, J., 80, 82
Tindal, M., 81
Toffler, A., 14
Toland, J., 80f
toleration, 68, 79f, 192
Toynbee, A., 32, 44f
Trinity, 107, 136, 294
Troeltsch, E., 237–42, 245–7, 254
Tucker, R., 158

Uniformitarianism, 176f
Upanishads, 31, 40
Ussher, Bishop, 175

van de Pol, W. H., 209, 218
Vatican I, 65
Vatican II, 50, 62, 247f
Vedas, 17, 31, 245, 289
Vivekananda, Swami, 237
Vogel, M. H., 132
Voltaire, 83f, 150, 191, 322n

Walpole, H., 190
Ward, H. Mrs., 183
Watson, J. B., 213
Weber, M., 36, 42f, 278, 282
Weiss, J., 130
Weizsäcker, C. F. von, 279
Werblowsky, R. J. Z., 15
Whiston, W., 321n
Whitehead, A. N., 279
Wilson, B., 261
Woolston, T., 83
Wundt, W., 211f

Zarathustra, 32f, 40, 314–15, 318
Zionism, 281